Integrated Marketing Communications in Risk and Crisis Contexts

Integrated Marketing Communication

Series Editor: Jeanne M. Persuit

University of North Carolina Wilmington
Integrated marketing communication (IMC) is a holistic approach to the areas of advertising, public relations, branding, promotions, event and experiential marketing, and related fields of strategic communication. This series seeks to ground IMC with communication ethics in order to take the theory and practice of IMC beyond a critical and deconstructive understanding and into new areas of productive inquiry. We seek to advance the scholarship of IMC in a manner that influences and informs future practice. Submissions may rely on varied methodologies and relate to the study and practice of communication and its theoretical diversity, including but not limited to the areas of rhetoric, visual communication, media ecology, philosophy of communication, mass communication, intercultural communication, and instructional communication. We welcome submissions addressing all facets of IMC and its relationship with communication ethics. While edited volumes will be considered, we encourage the submission of scholarly monographs that explore, in-depth, issues in IMC as related to communication ethics.

Titles in the series:
Integrated Marketing Communications in Risk and Crisis Contexts: A Culture-Centered Approach
By Robert S. Littlefield, Deanna D. Sellnow, and Timothy L. Sellnow
Integrated Marketing Communication: Celebrity and the American Political Process
By Jennifer Brubaker
Sport Teams, Fans, and Twitter: The Influence of Social Media on Relationships and Branding
By Brandi Watkins
Integrated Marketing Communication: Creating Spaces for Engagement
Edited by Jeanne M. Persuit & Christina L. McDowell Marinchak

Integrated Marketing Communications in Risk and Crisis Contexts

A Culture-Centered Approach

Robert S. Littlefield, Deanna D. Sellnow, and Timothy L. Sellnow

LEXINGTON BOOKS
Lanham • Boulder • New York • London

Published by Lexington Books
An imprint of The Rowman & Littlefield Publishing Group, Inc.
4501 Forbes Boulevard, Suite 200, Lanham, Maryland 20706
www.rowman.com

6 Tinworth Street, London SE11 5AL, United Kingdom

Copyright © 2021 The Rowman & Littlefield Publishing Group, Inc.

All rights reserved. No part of this book may be reproduced in any form or by any electronic or mechanical means, including information storage and retrieval systems, without written permission from the publisher, except by a reviewer who may quote passages in a review.

British Library Cataloguing in Publication Information Available

Library of Congress Cataloging-in-Publication Data

Library of Congress Control Number: 2020950416
ISBN: 9781793618771 (cloth) | ISBN: 9781793618795 (pbk)

Contents

List of Illustrations		vii
Acknowledgments		ix
Introduction		1
1	Situating Culture and Integrated Marketing in Risk and Crisis Communication	7
2	The Cultural Imperative in Risk and Crisis Communication Best Practices	27
3	Building the Cultural Model of Risk and Crisis Communication	41
4	The IDEA Model of Instructional Risk and Crisis Communication	59
5	The Culture-Neutral Approach	75
6	The Culturally Sensitive Approach	91
7	The Culture-Centered Approach	109
8	Implications of Emphasizing Culture in Risk and Crisis Communication	123
9	The Need for an Ethical Framework	145
10	Future Directions for Situating Culture in Risk and Crisis Communication	163

References 173
Index 191
About the Authors 199

List of Illustrations

FIGURES

1.1	Stages of Integrated Marketing Communications	12
1.2	Single Spokesperson Model of Crisis Communication	21
1.3	Multiple Spokesperson Model of Crisis Communication	22
2.1	Risk and Crisis Communication Best Practices	29
4.1	Symbolic of Most Serious Warnings in Western Cultures	62
4.2	Symbolic of Most Dangerous Weather Condition	63
4.3	Drop, Cover, Hold On Action Step Exemplar	68
4.4	How to Help	69
6.1	Hurricane Dorian Probable Path of the Storm	100
6.2	Hurricane Dorian Spaghetti Model	103
7.1	Culture-Centered Unlimited Feedback Model	112
7.2	Culture-Centered Multiple Spokesperson Model of Crisis Communication	114
8.1	Involvement of Cultural Agents in Stages of Integrated Marketing Communications	126

TABLES

2.1	Comparison of Strategic Planning Best Practices with Stage 1 of Integrated Marketing Communications	32
2.2	Comparison of Inclusive Approach Best Practices with Stage 2 of Integrated Marketing Communications	33
2.3	Comparison of Responsible Communication Best Practices with Stage 3 Integrated Marketing Communications	34

2.4	Comparison of Corrective Action Best Practices with Stage 4 Integrated Marketing Communications	35
3.1	Perspectives of Control of Cultural Characteristics on Approaches to Risk and Crisis Communication	53
3.2	Timeline of Public Communication about ZIKv Outbreak	55
3.3	Timeline of Hurricane Dorian	56
3.4	Timeline of PEDv and ASFv Outbreaks	58
6.1	Location of Land Areas Directly Affected by Hurricane Dorian	98
6.2	Examples of Emotive Language Used by NHC	101
6.3	Weather Warnings Included in NHC Bulletins and Their Meanings	104
8.1	Comparison of Communication Elements in Cultural-Neutral, Culturally Sensitive, and Culture-Centered Approaches	127

Acknowledgments

We thank Dr. Jeanne Persuit for helping us to conceptualize our book proposal and the final product. She is a leader in IMC research and her insights have been valuable throughout the writing process. We acknowledge the support of colleagues at the University of Vermont, the University of Central Florida (UCF), and North Dakota State University where the five-year NIFA Coordinated Agriculture Project of the U.S. Department of Agriculture entitled "A Human Behavioral Approach to Reducing the Impact of Livestock Pest or Disease Incursions of Socio-economic Importance," was supported, under award number 2015-69004-23273. Victor Martinez Rivera in the Nicholson School of Communication and Media at UCF provided creative expertise; and a final word of appreciation is extended to Kathy Littlefield for her encouragement, patience, and support throughout the project.

Introduction

The year was 1919, described by historian Alfred W. Crosby as possibly "the worst year in American history" (Little, 2020). The country had just fought in a World War and was in a deep recession. White mobs were violently attacking Black communities over jobs and economic disparities, and many of the Black soldiers who had fought in the war were tired of their *unequal citizenship* and were fighting back. The Red Scare was a political reality with the rise of communism and anarchist bombings were frequent.

Amid this backdrop emerged the deadliest flu in modern history, or what later came to be poorly named the Spanish Flu, as it was frequently known (Jordan, 2019). First identified in March 1918, at a U.S. Army camp in Kansas, this mysterious flu caused by the H1N1 virus with genes of avian origin ultimately infected 500 million people and claimed 50 million lives worldwide, including 657,000 deaths in the United States (Johnson & Mueller, 2002; USDHHS, 2018). The virus had "the power to kill a perfectly healthy young man or woman within 24 hours of showing the first signs of infection" (Little, 2020). The virus caused high temperatures and nasal hemorrhaging pneumonia, and as the body's immune system overreacted to the virus, causing severe inflammation, "the patients would drown in their own fluid-filled lungs" (Little, 2020).

Several factors contributed to the virulence of the Spanish Flu pandemic from 1918 to 1920. One major factor causing the worldwide spread of the virus was the movement and mobilization of troops in World War I, putting soldiers in close contact with each other in overcrowded conditions. Once contracted, little could be done to counter the virus due to limited health services resulting from a shortage of doctors and nurses. A second factor was the level of medical knowledge and technology available at that time. Medical technology and countermeasures were limited or non-existent. There were no diagnostic tests, no vaccines, no antibiotics (penicillin was not developed until 1928), no antiviral drugs, and no critical care measures available (intensive care units and ventilators). The only controls to the virus were non-pharmaceutical interventions (e.g., isolation, quarantine, good personal hygiene, use of disinfectants, and limitations of public gatherings). The third factor contributing to the spread of the virus was the lack of a coordinated plan to confront a pandemic. The federal government had no centralized plan and there was little federal help to initiate an intervention to stop the spread of the virus. Some local communities closed schools, banned public gatherings, and gave isolation or quarantine orders (Jester et al., 2019). But, without coordination, people relied on their own measures to protect themselves and they buried their dead.

Fast forward to 2020, to what has been described as the worst year ever (Brandus, 2020; Delaney, 2020). Natural disasters, an economic meltdown, soaring unemployment, racial violence, and political turmoil, on top of the novel COVID-19 pandemic, have produced major challenges for the global community. From the mega-wildfires that destroyed Australia's wildlife and threatened its population; to the global economic challenges faced by nations due to shutdowns and quarantine mandates, including having more Americans out of work than in the Great Depression; to the social and racial violence and protests globally following the killing of black citizens by police and citizens acting as vigilantes; to the political turmoil spawned by the Trump impeachment and deconstruction of relationships and agreements with America's global partners; to the COVID-19 pandemic with all of its societal disruption and public health challenges, the compounding effect of these crises appears to provide some truth to the forecast offered by Jordan (2019): If the crises of 1918 happened today, the situation would still overwhelm the world, only on a greater scale due to population growth and technological changes.

The COVID-19 pandemic has placed the United States at the top of many lists of countries experiencing crisis associated with the virus, including cases testing positive and the number of deaths resulting from the virus. While the total number of positive cases in the world continues to climb over 70 million, with more than 1,500,000 actual deaths, the total of U.S. confirmed cases has exceeded 16 million, with deaths continuing to climb over the 300,000 mark (Kaiser Family Foundation, 2020). These totals exceed other countries experiencing the effects of the virus.

In addition to these growing statistics, the combination of health, economic, racial, and political exigencies has challenged state and local governments to manage the crisis by allocating hospital beds, acquiring personal protective equipment, and implementing risk reduction policies (e.g., stay at home orders, school closures, and business closures), to name the major categories (Risk and Social Policy Group, 2020). Decision-makers at all levels have been called upon to provide strategies in response to these crises and to communicate their plans effectively to multiple publics. Across the board, organizations and businesses have faced conflicting perspectives on what to do to bring back a sense of normalcy to their operations.

Within this context, we introduce a cultural approach to decision-making and communication that is centered on the strategic inclusion of consumers, potential customers, and multiple publics into the process of designing and disseminating messages. This approach reinforces the outside-in orientation of integrated marketing communications (IMC) because the perspective of the customer or consumer is the basis upon which campaigns are developed and launched. The cultural approach enhances the dissemination of instructional messages through readily internalized, appropriately explained, and realistically actionable content. The culture-centered (CC) approach is rooted in the community and provides a pathway for effective communication with culturally diverse publics—at home and abroad—to reduce risks and mitigate crises.

ORGANIZATION OF THE BOOK

This book is part of the Lexington Books Integrated Marketing Communication (IMC) series and presents a model for examining risk and crisis communication within the context of IMC to provide a more robust understanding of myriad cultural variables affecting the perception of risk and crisis messages and the means by which these messages are processed by different publics, particularly multicultural and international groups. While the conceptualization of what constitutes IMC has been broad, from the perspective of risk and crisis communication, the focus is quite specific: all communication and messages created and disseminated during a risk or crisis must be carefully linked and strategically presented if the intended outcomes associated with the publics' responses are to be realized by the organization sending these messages.

The application of culture to the IMC model in risk and crisis situations is particularly useful. IMC acknowledges that every organization has multiple publics with different needs and perspectives. The CC model of risk and crisis communication within the context of IMC begins with the publics involved and works back to the organization's decision-makers to determine which marketing and communication tools should be used to effectively create and disseminate the messages. When IMC is CC, it is strategic, not tactical. It identifies the objective and matches it to the appropriate communication strategies to achieve the greatest success. If the objective is public awareness of an impending crisis, then a CC strategy would have involved the publics earlier to determine which message strategy would be most appropriate to reach the greatest number of people in a timely manner. If credibility about crisis information is the objective, then a CC public relations strategy would have identified opinion leaders from the affected publics earlier in the process to provide credible information in the face of an impending crisis presented itself. Collaboratively constructed, congruent messages delivered in this manner will have more impact than several divergent ones. Through an integration of push-and-pull CC strategies, risk and crisis communicators can focus the publics' attention on what is most important by integrating motivational appeals to internalize the crisis, explaining essential information accurately as well as translated in ways that are easily understood, and offering specific action steps to mitigate harm and perhaps even save lives. To be most effective, these messages ought to be distributed by a variety of credible sources through multiple communication channels. Through IMC, publics are informed, persuaded, reminded, and reinforced about what they need to know in risk or crisis situations. The CC model involves the publics in the process at each stage of the crisis to create a synergistic approach to IMC.

This book is divided into three parts. Part 1 provides a general introduction to risk and crisis communication within the context of IMC, the cultural variables at play in risk and crisis situations that influence message creation and reception, and an introduction to the CC model. In part 2, the framework for the IDEA Model of Instructional Risk and Crisis Communication is provided as an effective means for conveying messages to disparate publics. Each component of the model is presented: culture-neutral (CN), culturally sensitive (CS), and culture-centered (CC). The components of each approach are identified and case studies provided to demonstrate the model's utility in IMC, as well as potential limitations. In addition, research findings add a unique feature to the book and contribute to a more robust understanding of how risk and crisis messages are influenced by and affect diverse cultural groups. Part 3 completes the discussion of the model by identifying the lessons learned through the various cases, the need for an ethical framework when communicating with multicultural publics, and potential areas for further investigation as cultural variables are identified in our increasingly globalized environment.

Part 1

In chapter 1, culture and IMC are situated in risk and crisis communication. How organizations and spokespeople view themselves and their stakeholders, how stakeholders perceive messages, how multiple audiences respond to single and multiple spokespeople, and how context affects understanding are viewed using cultural variables. A review of current research in risk and crisis communication adds the foundation upon which the current work is framed to highlight how attention to cultural variables enhances communication effectiveness.

Chapter 2 presents the best practices of risk and crisis communication within the context of IMC and provides a framework for understanding why messages are more-or-less effective with different culturally diverse groups. The influence of culture and the challenge of globalization are offered to explain how groups perceive messages. Conflicting worldviews are identified to demonstrate how best practices reflecting managerial perspective are not valued universally. The recognition of culture as an inherent variable in crisis communication is described as essential, particularly in the context of IMC.

Chapter 3 completes part 1 by introducing the CC model of risk and crisis communication through three approaches: CN, CS, and CC. Through a discussion of fundamental assumptions, functions, and examples, each of these approaches is defined. The three crises selected to showcase these approaches are introduced in this chapter. The messages about the 2016 Zika virus (ZIKv) crisis are reflective of a CN approach because the World Health Organization (WHO) controlled the narrative with objective, scientific, and culture-free information. The warning messages about the Hurricane Dorian crisis that wreaked destruction on the Bahamas and the southeastern United States in 2017 were selected as the example of a CS approach because the government appealed to key characteristics of the affected publics to create and disseminate messages that appeared more sensitive to them. The creation and dissemination of messages about the African Swine Fever virus (ASFv) of 2018 is an example of the CC approach because members of the swine industry and producers were brought into the decision-making process and used as cultural agents to create and disseminate information to the affected producers.

Part 2

This section of the book begins with chapter 4, where the IDEA Model of Instructional Risk and Crisis Communication is described in the context of IMC. The model is broken down by its four elements: *I*nternalization, *D*istribution, *E*xplanation, and *A*ction. Through a variety of national and international contexts, the model is shown to provide a practical and effective guide for developing risk and crisis messages that will resonate with multiple publics. Additionally, the model is applied to IMC and its application to cultural approaches previewed.

Chapter 5 offers a more in-depth description of the culture-neutral approach within the context of IMC. Five dimensions of the CN approach are used for comparative purposes with the other two approaches. Using the ZIKv crisis as an example, the analysis shows when CN communication was used, how CN messages were presented, responses to the CN messages, how the CN approach facilitated effective communication, and what limitations to the CN approach were evident.

In chapter 6, an in-depth description of the CS approach is provided within the context of IMC. We do this by arranging our explanation via the IDEA model. Six dimensions of the CS approach provide the basis for a comparison with the other approaches, with cultural adaptation being the added sixth dimension. The Hurricane Dorian example provides examples showing when CS messages were used, how CS messages were presented, the responses to the CS messages, how the CS approach facilitated effective communication, and what limitations to the CS approach were evident.

The ASFv provides an example of a CC approach in chapter 7. Within the context of IMC, five dimensions of the CC approach are used to compare with the other two approaches. The same pattern of exposition shows when CC messages were used, how CC messages were presented, the responses to the CC messages, how the CC approach facilitated effective communication, and what limitations to the CC approach were evident.

Part 3

The third section of the book provides takeaways from using cultural approaches within the context of IMC to communicate in risk and crisis situations. In chapter 8, the lessons learned from the three cases involving CN, CS, and CC approaches are discussed using spheres of ethnocentricity as a framework for identifying why certain messages may be received differently depending upon the context of the communication. Differing cultural views about what constitutes a crisis and what appropriate responses might be are presented, along with tips for practitioners and business/industry leaders seeking to move their organizations from CN to CC orientations.

Chapter 9 essentializes the need for an ethical cultural framework when communicating risk and crisis messages within the context of IMC. Existing models of ethical decision-making are presented, including a CC model developed within the IMC context. Multiple sources and competing worldviews complicate achieving convergence, creating the necessity for establishing precedence. The principle of social utility (PSU) and the ethic of significant choice are introduced, along with a model for ethical CC decision-making. Accounting for cultural sensitivity and translational accuracy is pivotal to maintaining an ethical approach to risk and crisis communication.

Finally, in chapter 10, future directions for situating culture in risk and crisis communication are provided, predicated upon the belief that a CC approach is advantageous when communicating with multiple publics. The limitations of immediacy when a crisis strikes challenge the usefulness of the CC model when lives are at stake. Areas for future study are suggested to reveal how giving voice to those most affected by crises can be transformative and advantageous.

Chapter 1

Situating Culture and Integrated Marketing in Risk and Crisis Communication

The concept of culture is complex, even for anthropologists who study culture from every conceivable dimension. Johoda (1984) considered *culture* an elusive term, suggesting that the number of books devoted to this topic would fill many library shelves. Over time, others have concurred. But, when culture is introduced into the mix with IMC, and risk and crisis communication, the result is, figuratively speaking, the construction of a multi-lane expressway, with multiple entrances and exit ramps leading to myriad destinations ready for voracious exploration. Quite simply, the complexity and impact of culture on how informative and persuasive risk and crisis messages are created, disseminated, and received cannot be overstated.

Here is where we begin our examination, situating culture and integrated marketing within the domain of risk and crisis communication. Then, we offer a review of communication theory, spokesperson models, and interacting arguments to illustrate how culture both affects and reflects the senders and receivers of crisis messages in the IMC context.

CULTURE AND INTEGRATED MARKETING COMMUNICATIONS

To situate culture within IMC, both must be defined and briefly explained to provide context for what is to follow and to demonstrate how cultural perspectives influence the way organizations and spokespeople view themselves and stakeholders. Culture is characterized by its nonmaterial and material dimensions. Culture is reflected in society through its nonmaterial cultural dimensions (e.g., beliefs, values, symbols, and language), as well as by its material culture (e.g., physical objects, technology, and forms of dress).

IMC, a major communication development in the late twentieth century, is a process whereby all communication messages used in a campaign are linked to maximize communication effectiveness with stakeholders. The marketing elements included in IMC are advertising, sales promotion, direct marketing, marketing public relations, sponsorship, the internet, and World Wide Web (Kitchen & De Pelsmacker, 2004).

The Effects of Culture on Communication

While the number of cultural factors affecting communication is staggering, Sarbaugh (1979) identified four general categories of a taxonomy that organize the discussion of culture's effects on communication, particularly when applied to messages communicated to diverse publics. These categories include code systems, perceptions about relationships and intent, knowing and accepting normative beliefs and values, and worldview.

Code systems, or language variations, present a major challenge for effective communication. Within cultures, distinctive language features (e.g., rules of grammar and common usage) make it difficult to even suggest that a single culture has a common language. By extension, the "arbitrariness, abstractness, meaning-centeredness, and creativity" of language makes communication across cultures a complex undertaking (Ting-Toomey & Chung, 2005, p. 141). Because language affects how people think, speak, and interact, the presence of first language and second language usage further complicates the communication process. The verbal style used by spokespeople also influences how messages are perceived. For example, Gudykunst and Ting-Toomey (1988) explained four variations of verbal communication styles that affect levels of understanding (e.g., direct versus indirect, elaborate versus succinct, personal versus contextual, and instrumental versus affective). Other scholars have provided insight into code systems and language choices more specific to specific cultures (Klopf, 2000; Neuliep, 2003). These various perspectives pertaining to differing language styles and code systems serve as guidelines for individuals engaged as spokespersons to follow.

The way individuals view their relationship with members of cultures, as well as the corresponding intent demonstrated by these communicators, can affect how messages are received. Hofstede (1991) identified four broad cultural patterns that influence how individuals perceive each other and respond to intercultural communication (e.g., power distance, other-orientation, uncertainty avoidance, and gender-identity). The effect of this variable is evident by the degree to which the spokesperson establishes a relationship based upon authority and power. For example, if a spokesperson fails to consider the cultural perspectives of the publics, this CN position may alienate the spokesperson from the communities and reduce the probability that they will respond positively to the message.

Another aspect of intercultural communication involves the receptivity of the communicators to know and accept each other's beliefs and values. When the beliefs and values are known and accepted, positive intercultural communication is the result. If beliefs and values are not known or not accepted, misunderstanding and distrust occur. Thus, the manner of communication may be directly influenced. For example, in a high-context culture, beliefs and values are understood and accepted without explicit explanation. In a low-context culture, explicit information about the beliefs and values must be shared if there is to be knowledge and acceptance (Hall, 1976). Ting-Toomey and Chung (2005) classified these high- and low-context communication patterns by how they affect levels of connection and understanding between the senders and receivers. As every characteristic of a culture has the potential to influence as it reflects beliefs and values, the need for attention to this area of cultural variability is paramount.

Communication between cultures is complicated further by the various ways people perceive and act in the world around them. How people experience their reality (nature of life), focus their attention (purpose of life), and use their agency to affect change (place in the cosmos) contributes to an individual's worldview (Sarbaugh, 1979). For example, humans may be subjugated to nature, equal with nature, or attempt to dominate nature. From another perspective, individuals may feel controlled by, effectively manage, or want to control a situation. Ishii et al. (2006) discussed this in the context of fatalism versus agency.

Religious orientations that reference sacred writings, authority figures, rituals, speculation, and ethical perspectives also contribute to how people identify and understand messages related to their well-being (Samovar et al., 2014). Some scholars suggest that value orientations contribute to worldview and have a powerful influence on the way members of a culture perceive and respond to communication (Kluckhohn & Strodtbeck, 1961). Klopf (2000) goes on to suggest that the way members of a culture perceive, think, and speak is influenced by the manner in which they view the world around them. Thus, how individuals view their values in relation to other values reflects their value priorities (Schwartz, 1992).

The complexity of culture as characterized in this taxonomy reflects the challenges facing decision-makers using IMC to promote products or ideas, and risk and crisis communicators intent on saving lives. The language or code system used to convey the message must account for the ability of the receivers to understand and respond as desired. How groups perceive the intent of the sender as helpful, hurtful, or neutral toward them and their needs will affect how they respond to messages. How groups handle tolerance for ambiguity will also affect their reactions. To clarify, while some cultures may be more holistic in their response to a stimulus, others may respond better to direct and sequential messages to follow instructions about how to proceed.

Senders should not ignore the cultural beliefs, values, and assumptions of their customers, stakeholders, or publics. While decision-makers may know some elements of their publics' cultural values, without input from the groups to provide context for those values, the decision-makers' messages may not be perceived as they were intended. Even more importantly, differing worldviews may complicate communication between senders and receivers. Not all groups have the agency to make changes or take charge of the situation. Some groups may be fatalistic and unable to respond due to religious perspectives that the crisis is *god's plan*. Whether through differences in language, relational intent, tolerance for ambiguity, knowledge and acceptance of values, or through worldview, the complexity of culture can make effective IMC or risk and crisis communication a challenging endeavor.

In the area of communication, how groups present and represent themselves through their culture demonstrates what they value. Cultural variables shape not only how messages are created, but their dissemination and reception, as well. Studies abound with results supporting the conclusion that the cultural backgrounds of senders and receivers of messages influences how effectively those groups communicate with each other. When senders do not account for the cultural perspectives of those receiving their messages, they are—in effect—CN, or what is also referred to as culturally insensitive. When the sender makes an effort to tailor the message in ways that acknowledge norms and values of the receiving culture, it is an improvement. But, when senders use the cultural preferences of the receivers as they construct and disseminate messages integrating members of the cultural group, this CC approach creates the greatest opportunity for success in achieving the intended outcome. In addition, these cultural variables affect the ability of people from different groups to know and accept each other in the process of developing relationships.

The audience-focused attention to culture can be applied to approaches used in marketing. IMC is a relatively new marketing approach used to build relationships between a company and its consumers. By definition, "[IMC] is the coordination and integration of all marketing communications tools, avenues, and sources within a company into a seamless program that maximizes the impact on consumer and other end users at a minimal cost" (Clow & Baack, 2007, p. 8). As IMC has evolved, its elements have remained focused on advertising, sales promotion, personal selling, direct response marketing, and public relations.

The need for IMC grew as the availability of social media exploded around the world. As user access to media increased, media outlets expanded to provide alternative channels for reaching current and potential consumers. With the expansion and fragmentation of the media, marketing became exceedingly difficult. Because consumers received so much information from marketers, to build customer loyalty, companies needed a strategy dependent upon consistent messages that could be placed on the media platforms across the spectrum. In this way, through consistent and coordinated messaging, businesses could build strong bonds with consumers by tying together and reinforcing the images and messages using integrated marketing (Kotler, 2005).

The intersection of culture and IMC with risk and crisis communication is the central focus of this book because both IMC and risk and crisis communication are audience-centered concepts. McKendree (2016) explains that because IMC demands that organizations communicate with "consistency, coherence, clarity, and continuity within and across formal organizational boundaries," following an IMC approach can diminish or remove the "risk and uncertainty associated with crisis events" (p. 131). Within the audience-centered context, culture must be a primary variable in message creation because developing and deciding how and when and by whom messages should be disseminated makes a difference in how these messages are received by publics. Because IMC relies on a coordinated approach to promoting a product, decision-makers must account for multiple stakeholders and carry the consistent brand over multiple channels. One standard message may not have the same effect on all customers, but elements of the message that are consistently disseminated across a range of platforms will draw the publics to the product.

Similarly, when crises occur, decision-makers are challenged to provide consistent messages to multiple publics with differing cultural perspectives, particularly in the pre-crisis stage when the credibility of the spokesperson may be a factor. Persuit (2013) sees IMC as an enabling consideration of multiple perspectives in responding to crises and thereby engaging multiple audiences in "productive discourse" (p. 87). To meet this potential, vital information must be conveyed, with sensitivity toward the cultural perspectives of the publics, to achieve intended results. Whether in the promotional mix used to reach potential customers (in the case of IMC) or in messages designed to provide life-saving information to distressed publics (in the case of risk or crisis), decision-makers ought to account for the cultural perspectives of receivers to achieve their goals. If not, they risk losing potential customers or losing lives of victims needing critical instructions for self-protection.

The Process of Integrated Marketing Communications

For the public relations practitioner, IMC means that all the promotional tools available will be linked and function harmoniously in the creation and dissemination of a message. In this integration, every point of contact is a communication opportunity as elements are combined, integrated, and synergized in the promotional mix so to consumers, all messages look, sound, and feel alike. Practice tells us that when all tools are used together, they are more effective than if the tools are employed in a haphazard or uncoordinated way.

Schultz and Kitchen (2000) were among the first to identify the stages of IMC development in an organization. These stages move sequentially (figure 1.1).

In stage 1—tactical coordination of marketing communication—a high degree of interpersonal and cross-functional communication is needed both internally and externally. This stage is led by the business or organization, not by external agencies. For IMC to be implemented at stage 1, no real attempt is made to understand the consumer, customer, and prospect dynamics (Kitchen & De Pelsmacher, 2004). Additionally, no investment has been expended to build databases or apply information technology. Essentially, for businesses who anchor in this stage, IMC may be nothing more than ensuring that the promotional mix of elements is consistent. Most stage 1 businesses eventually move to stage 2—redefining the scope of marketing communication—where extensive information about their customers is gathered from external sources and evaluated. In this stage, the business aligns with external agencies to redefine the scope of the marketing communication based upon the available data that are collected. In stage 3—application of

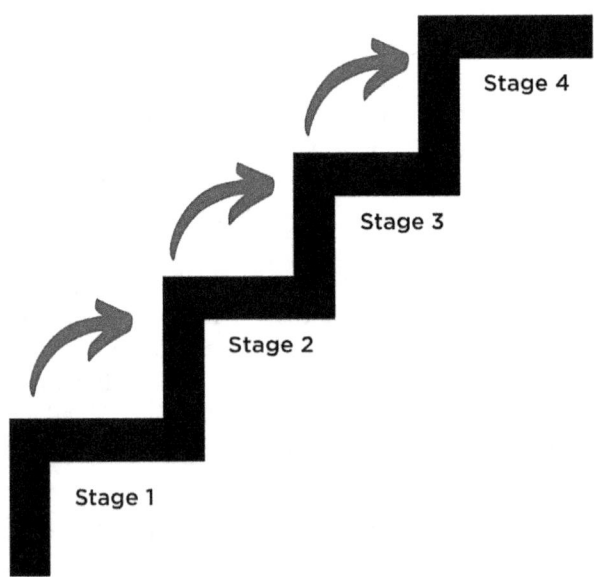

Figure 1.1 **Stages of Integrated Marketing Communications.**

information technology—databanks are built and maintained to segment publics. Data about different publics are converted into customer knowledge, ultimately affecting communication planning and implementation. To reach stage 4—financial and strategic integration—the business leader(s) constantly must monitor performance from a return on investment perspective. Information linked to each of the publics is analyzed on a global scale and used in the decision-making process when adapting to market forces or customer demand. Businesses that move through all four stages are using a comprehensive IMC approach.

By the end of the twentieth century, IMC was being adopted widely by public relations practitioners and businesses due to the explosion of all forms of media and the growth and development of niche and single media markets. As multinational and global entities expanded their influence over economic and political systems, digital technology played a major role in diffusing information and building corporate identities. With the growth of information technology, access to and use of large consumer databases became a tool for marketing programs of all types. As access increased, IMC strategies to build consumer loyalty for the organization's brand expanded.

Early proponents of IMC promoted its utility for others seeking to develop more effective relations with their publics. The components needed for IMC to function included consistency, interactivity, and mission. *Consistency* helps information to fit together to create an impression with publics. Although messages may be tailored for different audiences, a thread exists to link messages together and contributes to the collective brand. Another component is *interactivity*, whereby businesses use databases to identify publics who are given the opportunity to initiate communication and provide feedback. Providing for publics to engage with the company builds loyalty and strengthens the connection with their *mission* or stated purpose.

In particular, just as all communication messages must be linked for a promotional campaign to be success; in crisis situations, all of the messages must be coordinated and work in harmony in order to reach the publics with the information they need to mitigate the crisis and avoid personal harm. For example, governmental agencies must work with local community governments; emergency management efforts must be communicated with local community groups; health, environment, and education systems in a community must share information to bring needed resources to members of the community who need them. To be effective, risk and crisis communication must involve constant review and coordination during the pre- and post-crisis contexts.

IMC involves different levels of integration to reach targeted populations. These integration levels strengthen the effectiveness of the communication because their shared goal is the adoption or acceptance of the product or idea by consumers and stakeholders (MMC Learning, 2019).

In IMC, *horizontal integration* occurs when marketing crosses multiple departments in determining what actions must be taken and how messages are sent to stakeholders. In risk and crisis contexts, horizontal integration describes inter-agency coordination, one of the best practices necessary to ensure that relevant information being shared with the publics is consistent and immediate (Seeger, 2006).

Data integration in IMC involves different departments collecting and sharing information collaboratively to effectively and consistently integrate all the promotional tools used to promote a message. For risk and crisis, data integration involves entities sharing relevant information to minimize conflicting messages coming from different levels of crisis management.

Vertical integration suggests that IMC is consistent with higher-level objectives within the corporate structure and supports the mission. For example, if an organization supports corporate social responsibility (CSR), vertical integration focuses on making sure all messages from every level of the organization support that mission. In the case of crisis messaging, when applying IMC principles, one would expect to find consistency between corporate objectives and what organizational leaders were communicating through their messages.

IMC requires all staff to be informed and motivated to promote new product developments, new service standards, or new partnerships. Hence, everyone is responsible for knowing what is happening to fully market new ideas or outcomes; consistent *internal communication* is essential. For crisis situations, effective intra-agency communication is essential to functionally operate with a consistent message. Intra-agency communication enables an organization to retain its credibility by maintaining consistency about what is happening to mitigate the effects of the crisis on the publics.

Finally, IMC requires *external integration* to attain the goal of cohesive and integrated communication with outside entities. In this context, when multiple agencies are involved, there is a need to work together to deliver a seamless solution. For risk and crisis communicators, this goal becomes controlling the narrative. When multiple voices are presenting critical information in advance of or during a crisis, members of the publics need to know that their source of information is providing the complete message they need to survive.

Advantages of IMC

IMC offers many benefits to organizations when promoting their products or services. These include, for instance, being customer-centered, producing a consistent and credible message, controlling the narrative, responding to timelines, and being cost- and time-effective.

Customer-centered communications is at the heart of integrated marketing, guiding the customers through the buying or acceptance process. The customer-centered approach mirrors what Dutta (2008) termed the CC approach, whereby the perspective of those receiving the information guides the decision-makers when they create and disseminate their risk and crisis messages. When relationships are culture-centered, images and relevant information will have been identified from the intended publics. By using these images and information, risk and crisis communicators will know precisely what the publics need to know, when they need to know it, and from whom they should be getting it.

As IMC helps an organization build loyalty with its customers, it also opens spaces to help publics sort through conflicting risk and crisis messages, focusing on those that emanate from the most trusted and credible sources.

The *consistent and credible message*s that are characteristic of IMC are more effective in cutting through the noise from other messages and keep the customers unified in their support of the organization. Creating one consistent and credible message is the goal of IMC because it has more impact with multiple messages that may or may not have persuasive elements appealing to a broad population. This characteristic is consistent with the best practice of risk and crisis communication that calls for controlling the narrative through a single source (Seeger, 2006). When life or death is hanging in the balance, the publics want to know that the message they receive is the one to which they should be paying attention. If disjointed messages are presented in the face of crisis situations, the publics may become confused, frustrated, or anxious. The development of consistent messages presented in the face of a crisis sends a message of reassurance and order to the publics.

Customers are typically influenced more when shared messages are unified. Message consistency is enhanced in IMC by using images across different communication tools and modes of distribution to create more avenues for customers to be exposed to the product and decide about purchasing the product or idea. This is evident when a logo or image is used across multiple platforms and packaging options. Similarly, message consistency is a critical component of risk and crisis communication because, like IMC, having multiple agencies referencing the same information in the same or similar way is advantageous and is reaching multiple publics preferring different sources or modes of delivery.

As one might expect, as messages become more consistent, their credibility in the buyer's mind is enhanced. IMC seeks to reduce uncertainty about risks associated with the product or idea being promoted. *Controlling the narrative* and being credible are equally important for organizations disseminating information in risk and crisis situations. As the spokespeople present their messages, reliance on credible sources will enable them to appear more consistent and a source that people can trust to provide them with accurate information.

When IMC is implemented, messages are linked and sequenced to provide reminders to the customers about updated information and special offers to guide them to the buying process. The *timeliness* of these messages serves to direct the customers to keep moving toward the completion of a transaction. In risk and crisis situations, the timeliness of the warnings and updates is equally critical in the process of informing the publics affected by the crisis about steps they should take to get out of harm's way or mitigate the impact of the situation on their lives and livelihoods.

As a final consideration, IMC eliminates duplication of effort because all elements of the promotion are shared across the organization. These elements find their way into all advertising, exhibits, and sales literature, to name a few. A single department being responsible for IMC saves money for the organization through a reduction of duplication (e.g., advertising, time spent in meetings, creative sessions, and workload). Similarly, in risk and crisis situations, saving time and effort is critical when lives are at stake. Risk and crisis communication are enhanced when all aspects of the communication messages are being coordinated and disseminated by an identified spokesperson and strategic team.

Barriers to IMC

IMC has several barriers that limit an organization's ability to successfully communicate with target audiences, including what have been called *functional silos* within the organization. Silos are artificial walls or obstacles that stifle creativity, produce conflicts, and challenge decision-makers.

Within some organizational structures, departments exist with managers who have as a primary goal the protection of their turf, including both budgets and staff. Because multiple departments are involved when IMC is implemented, if information is not shared across departments, efficiency and cost savings may not be realized. In addition, managers often do not communicate with each other to avoid giving the appearance of being influenced by someone from another department. Public relations departments may not report to marketing; while sales departments may meet with advertising staff about new promotional offers. Instead of generating creative ideas to be used across IMC, departmental staff refrain from adopting or developing ideas generated by other units for fear of appearing to lack creativity themselves.

This limitation is not unique to IMC because in risk and crisis situations, similar turf wars exist between agencies seeking to mitigate the harms of the situation. Multiple entities are involved in crisis situations, including different levels of elected government, non-profit organizations, emergency management entities, communication specialists, news agencies, health and safety offices, environmental agencies, and community action groups, to name a few. The same silos that exist in IMC can prevent crisis responders from sharing information and result in less efficiency and cost overruns. Multiple agencies make it possible for crisis managers to avoid communicating regularly or completely with each other. Without a central command to bring the involved parties to the table to develop a comprehensive strategic crisis plan of action, the impact of their collective efforts will be limited.

IMC can have the effect of stifling creativity because once the coordinated marketing plan has been agreed upon and is in place, spontaneous creativity is eliminated. Making creative adjustments to IMC limits its effectiveness because of the coordination required to convey the adjustments across the organization. For example, the spontaneity of responding to declining consumer purchases with a new promotion to boost sales would be unlikely if an overall IMC did not allow for such modification. For risk and crisis communicators, the example of an organization developing its crisis plan and then failing to use it during a crisis runs parallel with IMC. For example, just as the dynamics of consumer response may prompt a change of strategy, the dynamics of crisis situations make constant adjustments a necessity. If the crisis managers are not agile and creative in their responses to changing dynamics during a crisis, they may limit their ability to respond in ways that will have a greater impact on reducing the threats to lives and livelihoods.

Finally, a threat to the effective implementation of IMC is the lack of familiarity among managers to the concepts of coordinated marketing. Because most public relations agencies are single discipline in their focus, they lack experience across the marketing disciplines and lack commitment to implementing a way of promotion that limits their individual influence in favor of a more collective decision-making strategy. Similarly, in risk and crisis situations, individuals bring their own training and expertise into their decision-making regarding how to reach the affected publics. Communications specialists may focus on the development of the message and how it is disseminated, while emergency managers may assume that their plans will be carried out without concern for how those plans are conveyed to the publics. Developing a CC, collaborative communication and management approach to risk and crisis communication is a goal worthy of pursuing.

Implementing Integrated Marketing Communications

As with any marketing system, there are challenges to implementing IMC effectively. Similarly, risk and crisis messages to be effective must also build upon strengths while overcoming the challenges. These best practices in both contexts focus on management, organizational climate, communication strategy, budget, and customer orientation.

For IMC to succeed, senior management must believe the benefits outweigh the drawbacks. IMC requires leadership from the top that is integrated at different levels throughout the organization. Discussing integration at every meeting, whether vertically or horizontally, as well as internally or externally, the focus must be on developing a consistent message and ensuring that all groups within the organization convey the message. As crises occur, they also require decision-makers with authority to use an overarching strategy that acknowledges the tensions associated with developing and disseminating a message that can be maintained consistently within the organization at all levels, and eternally from the organization across different populations (Littlefield, 2020b).

The organizational climate for IMC to succeed must be inclusive of all units. Information must be shared across departments so that all can benefit and use it successfully. Artwork and other media must be developed together and shared in all mailings, exhibitions, press releases, websites, and even holiday cards. The brand book and design manual should be used to maintain common visual standards across all promotional materials, and internal marketing of the promotional campaign must be carefully planned and consistently reinforced. In crisis situations, all entities responding to the crisis must exhibit the trait of shared authority and cooperation to make sure that brands and information are shared to provide consistent and recognizable messages. Images and designs must be consistently used and appropriate to the publics who view them.

Developing a marketing strategy involves having clear communication objectives and position statements. The vertical integration of the corporate vision must transcend levels in the organization. Linking the core values into every message will strengthen the impact of the campaign on the publics who experience them. Controlling the narrative is an essential task that risk and crisis decision-makers must complete to assure the publics that the goal of saving lives and mitigating the crisis takes top priority. Without such a strategy, the objectives of the crisis decision-maker are unclear, and the vision is inconsistently acknowledged.

In IMC, the budgeting process for organizations always begins from a zero base because the marketing is developed for the client. Thus, with each objective comes the budget needed to accomplish the intended objectives. An awareness of the preferences of intended customers also impacts the budget to develop uniquely tailored strategies designed to gain compliance or adoption. Similarly, developing a crisis plan is necessary for the decision-maker because budget estimates can be made that are built upon achieving objectives. If disseminating information to residents in an area requires multiple modes of distribution, providing budget authority for those distribution expenses will enable an organization or community to make plans prior to a crisis to have funds when needed.

Making CC decisions in IMC keeps the customers first. By considering the stages a customer goes through before, during and after a purchase, the appropriate communication tools can be selected for each stage. The sequence of communication will guide the consumer through each stage of the purchase or adoption process. Within the risk and crisis phases, the pre-crisis phase provides warnings and instructional messages appropriate to preparing for the crisis. When the crisis presents itself, a different series of messages must be used to help publics deal with the realities of the crisis and take action to save their lives or livelihoods. Once the crisis passes, in the post-crisis phase, messages of recovery and learning provide insight into actions the publics should take to avoid experiencing similar crises in the future. The CC risk and crisis messages developed for multiple publics provide a broad range of strategies with a broad range of appeal.

Establishing a Theoretical Baseline

Understanding how organizations communicate with their publics to market their products, promote ideas, or provide information about how to prevent harm or mitigate a crisis is essential. Using relational dialectics theory (Baxter, 2006; Baxter & Montgomery, 1996), Littlefield (2020b) argued that the prioritization by decision-makers of strategic responses to perceived tensions associated with a crisis influences how messages intended to maintain positive relationships with their publics are created and disseminated. Despite the different contexts in which such relational messaging occurs, the elements in the communication model are consistent. The sender of the message must conceive, develop, and disseminate the information via available channels to receivers who identify, understand, and respond immediately through feedback to the source of the message. While this process is underway, distractions may create noise for the receiver that blocks or impedes some of the message from being conveyed successfully.

If the sender understands the audiences' needs and is aware of how cultural elements may influence the audiences' receptivity, the message will likely be perceived as relevant and, thus, more persuasive. For example, knowing when to promote a product with more overt or more subtle messages may help the sender to craft a message that is more likely to be acted upon by the receiver (Sellnow & Sellnow, 2019). If the spokesperson knows how to interpret the feedback, the message may be modified, or additional strategies may be employed to entice the receiver to act as instructed.

There are several IMC approaches used to diffuse information or products into a social system. Sellnow et al. (2009) discussed and evaluated the effectiveness of these spokesperson models. The single-step model is very direct and proceeds from the sender to the receiver. This model can be face-to-face or involve social media, as evidenced by Twitter and Instagram enabling senders to market in real time directly to consumers. When more than one person is involved in the process, the multiple-step message may be transmitted via an opinion leader, or someone who is trusted by the receiver. The sender and the opinion leader have an established relationship that enables the message to move more directly than through some other form of media. In addition to using an opinion leader, IMC relies on multiphase communications to market comprehensively through mass media.

When publics process information, they select from a variety of communication channels over time, necessitating that marketers provide information at every stage of the diffusion process across the spectrum of choices. IMC draws its advantage from coordinating the promotion of the message horizontally and vertically as earlier discussed. In the case of securing buy-in from the customer, *knowledge* or familiarity with the product or idea is necessary. Once the consumer is aware, the *persuasion* phase incorporates both interpersonal and forms of mass communication to move toward the *decision* to respond as the sender instructs. The decision is not made in a vacuum, as the consumer must *confirm* it over time as conflicting messages or experiences challenge the original decision. The *implementation* of the decision enables to consumer to bring the diffusion process to its conclusion (Rogers, 2003). While this process appears to be linear; in reality, consumers often loop back and forth between the stages based upon how they perceive the relative advantage of the product or course of action.

Knowing when and how to use communication strategies is necessary for marketers to be successful. The use of specific strategies may be more effective in different situations based upon whether raising awareness or gaining acceptance is the goal. For example, an advertisement may provide the information uniformly to all consumers, but providing a sample may be more effective in ultimately securing the adoption of the product or idea by the consumer. In crisis situations, communication may come in the pre-crisis stage as warnings about the crisis; during the crisis stage in the form of instructional communication about how to mitigate or avoid harm, or in the post-crisis stage to share information that assesses the damage, determines levels of effectiveness; and plans for future crises.

The Role of the Spokesperson

Culturally identifying with a spokesperson helps the publics connect with the need or crisis event and contributes positively to the dissemination of crisis information. Weick (1988) wrote, "[I]nitial responses do more than set the tone; they determine the trajectory of the crisis. Since people know what they have done, only after they do it, people and their actions rapidly become part of the crisis" (p. 309). We argue that relationships must be built in advance during the pre-crisis phases with members of disparate populations to avoid the miscommunications that can arise.

The position of using a spokesperson affiliated with the ethnicity of the population is supported in the literature. Littlefield and Thweatt (2004) extended the work of Arpan (2002) and found that publics felt more comfortable receiving information from a cultural agent or spokesperson when discussing information related to their health or safety. Arpan initially argued that the ethnic identity of an audience should be considered before selecting a spokesperson to maximize receptivity.

The assumption behind the single spokesperson model (figure 1.2) is that one person presenting one message will be more effective in communicating information about how to respond to a crisis. This speaker-centered approach draws strength from what Klopf (2000) termed "projective cognitive similarity," or the belief that "the person with whom we are talking perceives, judges, thinks, and reasons the same way we do" (p. 223).

This perspective provides some assurance that the public will receive a consistent message in times of crisis, which is essential for success (Rogers, 2003). While this theoretical position seems logical, in reality, it is not practical because there is not just one universal public receiving a crisis message. Instead, there are multiple publics represented by a wide range of ethnic and cultural groups who are asked to receive the cross-cultural message uniformly and respond accordingly (Perelman & Olbrechts-Tyteca, 1958/1971).

Unfortunately, due to sociocultural variables, the publics' responses are often far from uniform. Scholars in intercultural communication recognize the diversity of the multiple publics and have identified factors that affect how culturally diverse groups send and receive messages (Abramson & Moran, 2018). These factors range from macro to micro in scope, but all can change the way a crisis message is received. Since each individual culture has specific elements associated with language, the use of one crisis message transmitted across cultures is an ineffective way to motivate individuals to respond appropriately to the crisis. Language differences and styles of communication are likely to increase misunderstanding or result in

Figure 1.2   Single Spokesperson Model of Crisis Communication.

non-compliance when crisis messages are transmitted unless these variables are considered. With only the single spokesperson presenting one message cross-culturally, individuals in the different cultural groups are unlikely to respond as directed.

Samovar et al. (2014) suggested that to communicate effectively with people from diverse cultural backgrounds, an individual must have knowledge about the people from other cultures and respect for their diversity. This said, the need to rethink the single-spokesperson model of crisis communication seems apparent. Under the established model (figure 1.2), the single spokesperson presents the message to the public. Because the public is seen as a homogenous group, the single spokesperson is confident that the crisis message will be received as it is intended. The reality of multiple publics complicates this model because of the cultural variables that may influence how the crisis message is perceived and acted upon by the publics.

In figure 1.3, during the pre-crisis phase, relationships should be established with cultural agents drawn from the diverse publics who will be part of the message transmission if the risk becomes a crisis and a response is needed. The single spokesperson can still be at the center of the crisis and will likely serve as the contact person for the cultural agents who are ultimately responsible for presenting the crisis message in a meaningful way to members of their respective cultural groups. This alternative approach is audience-centered and responds to the needs of people to get information from those who seem more closely affiliated with them. We propose that when communicating with diverse publics, using multiple spokespeople who represent and speak in patterns associated with the intended audiences, and

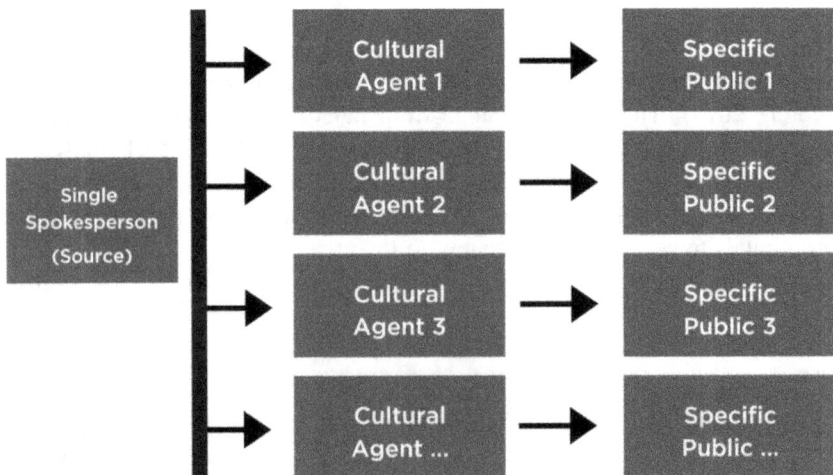

Figure 1.3 Multiple Spokesperson Model of Crisis Communication.

using language representative of these groups, will enhance the receptivity of those who receive the messages.

Interacting Arguments

While multiple spokespeople can have a positive impact when seeking to reach different groups within a social system, with more voices comes the potential for different, conflicting views. These differences may result in oppositional perspectives or arguments that must be evaluated by audiences who may not share the same level of technical expertise to recognize the merit of the information being presented. Accounting for the publics' understanding of the interacting arguments necessitates an audience-centered approach, whether through IMC or in risk or crisis messaging.

Perelman and Olbrechts-Tyteca (1958/1971) introduced the concept of interacting arguments affecting universal and particular audiences and described a means by which audiences might evaluate them. In their treatise, differentiated forms of interaction were identified, as follows: interaction occurring between arguments (e.g., X is a better solution than Y); interaction between arguments and the overall situation (e.g., X is a better solution than Y, given the current situation); interaction between arguments and their conclusion (e.g., X will achieve the preferred result more quickly than Y or other alternatives); and interaction between the arguments in the discourse with those about the discourse (e.g., X may be better solution than Y, but neither address the systemic cause of the problem). They suggested that when arguments interact, audiences or stakeholders make judgments based upon the strengths of the different arguments (e.g., source of the information, the strength of the claims, and their value).

Because opposing arguments are dynamic and shift as the argumentation proceeds, Sellnow et al. (2009) portrayed competing arguments as interacting through convergence, congruence, mutually exclusivity, or dominance. As claims are presented in the ongoing argumentation, the publics may find some merit in each of the competing arguments and be unsure about which claim is the best option. With the addition of multiple sources of information, convergence is the primary objective for organizations seeking to bring competing arguments to a single conclusion that is recognized by the publics as making sense. The convergence of competing perspectives into a coherent and cohesive argument intersects the assumptions underlying IMC. To move toward a context where potential customers collect and contemplate multiple messages about a product or idea, conflicting perspectives must converge into a single conclusion. Similarly, once that conclusion is reached, it becomes a part of the broader interaction between multiple groups who may or may not share that perspective.

Considering Culture in Crisis Stages

When decision-makers are confronted with a crisis and must decide how to respond, or businesses seek to promote a product or idea using IMC, developing a coherent message to influence publics or secure customers requires an awareness of the communication process. Messages are created and disseminated; receivers hear, interpret, and respond accordingly. The goal is to gain compliance or acceptance. When crises strike, keeping culture at the center of the decision-making process is essential because, with an audience focus, the decision-maker or communicator will tailor responses in such a way that the intender receivers of the message are willing to accept.

In the pre-crisis stage, communicators invite members of cultural groups to be part of the discussion. In this stage, there is time to develop trust and learn what the groups want or need to know, how they prefer to receive the information, and from whom. Enlisting the support of cultural agents who are already trusted by the group can enable senders to understand how messages should be presented for greatest impact. In this stage, multiple arguments are introduced, and the effective communicator will seek convergence to find the most effective means to market the information.

In the crisis stage, there is no time for trust building because messages must be presented directly, consistently, and credibly to save lives and mitigate the harms emanating from the immediacy of the crisis. Using knowledge gained during the pre-crisis stage, communicators use the trusted spokespeople and opinion leaders to convey the important information in a way that will be culturally synchronous with the preferred ways of communicating. The goal is to make sure the critical information is shared with the affected publics in such a way that they will respond and act according to what is suggested.

In the post-crisis stage, listening and responding to the cultural groups affected by the crisis is essential if organizations are going to learn how to do a better job of communicating when the next crisis occurs. Bringing members of the cultural groups or community into the decision-making process within an organization will build trust and establish credibility. Ultimately, cultural groups will be more likely to demonstrate loyalty to the organization if they believe the focus of interest for the organization is genuinely on them, rather than on itself.

SUMMARY

This chapter has revealed how dimensions of culture are reflected in the communication process and the study of IMC, as it intersects with risk and crisis communication and benefits from the inclusion of culture in the conception, dissemination, and reception of informative and persuasive risk and crisis messages. A review of related communication theories, spokesperson models, and interacting arguments provided the conceptual framework for the inclusion of culture and IMC in the advancement of effective risk and crisis communication. Our discussion of pre-crisis, crisis, and post-crisis stages supports the need to include elements of culture in the crafting and transmission of messages, as well as an understanding of cultural beliefs, values, and practices affecting the way crisis messages are received. In chapter 2, we propose our rationale for using culture to enhance the best practices of risk and crisis communication, along with a discussion of how differing worldviews may serve to mitigate the realization of strategic planning designed to save lives and livelihoods.

Chapter 2

The Cultural Imperative in Risk and Crisis Communication Best Practices

Chapter 1 focused on how interacting arguments function to develop a consistent and coherent message in IMC or in risk and crisis communication. In either case, dialogue among stakeholders must culminate to conceive an informed and mutually beneficial decision that establishes and maintains the relationship. This chapter presents risk and crisis communication best practices within the context of IMC as a framework for understanding why messages are more-or-less effective with culturally diverse groups. A common thread impacting how these messages are perceived is the influence of culture and the challenge of globalization.

INTEGRATED MARKETING COMMUNICATIONS

The four sequential stages of marketing introduced in chapter 1 lead to fully IMC. Specific steps must be taken within each of these stages to prepare the organization for promoting a product or idea to potential consumers.

Stage 1 focuses on the *tactical coordination of marketing communication* in preparing to launch the campaign. Within the organization, internal communication centers around making sure everyone knows about and understands what is being planned for the campaign for intra-organizational consistency. Horizontal coordination across departments and divisions provides coherence about what actions must be taken to prepare, disseminate, and evaluate messages for the campaign. Vertical coordination establishes the priorities associated with the promotional campaign because from the chief executive officer (CEO) to the public-facing information officer, in the tactical stage, all levels of the organization must buy into the values and priorities underlying the campaign. Because IMC may involve external entities, data need to be shared prior to launching the campaign to minimize the potential for conflicting messages. Preparing to control the narrative with a consistent promotional mix of messages is essential. With this preparation, little to no emphasis is placed on learning about the customer. Rather, the focus is quite simply on planning the campaign. Some businesses may never move beyond stage 1. That is, they may remain self-focused in an attempt to ensure that their promotional mix of communication speaks with one voice, rather than being other focused on tailoring those messages to the receivers represented in their stakeholder publics (Littlefield, 2020b).

As organizations shift their focus from self to others, they enter stage 2. In stage 2—*redefining the scope of marketing communication*—agents gather as much information as possible about customer preferences. They begin to use intelligent automation to increase efficiency and accuracy as they seek more and more information and evaluate feedback. In stage 2, a real effort is made to understand consumer dynamics and then to redefine strategies accordingly. At this point, the business also begins to reach out to other agencies that may have useful information about the customers to be integrated into the promotion of the product or idea. This alignment with other businesses or agencies serves to share resources and build brand loyalty to a range of related products or ideas.

Once the data are collected and inter-agency shared, the business is ready to move into stage 3, where the *application of information technology* is used to build larger audiences for the products or ideas being promoted. Acquiring several data sources enables businesses to create databases that can be segmented globally and maintained. With customer data available to analyze, businesses or organizations gain knowledge about the customers and can plan and implement campaigns to reach segmented groups.

As their capacity to monitor the efficiency and accuracy of automated customer databases and to process feedback from consumers grows, business executives begin to make decisions based on potential return on investment. Information and knowledge about each segmented group is used to make these strategic choices. Applying knowledge about customers or publics requires technical and financial resources, as well as reasoned executive management to be effective. In stage 4, the *financial and strategic integration* of all aspects of the campaign are constantly reviewed and revised to meet changing demand for the products or variables that previously were not identified.

When all four stages function with integrated tactical coordination, redefined scope, application of information technology, and financial and strategic management, an organization can be described as fully utilizing IMC. Next, best practices of risk and crisis communication are applied, using these stages of the IMC framework as a guide.

BEST PRACTICES OF RISK AND CRISIS COMMUNICATION

When evaluating how organizations respond to risk or crisis situations, scholars have identified practices that proved effective in mitigating negative impacts and maintaining positive relationships with relevant publics. These best practices (Seeger, 2006) drawn from previous crises provide principles for organizations to follow when facing similar situations. In addition, they form a baseline for analyzing communication strategies and informing decision-makers as they manage communication before, during, and following a crisis.

As figure 2.1 illustrates, the grouping of practices in the categories of strategic planning, proactive strategies, and strategic response loosely adhered to the pre-crisis, crisis, and post-crisis stages experienced by an organization or community facing a traumatic event. However, in reality the best practices were used as the situation called for them.

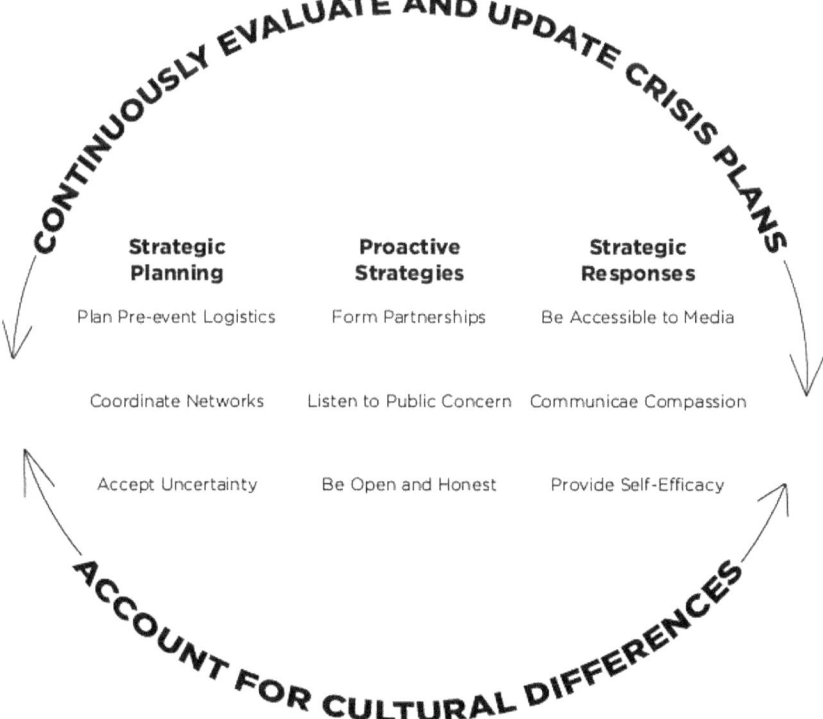

Figure 2.1 Risk and Crisis Communication Best Practices. *Source*: Seeger, 2006; Sellnow & Vidoloff, 2009.

In the pre-crisis stage, best practices associated with strategic planning include pre-event planning, coordinating networks, and accepting uncertainty. Proactive strategies involve forming partnerships, listening to public concerns, and being open and honest while communicating about the crisis. As the crisis evolves, best practices involve remaining accessible to the media, communicating with compassion and empathy, and providing suggestions for self-efficacy.

Because these practices may be relevant during more than one stage of the crisis, plans must be evaluated and updated continuously. An eleventh best practice to account for cultural differences was added later to reflect the importance of audience-focused messaging when informing or persuading the publics during a crisis (Sellnow & Vidoloff, 2009).

In 2020, the best practices were revisited by scholars seeking to determine if they remained sufficient and relevant after over a decade of application and study (Veil et al., 2020). They began with a review of the original best practices after determining that even though risk communication and crisis communication were sufficiently different in purpose and form, in the context of best practices, keeping them connected demonstrated an "inherent duality" (p. 379).

Their analysis provides a more robust description of best practices associated with the pre-crisis stage to include planning ahead for a prompt response, establishing a crisis communication network with credible sources, and accepting uncertainty and ambiguity as an inherent aspect of responding to risk and crisis situations. In the crisis stage, forming partnerships with the publics; listening to the publics' concerns; and communicating with honesty, candor, and openness remained ways to involve the publics in the communication processes throughout the crisis. As the crisis changes, meeting the needs of the media to remain accessible; communicating with compassion, concern, and honesty; and providing suggestions for self-protection reflected a more specific focus for the message's purpose. Just as Seeger (2006) suggested that crisis plans should be continuously evaluated and updated, and Sellnow and Vidoloff (2009) accounted for cultural differences, these best practices were confirmed as contributing to the creation of more effective risk and crisis communication.

In addition to confirming the validity of the initial set of best practices, Veil et al. (2020) identified several additional ones. These practices focus on prioritizing the safety and well-being of the public; tailoring messages to affected audiences and providing instruction for self-protection; acknowledging and accounting for vulnerable populations; accepting uncertainty and avoiding public speculation; and completing and communicating recovery efforts. Prioritizing the safety and well-being of endangered publics is an aspect of the tensions of strategic communication decision-making that encourages decision-makers to be other-focused throughout the crisis to assure publics that their interests are the priority (Littlefield, 2020b).

To reflect a CC perspective, messages must be tailored and include instructions for self-protection and have input from members of the affected publics (Littlefield, 2013). Moreover, acknowledging vulnerable groups as encompassing more than race, ethnicity, language, and religion is critical (e.g., socio-economic status, physical ability, technology access, and education level) to success. The practice of avoiding speculation was integrated with accepting uncertainty to become an enhanced best practice because of the effects unsubstantiated information can have on the perceptions of those receiving the messages. Finally, recovery efforts should be completed and communicated to bring closure for publics who experienced the crisis.

To reframe the best practices, Veil et al. (2020) compiled 15 Essential Guidelines for Ongoing Risk and Crisis Communication. These guidelines are grouped into four areas that clarify how decision-makers should communicate. The first group includes practices to prepare prior to the crisis. Strategic planning includes, for example, preparing ahead for a prompt response, establishing a crisis communication network, and prioritizing the safety and well-being of the public. The second area is very audience-focused in that it addresses the need for inclusivity by listening to public concerns, acknowledging and accounting for vulnerable populations, acknowledging and accounting for cultural differences, forming partnerships with the public, meeting the needs of the media, and remaining accessible to the media. Next, the sender-focused strategies demonstrate responsible communication by accepting uncertainty and avoiding public speculation, providing instructions for self-protection, tailoring messages to affected audiences, communicating with honesty, candor, and openness, and communicating with compassion, concern, and empathy. Guidelines in the fourth area focus on completing and communicating recovery efforts and continuously evaluating and updating crisis plans. In this post-crisis phase, these guidelines reflect the learning that occurred to be better prepared for the next crisis.

COMPARING STAGES OF IMC WITH BEST PRACTICES

Strategic Planning and Stage 1 Tactical Coordination of Marketing Communication

The best practices associated with strategic planning are applicable to what occurs during stage 1 of the IMC process, where organizations are pulling together the resources in preparation for a coordinated campaign. In table 2.1, the characteristics of the two stages reflect a similar focus. The best practice

Table 2.1 Comparison of Strategic Planning Best Practices with Stage 1 of Integrated Marketing Communications

Strategic Planning	Stage 1—Tactile Coordination of Marketing Coordination
Plan for a prompt response	Horizontal integration
Establish a communication crisis network	Internal coordination
Establish a communication crisis network	External coordination
Prioritize the safety and well-being of the public	Vertical integration

of planning ahead involves confirming that all departments across the organization are familiar with and ready to share information and proceed in the presentation of a coordinated and coherent marketing campaign. To establish a crisis communication network, communication within the organization must be coordinated so that all messages reflect the core themes of the marketing campaign. Similarly, making connections with external entities that may contribute to the campaign either directly or indirectly is necessary to adhere to the best practice of establishing a crisis communication network. The additional best practice of prioritizing the safety and well-being of the public is reflected in the need for vertical integration on stage 1 of IMC. The values of the company must be initiated from the leadership and move through every level of management and to every member. Prioritizing the safety and well-being of the public is other-focused. The tension of focus of interest faces every decision-maker (Littlefield, 2020b) and makes vertical integration essential if this priority is going to be coherently and consistently communicated to customers or publics.

Inclusive Approach and Stage 2 Redefining the Scope of Marketing Communication

For the best practices associated with what Veil et al. (2020) describe as an inclusive approach, a CC perspective must guide the best practices associated with stage 2 of IMC shown in table 2.2.

To listen to concerns and form partnerships with the public, businesses using IMC must seek public information and evaluate feedback from the public to tailor their marketing message in such a way that customers will recognize and respond positively. Partnerships formed with publics prior to a crisis lead to more effective communication during a crisis. However, these relationships must continue throughout a crisis and be inclusive of publics' perceptions as they change during a crisis. Arnett et al. (2017) see this dimension of crisis communication as a negotiation among stakeholders to collectively create "mutually creative solutions" (p. 28). Seeking and evaluating

Table 2.2 Comparison of Inclusive Approach Best Practices with Stage 2 of Integrated Marketing Communications

Inclusive Approach	Stage 2—Redefining the Scope of Marketing Communication
Listen to public concerns	Seek public information and evaluate feedback
Forming partnerships with the public	Seek public information and evaluate feedback
Meet the needs of the media and remaining accessible	Seek public information and evaluate feedback
Acknowledge and account for vulnerable populations	Consumer research of customer preferences
Acknowledge and account for vulnerable populations	Intelligent automation of information processing
Acknowledge and account for cultural differences	Consumer research of customer preferences
Acknowledge and account for cultural differences	Intelligent automation of information processing

feedback is how organizational leaders include consumer preferences in IMC. Littlefield (2020b) confirmed this conclusion, suggesting that decision-makers who modify their communication with publics as the dynamics of a crisis change are more successful in maintaining their relationship with publics.

The need to remain accessible and provide media with information was one of the best practices identified by Seeger (2006). Being responsive to media as a partner in the process of disseminating messages during a campaign or crisis helps organizations control the narrative. When media trust the source of the information that is needed by publics to respond as encouraged or directed, they will return to that primary source and be able to disregard messages coming from less trusted sources. This represents a flow from source through media to publics.

When Veil et al. (2020) identified partnerships with the media as part of an inclusive approach to risk and crisis communication, they broadened the inclusion to be more than that of a pre-crisis arrangement. Instead, they suggested that media must remain included throughout the duration of the campaign or crisis. When considering this within stage 2 of IMC, as organizations or businesses seek information about publics and consumers, they use media as sources providing consumer information and insight into the cultural preferences needed for organizations to develop their marketing or crisis messages.

Veil et al. (2020) also emphasize acknowledging vulnerable populations. While consumer research of customer preferences in stage 2 provides decision-makers with insight about which vulnerable populations may be part of their consumer base, the need for organizational leaders to acknowledge and communicate through vertical integration why the most vulnerable publics should be accounted for is necessary. In contrast, to acknowledge and account for cultural differences, decision-makers must enact horizontal integration to ensure that the strategic messages embedded within the marketing reflect the cultural differences identified through the extended information gathering during this stage of IMC.

Responsible Communication and Stage 3 Application of Information Technology

The guidelines for responsible communication as essential best practices (Veil et al., 2020) are source-centered in that they focus on what decision-makers should consider when developing and marketing their communication plans. Doing so requires decision-makers to apply what they know to achieve maximum effectiveness. As depicted in table 2.3, this corresponds directly with stage 3 of IMC because in this phase, the data acquired in stage 2 is built into globally segmented databases that are used to plan and implement communication strategies to market the ideas or crisis messages.

Organizations that take their role to provide information seriously adhere to the best practice of tailoring messages to affected audiences. When receivers fail to see the relevance of messages, they will disregard them, which may lead to negative outcomes. One way to convey relevance in IMC is by segmenting the database as messages are conceived and developed.

Table 2.3 Comparison of Responsible Communication Best Practices with Stage 3 Integrated Marketing Communications

Responsible Communication	Stage 3—Application of Information Technology
Tailor messages to affected audiences	Create segmented databases
Tailor messages to affected audiences	Plan integrated marketing campaign
Communicate with compassion, concern, and empathy	Implement integrated marketing campaign
Provide instruction for self-protection	Implement integrated marketing campaign
Communicate with honesty, candor, and openness	Implement integrated marketing campaign
Accept uncertainty and avoid public speculation	Analyze data
Accept uncertainty and avoid public speculation	Plan integrated marketing campaign
Accept uncertainty and avoid public speculation	Implement integrated marketing campaign

The responsible best practices for crisis spokespersons include communicating with compassion, concern, and empathy; communicating with honesty, candor, and openness; and providing instruction for self-protection. Compassion, concern, and empathy focus on sender attributes. If the corporate image is other-centered, the message will use language and images that are familiar and relevant to their audiences. Honesty, candor, and openness are source-specific in that they reveal the true character of the sender of the message. Spokespersons present their messages in such a way that audiences perceive them as being honest and open. When providing instructions for self-protection, organizations are well-served when they identify cultural agents or opinion leaders to actually convey them (e.g., a religious leader provides instructions to members of the congregation). In IMC, these best practices correspond with the implementation of marketing strategies because they occur as part of the dynamic process of disseminating the messages to customers and publics.

In the attempt, overtly admitting and accepting uncertainty is also a best practice to avoid public speculation and reduce confusion at a time when lives may be at stake (Veil et al., 2020). Stage 3 of IMC calls for analysis, planning, and implementation. These three steps enable decision-makers to build into their messages those elements that acknowledge only what is both known and unknown, along with a pledge to share additional information as it is discovered.

Corrective Action and Stage 4 Financial and Strategic Integration

The final group of risk and crisis communication best practices focuses on corrective action. This group corresponds with stage 4 of IMC, which is identified as financial and strategic integration (see table 2.4). Essentially, organizations can illustrate what and how they learned from the crisis regarding steps they will take to avoid similar crises or mitigate harm in the future.

Finally, effective communication also involves completing and communicating recovery efforts as a means to bring closure to a crisis event (Veil et al., 2020). Within IMC, as organizations move toward fully integrated marketing, decision-makers engage in monitoring performance on

Table 2.4 Comparison of Corrective Action Best Practices with Stage 4 Integrated Marketing Communications

Corrective Action	Stage 4—Financial and Strategic Integration
Complete and communicate recovery efforts	Monitor performance
Continuously evaluate and update crisis plans	Global evaluation of each segment served

a Return-On-Investment (ROI) basis. Another aspect of taking corrective action is the need for crisis managers to continuously evaluate and update their crisis plans to make sure that what was learned in a previous crisis has been used to modify past practices and update future plans. This monitoring and modification of plans corresponds with what IMC decision-makers must face when evaluating from a global perspective if each segment of the audience responded as expected and if the organization provided each segment with what was needed in order to achieve a successful marketing outcome.

Summary of Comparisons

This previous comparison of best practices (Seeger, 2006) or essential guidelines (Veil et al., 2020) with the stages of IMC is appropriate because IMC combines, integrates, and synergizes elements of marketing that generates a greater impact in a cost-effective manner (Kitchen et al., 2004). When risk and crisis communicators consider tensions associated with strategic decision-making, they also must employ practices that are most likely to produce the best results when developing and disseminating messages to save lives and livelihoods. IMC works backward from the customer to the organization to determine "the forms and methods through which persuasive communications programs should be developed" (Schultz, 1993, p. 17). Similarly, CC risk and crisis communication begins when publics are involved in all stages of message creation and dissemination. Clearly, using the stages of IMC to identify the chronological application of best practice guidelines provides for a more coordinated approach to achieving desired outcomes. However, what remains is an examination of how the culture impacts risk and crisis communication created using an IMC approach.

THE IMPACT OF CULTURE

Culture is ubiquitous and influences every aspect of life (Hofstede, 2001). A useful taxonomy for considering how culture impacts communication includes our code systems, our relationship and intent toward others, whether we know or accept the normative beliefs and values of those around us, and our worldviews. While each one influences how publics respond to risk and crisis messages, the worldviews of publics receiving risk and crisis messages carry the most weight because how individuals regard their agency to control the world around them may determine their receptivity to a message. The worldviews that determine agency relevant to this context include progressive, fatalistic, and holistic approaches.

First, publics with a progressive worldview have the most agency. These individuals have an "independent view of self" (Vignoles et al., 2016), believe that they can determine what happens to them, and put their welfare in the number one position. They view themselves as separate from others and prioritize themselves over others (Markus & Kitayama, 1991). If they feel insecure about where they live, they move to a new location. If they are unsure about how to do something, they seek out information or take a class. If the risk of a hurricane exists, they develop plans to stockpile the resources they will need to take care of themselves if utilities or services are not available for an extended period time. They regard themselves as self-reliant and individualistic (Triandis, 1993). Risk and crisis messages directed to individuals with progressive worldviews are likely to be met with receptivity because they see themselves as capable of managing their own affairs, and in their own self-interest, they will want to be sure they have what they need to survive the crisis.

Second, publics with a fatalistic worldview are unlikely to believe they have the agency to protect themselves. The origins of a fatalistic worldview come from the development of religious and philosophical thought and are reflected in cultural contexts (Solomon, 2003). Individuals who subscribe to a fatalistic worldview "believe that their destinies are ruled by an unseen power or are played out inevitably rather than by their will" (Maercker, 2019). They are influenced by their circumstances and often believe, "that's just the way it is." Fatalism also is perpetuated if efforts to change the circumstances have met with previous failed attempts. When the locus of control over what happens in life is believed to be out of reach, individuals must focus on living in the present. This makes responding positively to risk and crisis messages irrelevant because nothing they do will make a difference. The instructional risk and crisis messages may be received but will result in inaction.

Finally, publics that have a holistic worldview believe they have the agency to protect themselves and are concerned for the agency of others (Markus & Kitayama, 1991). They embody a collectivist worldview and value the welfare of all over self-preservation (Triandis, 1993). An element of self-sacrifice is inherent in this worldview because of the shared benefit necessary for all to be served. From a practical perspective, acting for the benefit of all influences the agency used by these individuals. For example, instead of stockpiling resources for their own benefit, they collaborate to make sure those resources are spread around, providing some level of security to the entire community. They see themselves as able to help those who lack the agency to act for themselves to protect their homes or property and they feel a commitment to others (Vignoles et al., 2016). This holistic worldview brings a practical orientation to problem-solving and shared decision-making.

Risk and crisis messages presented to publics with a holistic worldview are likely to be received and will be acted upon collectively for the greater good.

The examples of progressive, fatalistic, and holistic worldviews bring into focus how decision-makers must alter risk and crisis messages to achieve desired outcomes. The culture of publics with progressive worldviews are more likely to receive instructional risk messages positively and act upon them once they perceive the risk or crisis to be a threat to them or their livelihood. The certainty associated with the content of these messages and the credibility of the decision-maker controlling the narrative will influence those with progressive worldviews to act.

Those individuals with a fatalistic worldview are unlikely to act when receiving instructional risk messages because of their willingness to accept their fate, thus negating the need to exercise agency. The fatalistic worldview poses challenges for the communicator who will need to engage cultural agents or opinion leaders who are trusted to provide additional credibility for the message. If religious or spiritual leaders are included as part of the communication team, there may be a greater chance to influence followers to do what is asked of them. Showing empathy and sincerely reflecting other-serving focus will be needed to influence skeptical publics from challenging their fatalistic worldview. In addition, because the fatalist worldview keeps the focus of individuals on the present, communicators may find this group to be more responsive during the actual crisis because of the immediacy of the situation.

For those with a holistic worldview, instructional messages are likely to be met with receptivity because individuals have the agency to take steps to protect themselves. Just as with the creation of messages for those with the progressive worldview, when informing or persuading people with the holistic worldview, communicators must control the narrative and provide credible and timely information; and, to be most effective, communicators also must include other-serving messages because looking out for the welfare of the community will reinforce them to act. In addition, showing empathy for those who lack agency will enhance the effectiveness of risk and crisis messages.

Through the identification of these three worldviews, we have demonstrated how publics may be predisposed to perceiving and responding to crisis messages. However, it is important to note that even though worldviews may be shared by individuals within a social system, "individuals within the same system may adopt very different ways of fulfilling these broad 'cultural mandates'" (Vignoles et al., 2016, p. 969). Therefore, a CC approach to creating, disseminating, and receiving messages must be used. This approach will be sensitive to the differences inherent in publics receiving the messages and allow for individual responses based upon cultural orientations.

SUMMARY

Risk communicators seek to engage publics in interactive arguments to arrive at an informed and mutually beneficial decision to avoid a crisis. Crisis communicators strive to persuade publics to respond in a way that will prevent, mitigate, or manage a crisis. This chapter provided the best practices of risk and crisis communication within the context of IMC to provide a framework for understanding why messages are more-or-less effective with culturally diverse groups of people. The common thread of culture explains how worldviews can influence the way publics may be predisposed to perceiving and responding to crisis messages.

In chapter 3, the CC model of risk and crisis communication is introduced, along with the three crises that will be used to illustrate its components. As the fundamental assumptions and functions of the model are developed, the usefulness of considering cultural variables in risk and crisis communication is revealed.

Chapter 3

Building the Cultural Model of Risk and Crisis Communication

The previous chapter described the risk and crisis best practices and essential guidelines within the context of IMC to provide a framework for understanding why messages are more-or-less effective with culturally diverse groups of people. Culture is the common thread impacting how these messages are ultimately perceived. Thus, this chapter introduces a CC model of risk and crisis communication. More specifically, the CN, CS, and CC approaches are each defined followed by a discussion of fundamental assumptions, functions, and examples. In addition, each approach is clarified by applying it to one of three actual crisis cases.

THE CULTURE-CENTERED APPROACH

The role culture plays in effective communication has received increasing attention in recent years. This is particularly true in the context of risk and crisis situations. To be effective, these messages must be created, disseminated, interpreted, and acted upon by publics that may not share the same norms and values as those sending them. In essence, audience-focused communication is more effective than sender-focused communication in gaining compliance as participants grapple with tensions of strategic decision-making (Littlefield, 2020b). Despite the intuitive connection between audience-focused messages and positive outcomes, risk and crisis communication scholars and practitioners have traditionally prioritized a focus on the source of the message and have taken for granted that publics will interpret the situation as the crisis expert does. In other words, both scholars and practitioners have been too ethnocentric in their approach (Claeys & Schwarz, 2016). Ethnocentric messages tend to avoid cultural differences by denying their existence, raising defenses against them, or minimizing their importance (Bennett, 1993). The message source is placed at the center of the spheres as knowing the facts, with assumptions about the nature and severity of the crisis, and the application of potential solutions based upon the source's viewpoint. Other perspectives are marginalized as ethnocentric decision-makers justify choices based upon their own perception of what they believe is the best way to communicate.

The CC model is offered here to challenge this ethnocentric orientation of decision-makers by confronting the top-down perspectives reflected in message creation without taking into consideration the cultural dimensions of how those messages are received. This approach also confronts the erroneous assumption that publics are unwilling to take action to protect themselves in times of crisis. Noncompliance may not be due to apathy or even to a sense of not having the agency to act. The reason may be a result of different priorities based on unique cultural norms that would be violated if the actions conveyed in the crisis message were followed. For example, being instructed to engage in self-protective actions on a holy day could result in individuals choosing to follow their religious beliefs instead of the call to save themselves in a crisis. This reluctance to act may not make sense to the source of the message, who views self-preservation as essential to life; but for the receivers, the value conflict is real and complicates their willingness to comply.

CC approaches to communication are not unique to risk and crisis. Dutta (2008) introduced this approach in the context of health communication by focusing on how diverse publics assign meaning to health messages. Dutta considered the intersection of structure, culture, and agency as creating "openings for listening to the voices of marginalized communities, constructing discursive spaces which interrogate the erasures in marginalized settings and offer opportunities for co-constructing the voices of those who have been traditionally silenced by engaging them in dialogue" (p. 5). Essentially, in the context of health, social structures often limit the choices available to individuals seeking access to the services; culture provides the dynamic framework for conveying meaning about what and how to deal with matters related to the maintenance of health, and agency refers to the active capacity of individuals to act and negotiate the structures in which they live. Dutta concluded that structure, culture, and agency are intertwined because structures function in culturally situated contexts in communities, and agency is enacted as individuals struggle with the structures they face. When health messages are issued to publics, the established structures hinder individuals from accessing the necessary services they need to comply with the instructional messages being issued. The cultural context marginalizes individuals outside of the structures, limiting their agency to comply or take steps to protect their own or their family's health.

Dutta (2008) suggested that power, marginalization, context, stories, and resistance are key concepts that define the CC approach in health communication. *Power* is connected to the dominant actors who control the "discursive spaces supportive of the control they hold" (p. 13). Those who send messages have power over those who receive the messages. *Marginalization* occurs for publics who have limited access to resources and lack access "mainstream communication platforms on which they could articulate their questions and concerns" (p. 13). The *context* refers to the local situation and the lived experiences of the community members that are often overlooked by those disseminating messages proscribing actions that may be out of step with their lived experiences in the community. For Dutta, *stories*, "offer insights into the ways in which culture constitutes its meaning" (p. 14) and draw attention to how individuals continue and are transformed by experiences and events. *Resistance* reflects the ways the dominant structures and messages are challenged. Examples include not following directions, refusing to comply, protesting, and creating alternative ways of being outside of the formal structures.

These cultural concepts are relevant to risk and crisis situations. The ethnocentric approach inherently reflects the power assigned to the source of the message. The ability of the source to construct the message conveys power over the audiences who must receive and respond to it. The systems accessible to the message source provide additional power and imply that the message is accurate and pertinent to those who receive it. Those who have been marginalized due to socioeconomic factors or limited access to the media—used by those with the power to choose the channel for conveying the message—find themselves with less power and at greater risk of harm. The context shapes how receivers experience life and view their place in society. Failure to comply with messages instructing them to act may be ignored because they do not address the real needs and priorities that run counter to the ethnocentric values held by the spokesperson. When a crisis occurs and individuals do not respond to warnings as instructed, the resistance may come in the form of placing blame on the agency or organization for not listening to the needs of the public or for not showing empathy with the circumstances in which they live. Thus, the intersection of culture with communication reveals the strengths and limitations of approaches taken by decision-makers in organizations as they create, disseminate, and respond to messages in a crisis situation. The following sections describe three different communication approaches illustrating this connection with culture: CN, CS, and CC communication.

Culture-Neutral Communication

When a spokesperson is called upon to provide instructions to protect lives or mitigate harms, the CN approach dictates that the message should focus on verifiable facts and instructions that objectively stand as truths without exceptions. The underlying assumption in a CN approach is that instructional messages for preserving livelihoods and saving lives should be factually accurate and value neutral. In other words, cultural norms and perspectives are intentionally excluded (Haskell, 1990). Doing so creates a perception of objectivity and if all subjectivity is excluded—making the message neutral to all cultures—they can speak effectively to a universal audience (Perelman & Olbrechts-Tyteca, 1958/1971).

CN communication assumes the message will be based entirely on objective information and, thus, not subject to interpretation (Reiss & Sprenger, 2014). Facts are facts, and the assumption of objectivity portrays facts as positive. Those who value objectivity believe that more is better; that is, because facts are not subject to interpretation, the message can be trusted (Rykiel, 2001). CN communication is viewed as positive because of its universal applicability. Those who use CN communication assume that including cultural content would weaken the message because content reliability is challenged by the subjective interpretation of the facts. When considering the key concepts associated with communication directed at particular audiences (Perelman & Olbrechts-Tyteca, 1958/1971), a more robust understanding of CN communication is revealed.

In CN communication, the sender has the *power* in the relationship because the acceptance of facts as objective and the exclusion of cultural considerations places publics in the position of having to interpret the message through the sender's cultural context. The belief that objective facts are most persuasive and that adding cultural content weakens the message is itself a cultural value, negating the neutrality the label suggests. The language used by the sender reflects the power of the dominant cultural group. Even though the intent of the sender may be honorable, the intent may be interpreted as insensitive and even hurtful if target audiences do not interpret its meaning as intended. The exclusion of cultural dimensions in message creation limits the likelihood for shared understanding and interpretation. Even the sender of a CN message's worldview implies a power relationship because the message is intended to instruct or activate other people to do something. If individuals hearing the message adhere to a different worldview, they may reject the message as being irrelevant, the actions as impossible to accomplish, or the outcome as unattainable.

The values and beliefs of the publics receiving the CN message place them in a marginalized position. *Marginalization* occurs when publics are underserved and have been denied access to resources and opportunities to participate in decision-making (Dutta, 2008). Marginalized groups may speak a different language or multiple languages, live in close proximity to others who share their language(s), and subscribe to the collectivist characteristic of looking out for the group, rather than for themselves as individuals (Hofstede, 2001; Triandis, 1993). Marginalized publics may not trust messages conveyed by people representing the dominant culture if their previous experiences were negative. Ignoring cultural dimensions in the message content or distribution limits publics from understanding whether the dominant culture knows and accepts the values held by the marginalized group. For example, when the spokesperson disseminates what is believed to be a CN message but does so on a day that is sacred to members of the marginalized group, publics likely will assign negative attributes to the spokesperson and to the message. The worldview of the dominant culture to instruct or influence the marginalized culture to take necessary action reflects the power structure inherent in the relationship. Once the worldview of the dominant culture has been imposed, the marginalized publics are more likely to disregard the message intended to be helpful.

Target audiences may also perceive the *context* of the risk or crisis differently from that of the entity in power who is communicating using a CN orientation. To clarify, they interpret the context through a lens reflecting their worldview. Thus, the communicator framing a seemingly CN message believes members of the diverse publics simply need to follow the instructions as directed to mitigate the potentially harmful effects of the crisis. The CN (a.k.a. objective) message tells this group what they need to know, and they proceed to follow instructions to protect themselves. They are progressive, proactive, and self-focused. This may contradict the lived experiences of marginalized publics who may not have the resources or agency to follow the instructions as directed. The relational history the marginalized publics have with the CN spokesperson may also impact how they respond. If marginalized groups view the entity through their lived experience of being excluded from assistance during a previous crisis or provided less-than-adequate support, this predisposition will likely affect how they perceive the message in the current context. History may also reflect the level of acceptance marginalized publics received within the dominant community where they reside. Being placed in a relationship where marginalized publics are expected to act in one way while publics aligned with the dominant perspective are privileged to act in a different way may affect how messages are received. The context may bring the conflicting lived experiences into focus and influence the receptivity of both universal and particular audiences to the CN message.

In CN communication, the sender controls message content and the *stories* included tend to reflect ethnocentric perspectives. Sharing stories of lived experiences provides insight into the cultural perspectives of those involved. As stories are co-created, they provide meaning and have an impact on how participants respond. If participants identify with the stories and content in the messages, they will be more likely to internalize the message (Littlefield et al., 2014). However, when messages are stripped of culture, they lose the element of storytelling other than to reflect the perspective of the spokesperson. The use of objective language in CN communication minimizes the use of word choices reflecting the cultural nuances of the receiving publics. While excluding these personal references and familiar stories reflecting life experiences may be intended to convey cultural neutrality; in fact, the exclusion of the real stories of people impacted by a crisis may be perceived by publics as hostile because no effort is made to establish a personal relationship. Without stories to create meaning in a crisis, decision-makers convey their lack of knowledge about those being affected by the public. Without shared knowledge, the intended outcomes may be impeded, and lives and livelihoods will be at stake. Stories reflecting the worldview of the teller provide only one perspective of a crisis, leaving those who do not share that worldview with options unavailable to mitigate or protect them.

Unlike the other elements, *resistance* in CN communication has its locus of control with the receiver. Resistance, by its nature, reflects practices that challenge the control of the dominant perspective. For example, when communicators suggest strategies requiring the expenditure of funds to prepare for or mitigate a crisis, the lack of discretionary income to purchase the items needed to protect their safety may result in resistance as marginalized publics challenge the feasibility of spending their limited funds to prepare for what is being described as a risk or crisis, that may or may not be an actual danger or threat to life. Dutta (2008) described micro-processes and macro-processes of resistance. Micro-processes represented resistance offered by individuals, such as not responding as instructed to a crisis message. Individuals make independent decisions based upon their own circumstances. Macro-processes involved systemic, transformative action taken by groups, such as rallies, protests, or marches, to demonstrate resistance. Because of the immediacy associated with crises to the lives and livelihoods of those affected, micro-processes of resistance are more likely to occur in the pre-crisis and crisis stages, while macro-processes are more likely to occur in the post-crisis environment as communities assess the damages they experienced and prepare for future crises. Resistance may be directed at the content and language of the message, the manner of its dissemination, or the actions suggested to mitigate or reduce harm. If the relationship between the entity presenting a crisis message and the publics receiving the message has been influenced by previous contact, neutral messages may be perceived as ingenuine and lacking empathy. Without an indication that the spokesperson knows and understands the reality-facing marginalized publics, the resistance may hinder the spread of the message intended to protect the lives of those affected by the crisis. Because the worldview of the spokesperson emanates from a position of control, publics lacking all other aspects of agency may be left with only their decision to ignore or resist the CN messages.

In summary, CN communication originates from the perspective that objectivity gives weight to messages intended to convey instructions via facts about how to save lives in times of crisis. To suppress subjectivity, entities design their messages for the universal audience. However, the reality of the situation in times of crisis is such that multiple publics exist within the universal audience. These particular audiences view messages according to the categories associated with who controls the power, how marginalized publics are engaged, the context of the situation, how stories are used in the identification and meaning-making process, and the agency publics have as receivers of crisis messages. By keeping communication free from cultural subjectivity, the process is sender-oriented and likely to be resisted or ignored. To address this challenge, communicators have taken steps to examine cultures and identify characteristics of culture that will enhance the receptivity of their messages.

Culturally Sensitive Communication

CS communication provides for the integration of cultural characteristics, preferences, and stories into the processes of message creation, dissemination, and reception. Cultural sensitivity reflects an awareness that similarities and differences exist between cultural groups. In the context of communication, being culturally sensitive allows the message source to move from an ethnocentric orientation to one that acknowledges the benefits of accounting for how different groups may perceive messages differently. However, as Dutta (2008) suggests, the CS approach is built upon the contrast between the *expert* position and the *object* position. That is, the *expert* source of the message has the tools and knowledge to study the targeted cultural group and determine the best methods for creating CS content and disseminating messages that will achieve the intended outcomes. Inherent in this process is the cognitive bias of the source to determine what characteristics will be thought to be most effective. The *object* position in this relationship is represented by the marginalized cultural groups receiving the message. The taken-for-granted assumption of the CS approach is that culture is static and if certain cultural preferences or characteristics are addressed by the source of the message, the individuals of that culture receiving the message will recognize those cultural markers and be more responsive.

CS communication creates the appearance of adapting to the needs and preferences of specific cultural groups who are the objects of focus. Factors may influence this adaptation, including choice of language, understanding established relationships between groups, acknowledgment of beliefs and values, and consideration of competing worldviews. For example, if cultural groups speaking a second language are included in the audience, providing messages in the second language may represent sensitivity to those groups, garnering a positive response. However, printing messages in the second language may be ineffective if the individuals speak the language but do not read it. Using a spokesperson from the same ethnicity as the cultural group being addressed may be viewed as CS because of the identification that may occur. However, a spokesperson may reflect regional differences, socioeconomic status, and education levels, limiting effectiveness. The ability of the spokesperson to seek common ground with competing beliefs and values is further complicated by the tension between ethnocentricity and ethno-relativity. In the creation of CS content, the spokesperson, by virtue of having the power to construct the message, will select those beliefs and values reflecting the ethnocentric perspective. Acceptance and integration of alternative beliefs and values held by diverse publics is unlikely without considering alternative ways to accomplish the outcome of saving lives and livelihoods that will be more acceptable. For example, persuading American Indian women to seek preventive care for cancer in certain Nations was ineffective until the alternative value of remaining healthy to take care of the family was introduced. The adoption of the holistic worldview that expanded a broader concern for the community—in this case, the families of these American Indian women—reflected a more inclusive and collectivistic perspective that appealed to the audience (Littlefield et al., 2007).

The locus of *power* in the CS approach rests with the sender because the content is selected based on what is thought to be most significant or what will provide the greatest influence on the receivers. The decision-maker considers the static categories of the culture (e.g., language, ethnicity, religion, and worldview) and identifies the strategy to be used (e.g., choice of language, identification of spokesperson, timing, and nature and purpose of life). The process is transactional because the decision-maker makes choices based upon what is expected to be the appropriate response. The expectation of the relationship from the sender's perspective is such that if the sender shows cultural sensitivity, the receiver should recognize that sensitivity and respond accordingly. While the receiver is the object of the transaction, the choice of which cultural beliefs, values, and characteristics to emphasize or highlight remains with the source of the message. The worldview of the sender retains the agency to make the decisions about what should be most effective with the targeted publics.

The object of the CS communication addresses *marginalization*; that is, the marginalized public experiencing the risk or crisis. Within any crisis, multiple marginalized groups are underserved or underrepresented in their communities. Deciding which marginalized groups to identify or focus on in a crisis is controlled by the decision-maker who examines the context to determine where the greatest need or threat exists. Recognizing the marginalized groups through cultural content reflects sensitivity to language, relationships, values, and worldview of those groups, but the sender remains in the position to include or exclude groups, depending upon history, personal contacts, or individual preferences.

Regarding *context*, to be culturally sensitive, communicators must broaden their awareness of the lived experiences of individuals who are experiencing the crisis. This involves an investigation by the decision-maker to gather what is considered relevant information to inform the decision about how to address the crisis with the multiple publics in the context. Once marginalized individuals and groups are identified, decision-makers must expand their spheres of ethnocentricity to move beyond their own experiences to include those of their publics in the process of context construction (Littlefield, 2013). The result of this expansion is a shared context and engaging with publics where they live and how they experience crises provides for a more robust context. The intersection of what constitutes the reality between the expert and the object results in messages that are acknowledged as being sensitive to cultural considerations but not fully accepting of an integrated perspective where both groups share in the creation of meaning.

The messages of CS risk and crisis communicators must include the *stories* of the marginalized publics that have been added to the source's spheres of ethnocentricity. These stories, once introduced into the public discourse about the crisis, provide reliability and salience for the spokesperson because of their authenticity and relevance to the publics receiving the messages (Persuit, 2013). Cultural groups pass along stories that represent their communication practices (e.g., how they prefer to receive messages, when they prefer to receive messages, from whom they prefer to receive messages, where they prefer to receive messages). Their stories offer lessons regarding what messages were effective and ineffective, and why. While the decision-maker controls which cultural stories are utilized, the appeal to diverse publics may be enhanced when cultural content is added to the risk or crisis message.

Just as with CN communication, *resistance* to CS communication comes from the message receivers because the decision to act is left to them. While it is less likely that marginalized groups will resist messages that have been constructed to be CS, the potential for pushback exists nonetheless. For example, while American Indian Elders are respected across all tribal groups, their ability to influence often extends to the limits of their own tribal nation. Deciding to ask one Tribal Elder to speak to several American Indian communities representing different tribal nations would be unlikely to be considered as CS (Littlefield et al., 2006).

In summary, CS communication originates from the desire of the communicator to make risk or crisis messages more appealing and persuasive to diverse publics to save lives and livelihoods and to mitigate the harmful effects of a crisis. Through an examination of the publics that may be affected by a risk or crisis, decision-makers are in a position to determine which characteristics of the culture should be used as content in the instructional communication to make it more responsive and appealing to those who must understand and use the information. The sender has the power to make these content decisions based upon which marginalized publics are most affected. The context is shared because the decision-maker cannot construct content without experiencing the lived reality of the marginalized publics included in their spheres of ethnocentricity. Stories are shared by the publics with the sender to create meaningful content that is relevant and appealing. Resistance remains in the control of the publics who receive the messages and determine if the CS content reflects their beliefs, values, and worldview. The progression toward inclusivity is best exemplified in the CC model of communication that follows.

Culture-Centered Communication

The CC approach to communication is characterized as audience focused and dependent upon the inclusion of individuals from the community as full partners in the decision-making process. Because culture is constructed by its members, when representatives of the cultural groups share in the process of message creation and dissemination, the intersection of these differing perspectives produces a new, shared culture. Dutta (2008) offered characteristics of the CC approach that contributed to the full engagement of diverse groups in the construction of meaning on health in health communication. These characteristics include voice and dialogue, structure, context and space, values, and criticism; and their inclusion in this discussion of power, marginalization, context, stories, and resistance is helpful when describing CC risk and crisis communication.

When members of diverse publics are included as part of the communication team in the message creation and dissemination process, the decision-maker enters into a commitment with the marginalized publics to do more than hear their *voices and engage in dialogue* about how to create effective CC communication. They are co-equal in the decision-making process and their *power* is shared. The introduction of these diverse voices informs how risk and crisis messages are understood and acted upon by members of the community. By engaging in dialogue, new ways of conveying messages are identified and utilized. No longer are members of publics excluded from decision-making and a legitimate space for dialogue is created. Through this space, all members can identify the intent of the other and develop relationships where a helpful intent is recognized. The relationships that develop contribute to all members knowing the beliefs and values of the other, thereby enabling them to accept alternative perspectives. Including diverse publics gives them agency through their voice and dialogue within the structures that frame communication during a crisis.

A second characteristic of the CC approach involves *structure*. As Dutta (2008) proposed, "Structure refers to those organizations, processes and systems in society which determine how that society is organized, how it functions, and how individual members within it behave with respect to each other" (p. 62). In risk and crisis situations, organizations responsible for public safety and crisis mitigation are not easily accessible due to *marginalization* of diverse publics. Those operating within the structures of society have the agency to make decisions about what should be done in response to risks or crises. Outside the structures, there is little opportunity for marginalized publics to engage or have the agency to influence decision-making. Thus, the CC approach opens the structures to facilitate the dialogue between the traditional decision-makers and those who traditionally have been affected by those decisions. As co-participants in the process, agency is openly shared, and decisions reflect this status equality.

CC communication utilizes *context* and *space* when constructing a shared perspective by the decision-makers. Because cultural context involves the real-life experiences of individuals where they reside and interact with others, as Dutta (2008) suggested, "contexts are intertwined with the structures within which communities are embedded" (p. 63). This suggests that the lived experiences of a cultural group become part of a larger structure affecting everyday life. For example, the reality experienced by publics who have been excluded from receiving goods or services during a crisis becomes part of a larger context of poverty and social justice. In CC communication, the accessibility of marginalized groups to decision-makers inherently provides for the creation of a shared context that reveals the lived experiences of all participants. In addition to context, access to decision-making places all participants in the same geographic space. As co-participants in the process of creating and disseminating messages, interaction in the same space is required. In crisis situations, decision-makers often are removed from the geographic areas being impacted. Unlike the marginalized publics who often find themselves in areas most susceptible to crises, decision-makers have the agency to locate themselves in safer areas. From these different spatial vantage points, the voices of the decision-makers traditionally are heard; while the voices of the marginalized publics who reside in areas most affected by the crisis are ignored. When CC approaches are used by organizations, the co-participants in the decision-making process are brought into the same location. This provides for shared understanding and dialogue, reducing or eliminating the resistance that may have occurred due to misunderstandings or conflicting values.

Another aspect of the CC approach involves the values of those involved in the communication process. Beliefs and values are held by individuals, are reflected in the macro culture in which they live, and are shared through their *stories*. When the values of different cultural groups intersect through shared stories of real-life experiences, the power associated with one group over another is moderated. Values held by individuals or groups with agency are no longer prioritized because the macro culture affording them control within existing structures (e.g., government, financial institutions, and schools) are now accessible to the marginalized publics. The values of marginalized populations are no longer silenced or ignored. Thus, when decision-making is expanded to include representatives from marginalized publics, a new configuration of value priorities is established that accounts for what is important to everyone. The co-created values are shared through their stories and provide for the interactive arguments to produce meaningful dialogue, contributing to the development of effective risk and crisis messages.

The convergence of values reduces *resistance* because all perspectives have been accounted for in the process. Through a CC approach, Dutta (2008) described the benefits of, "a critical framework for interrogating the dominant theories and practices in health communication" (p. 65). Similarly, in risk and crisis communication, a CC approach requires reconsideration of the dominant decision-making process that produces and disseminates messages to diverse publics. The acknowledgment that decision-makers control the language, content, and distribution of messages confirms the sender-focused model and privileges the values of those in control. To acknowledge that existing structures have favored the values of those with agency, and that these structures have marginalized diverse publics and their values from having an equal voice in the decision-making process, provides both decision-makers and marginalized publics with the opportunity to critique and construct messages that will be more effective in reaching the publics affected by risks or crises.

In summary, the CC approach to risk and crisis communication engages the decision-makers and marginalized publics as co-participants in the process of designing and disseminating risk and crisis messages. The CC approach provides for shared power between the participants, and the distinction between dominant and marginalized groups is erased in the co-construction of a context that is shared. The values held by macro culture and marginalized cultures are shared through stories in a common space where differing views are accepted and acted upon for the betterment of those who will process and act upon the instructions they received in a situation of risk

Table 3.1 Perspectives of Control of Cultural Characteristics on Approaches to Risk and Crisis Communication

Perspectives of Culture	Culture-Neutral	Culturally Sensitive	Culture-Centered
Power	Sender control	Sender control	Shared control
Marginalization	Sender control	Sender control	Shared control
Context	Sender control	Sender control	Shared control
Stories and values	Sender control	Sender control	Shared control
Resistance	Receiver control	Receiver control	Sender control

or crisis. While complete eradication of resistance to instructions or messages designed to protect or save lives may be impossible, the CC approach offers the best option to include diverse perspectives during the pre-crisis stages when relationships and partnerships are needed to gain acceptance and compliance. The three cultural approaches to risk and crisis communication are compared in table 3.1, illustrating perspectives of control in relation to perspectives of culture.

SELECTED CASES FOR EXAMINATION

With these cultural approaches to risk and crisis communication in mind, we now introduce three contemporary crises that illustrate and explain the three cultural models just described. These crises include ZIKv, Hurricane Dorian, and ASFv.

Zika Virus

The detection and rapid spread of ZIKv in the western hemisphere, and how the WHO disseminated messages about this crisis to its global audience, prompted its selection as an example of an organization using a CN approach when communicating globally. ZIKv was chosen because it represented a mega-crisis that crossed geographic boundaries (Romero, 2016), constituted an international public health emergency (WHO, 2016d), and represented a threat due to the absence of immunity in the whole of Latin America and the Caribbean (Duffy & Brasileiro, 2016).

In 2015, an epidemic of ZIKv began in Brazil and quickly spread to other countries in the western hemisphere, particularly in South and Central America, but also in North America and the Caribbean. The WHO began its tracking of ZIKv in this region, and by 2016, an estimated 1.5 million people were infected in Brazil, with over 3,500 cases of microcephaly reported between October 2015 and January 2016 (WHO, 2019). This prompted the issuance of a Public Health Emergency of International Concern about ZIKv to the WHO member nations in the Pan American Health Organization (PAHO) and to the global community.

By way of background, ZIKv is transmitted primarily through the bite of infected aedes aegypti mosquitoes. Symptoms are typically mild, and include fever, rash, conjunctivitis, muscle and joint pain, and headache, lasting from two to seven days. Typically, hospitalization is not required. Contracting ZIKv during pregnancy can cause microcephaly and other congenital malformations in unborn fetuses. While most people who contract ZIKv are asymptomatic and can be treated with common pain and fever medications, rest, and drinking plenty of fluids (WHO, 2016a); an increased risk of neurologic complications such as Guillain-Barré syndrome, neuropathy, and myelitis accompanies the contracting of the virus (WHO, 2018).

ZIKv was first identified in Uganda in 1947 in monkeys; and later, it was identified in humans in 1952. While not the first outbreaks in the world—the first recorded outbreak of ZIKv was reported in 2007 in Micronesia and later in other countries in territories in the Pacific—the crisis in the Americas began in early 2015, when Brazilian health officials detected cases of fever and rash that were confirmed to be ZIKv. By late spring, the rate of contracting the virus exploded, eventually prompting Brazilian officials to stop counting the cases (WHO, 2016a). Soon after, evidence of transmission spread throughout the Americas was reported and confirmed by the WHO. By July 2019, Zika had been identified in eighty-seven countries and territories (WHO, 2019). In table 3.2, a general timeline leading up to the ZIKv outbreak in the Americas is provided.

Hurricane Dorian

Hurricane Dorian was a powerful natural disaster that devastated the Bahamas and caused catastrophic damage along the southeastern United States and Atlantic Canada ("Search for survivors," 2019) and ranks as the strongest landfalling Atlantic hurricane in recorded history with wind speeds peaking at 185 mph ("Atlantic hurricane best," 2020). In advance of this hurricane, the National Hurricane Center (NHC), the National Weather Channel, and regional and local meteorologists provided warnings to help nonscientific publics understand the complex weather information. The communication strategies used by these weather experts made this crisis a good example of how a CS approach helped distribute necessary information needed by multiple publics to save their lives and protect their property.

Table 3.2 Timeline of Public Communication about ZIKv Outbreak

Relevant Date	Observation
1947	First case isolated in rhesus monkey in the Zika forest of Uganda
1952	First case isolated in humans in Uganda and the United Republic of Tanzania
2001–2014	Average of 163 microcephaly cases annually recorded in Brazil
2007	First appearance of Zika strain in Micronesia and Malaysia
2013–2014	Four additional Pacific island nations document large Zika outbreaks
May 2015	First case of Zika confirmed in Brazil
December 2015	WHO and PAHO issue an epidemiological alert
January 17, 2016	First U.S. baby born with brain damage attributed to *Zika*
January 18, 2016	CDC issues travel warning for Caribbean region
February 1, 2016	WHO director-general convenes meeting of the Emergency Committee
	That issues a Public Health Emergency of International Concern (PHEIC)
	Brazil stops counting cases: Cumulative total of 5,280 cases of microcephaly or central nervous system malformations reported, including 180 deaths
February 4, 2016	The United States reports Zika case transmitted through sexual contact
February 17, 2016	Cumulative total of 48 countries and territories reported with local transmissions of ZIKv.

The origin of the Hurricane Dorian crisis began on August 24, 2019, when the NHC identified a tropical wave developing over the Central Atlantic Ocean that became a hurricane on August 28, 2019. It intensified rapidly, reaching its peak as a Category 5 hurricane by September 1, 2019. Dorian made landfall in the Bahamas on September 1, 2019, remaining stationary until it began moving to the northwest on September 3, parallel to the east coast of Florida (Weather.gov, 2019). In preparation for the storm, Florida, Georgia, South Carolina, North Carolina, and Virginia declared a state of emergency, with multiple coastal counties issuing mandatory evacuation orders. More specifically, Florida governor Ron DeSantis declared a state of emergency for twenty-six counties on August 28, 2019, extending the declaration to the entire state on August 29, 2019 (NPR, 2019). On August 28, 2019, Georgia governor Brian Kemp declared a state of emergency for coastal counties in Georgia, adding several more on Wednesday, September 4, 2019 (Rhone & Hansen, 2019). On August 31, South Carolina Governor Henry McMaster declared a state of emergency for the entire state after

Table 3.3 Timeline of Hurricane Dorian

Relevant Date (2019)	Observation
August 23	A defined area of low pressure consolidates in the Atlantic Ocean.
August 24	The tropical wave acquires sufficient organized convention over the Central Atlantic Ocean to be classified as Tropical Depression Five and later Hurricane Dorian.
August 27	Dorian makes landfall in Barbados.
August 28	Dorian becomes a Category 1 hurricane north of Greater Antilles and the U.S. Virgin Islands.
August 31	Dorian reaches Hurricane 4 status.
September 1	Dorian strikes the Great Abaco Islands as a Category 5 hurricane with maximum sustained winds of 185 mph. Dorian remains stationery over the Bahamas.
September 3	Dorian begins moving northwestward and weakens to Category 2 strength.
September 5	Dorian re-intensifies to Category 3 strength off the coast of South Carolina.
September 6	Dorian makes landfall on Cape Hatteras at Category 2 intensity.
September 10	Dorian dissipates near Greenland.

the path of Dorian shifted to affect South Carolina as a strong hurricane, announcing mandatory evacuations for several counties on September 1, 2019 (SCEMD, 2019).

The impact of Hurricane Dorian in lives lost and economic devastation was significant. A total of 84 people are confirmed dead and 245 persons remain missing (Associated Press, 2019; Avila et al., 2020; Bahamas Information Services, 2020), and the economic damage to the Bahamas, the United States, and Canada exceeding $4.68 billion. In the Bahamas, buildings were swept away, and large areas were submerged underwater, including runways at Marsh Harbour International Airport ("Hurricane Dorian Updates," 2019). Local animal shelters and a majority of the Humane Society of Grand Bahama were affected, with hundreds of dogs and cats died in the flooding. Prime Minister Hubert Minnis declared Dorian to be "the greatest national crisis in hour country's history" (Humayun & Ehlinger, 2019). In the aftermath, the United Nations projected that at least 70,000 people were homeless on Grand Bahama and the Abaco Islands (Blackwell et al., 2019). In the United States, the storm surge along the coasts produced damage in Florida and South Carolina. Tornados spawned by the hurricane damaged homes, and residents of islands in the Outer Banks of North Carolina had to be rescued from flooding. In table 3.3, a timeline of Hurricane Dorian reveals the path of destruction that began affected the entire eastern coast of North America.

African Swine Fever Virus

ASFv is a highly contagious disease that devastates animals in pork-production facilities. Although ASFv does not infect humans, this rapidly spreading disease has the potential to impact food security by hampering the production of pork, a major source of animal protein for many people worldwide. Clinically, ASFv is a severe and deadly virus affecting wild and domestic pigs of all ages. The virus spreads easily by animal contact, contaminated feed, and fomites such as specks of feces on clothing worn by people or on equipment moving among buildings where animals are housed. Once infected, few animals survive.

ASFv has so far defied containment. Since 2007, ASFv, for which there is no vaccine or efficacious treatment, has spread rapidly in Africa, Asia, and Europe (African Swine Fever, 2020). At present, the disease has not been reported in North America; however, the swine industry in the U. S. remains on high alert, encouraging producers to engage in heightened biosecurity to prevent contracting or spreading the disease. Biosecurity refers to strategic actions taken to prevent the spread of disease among humans and animals. IMC plays a critical role in the industry-wide effort to create a consistent narrative for biosecurity measures against ASFv. Furthermore, the global impact of the disease and the diverse stakeholders within the U.S. swine industry make cultural-centered communication essential in the formation of a consistent and meaningful narrative.

Comprehending and analyzing the risk and crisis communication about ASFv in the United States, however, requires a parallel discussion of porcine epidemic diarrhea virus (PEDv). Both diseases pose severe and ongoing threats to the pork industry worldwide. However, an outbreak of PEDv from 2013–2015 presented the U.S. pork industry with its greatest crisis in decades. PEDv had been seen previously in China, but it had never been diagnosed in the United States until the spring of 2013. While older animals can become ill and recover, piglets stand little or no chance of surviving PEDv. By 2014, PEDv was decimating the U.S. swine population by killing 100,000 piglets per day (Strom, 2014). Because the U.S. industry had no experience managing PEDv, extensive research was needed. This research effort was completed by the National Pork Board, American Association of Swine Veterinarians, and university extension offices. The conclusions were then translated into biosecurity recommendations that were shared broadly throughout the industry. By 2015, these biosecurity efforts resulted in PEDv being largely contained (see table 3.4).

The successful research collaboration and communication of a shared biosecurity narrative for PEDv provided the swine industry with a blueprint for engaging in effective crisis planning and communication focusing on ASFv

Table 3.4 Timeline of PEDv and ASFv Outbreaks

Relevant Date	Observation
2013	PEDv begins to spread throughout the U.S. swine industry
2014	The disease peaks with deaths of nearly 100,000 piglets per day
2015	PEDv cases decline due to intensified biosecurity practices
2019	Officials from Canada, Mexico, and the United States issue a joint statement on shared efforts to prevent the spread of ASFv to the North America
2020	Fifty countries in Africa, Asia, and Europe report outbreaks of ASFv

(USDA, 2020). Thus, our explanation of how the ASFv response aligns with IMC and culture-centered communication includes frequent references to the PEDv response.

SUMMARY

This chapter introduced the CC model of risk and crisis communication through a discussion of the CN, CS, and CC approaches. Each of these approaches was defined, followed by a discussion of fundamental assumptions, functions, and examples. The introduction of three recent crises lays the foundation for a more robust examination of how the CN, CS, and CC communication contributed to the level of effectiveness demonstrated by each of the entities that created and disseminated risk and crisis messages in response to the pre-crisis, crisis, and post-crisis events that occurred.

We now move to chapter 4 that provides a detailed description of the IDEA model, which focuses specifically on designing and distributing instructional risk and crisis messages in the context of IMC. The model consists of four elements and may be used to design messages in any risk, crisis, or emergency context, and provides a framework for messages described in the subsequent chapters focusing on the CN, CS, and CC approaches to risk and crisis communication.

Chapter 4

The IDEA Model of Instructional Risk and Crisis Communication

Chapter 3 introduced the CC model of risk and crisis communication as it informs effective communication in these contexts by providing the basis for the CN, CS, and CC approaches. With the ever-increasing mega-crises that cut across regional, national, and international boundaries, cultures, and co-cultures, an understanding of CN, CS, and CC messages is indeed critical to successful communication. This chapter focuses on the IDEA model of effective instructional risk and crisis communication as another key message design framework for achieving desired affective, cognitive, and behavioral learning in these contexts (Sellnow & Sellnow, 2019). We begin with a detailed description of the IDEA model in the context of IMC, and offer an explanation of how the IDEA model has been used in a variety of national and international contexts. We follow with a discussion about how the IDEA model intersects with IMC, as well as helps illustrate how the three cultural approaches interact with the IDEA model to create and disseminate effective instructional messages of risk and crisis.

COMMUNICATION AND LEARNING IN CULTURE-CENTERED IMC

As discussed in earlier chapters, IMC is essentially both receiver-oriented and outcome-based. Because it is receiver-oriented, tailoring messages in ways that appropriately integrate cultural norms and values of target audiences is critical. The CC approach provides a valuable means by which to make informed decisions because it integrates multiple perspectives into the process. For example, the presence of multiple languages or code systems used to convey messages affects a decision-maker's choices about how to communicate with intended publics. The intent of the decision-maker toward the cultural recipients of the message likely will have an effect on their relationship in the present or future. The spokesperson makes message content choices based on knowing and accepting the normative beliefs and values of the intended publics. Finally, the contrast between the worldview of the decision-maker and that of the intended publics as progressive, fatalistic, or holistic will influence how effective the communication between them will be. Outcome achievement is equally critical to communication success and can be measured based on three learning outcome achievements. In other words, the success of IMC may be determined based on the degree to which consumers, potential customers, and disparate publics learn.

Learning is achieved via mastering outcomes in three domains: affective, cognitive, and behavioral (Bloom, 1956; Dewey, 1938; Krathwohl et al., 1973; Simpson, 1972). The affective domain is based on an individual's attitudes and emotions about the topic as they motivate people to pay attention to and appreciate what is shared. The cognitive domain has to do with knowledge comprehension (e.g., facts, concepts, patterns, and procedures). The behavioral (a.k.a. psychomotor) domain is about efficacy regarding the application and performance of skills and concepts. These elements in the definition of learning run counter to a common misunderstanding that effective instructional communication is essentially information sharing; and, thus, learning is achieved when that information is understood by the learner. Hence, better instruction in any context—including IMC in risk and crisis contexts—is achieved by simply sharing more than merely information (Sellnow et al., 2017b).

Comprehensive learning is achieved when people not only understand information but also are motivated to remember and able to apply it. Thus, effective IMC campaigns must first motivate consumers to pay attention, convincing them of its value, relevance, and impact (affective learning); understand/comprehend the information shared both accurately and consistently (cognitive learning); and engage in appropriate actions as desired by the sender (behavioral learning). The IDEA model provides a framework for designing and distributing messages that achieve these outcomes.

THE IDEA MODEL

"IDEA" is essentially an acronym standing for each of the four elements of the model: *I*nternalization, *D*istribution, *E*xplanation, and *A*ction. Although effective instructional communication is achieved via a fluid and dynamic interaction among them (i.e., each one does not function in a vacuum), we explain each element as it may be employed ultimately in collaboration with the others to achieve affective, cognitive, and behavioral learning through IMC and in risk and crisis contexts.

I: Internalization

Instructional risk and crisis messages address internalization by answering the question: *How am I (or the people and things I care about) affected?* In IMC, this urgency to recognize a looming threat and prepare for it can be seen as timing of messages needed to provide warning and possibly prevent a crisis (Persuit, 2016). The goal is to motivate receivers to pay attention to and remember the information shared. In other words, receivers must be motivated to *want to* learn (Christophel, 1990; Richmond, 1990). Moreover, the explosion of technological affordances that has transpired in recent years has produced in a wealth of messages competing for our attention 24/7. Thus, receivers must make choices regarding on which of them to focus. For these reasons, keying in on relevance and utility is critical to gaining and maintaining receiver attention (Bolkan & Griffin, 2018; Frymier & Shulman, 1995; Mazer, 2017). Instructional communication research has generated a wealth of research confirming that "academic achievement, study stills, and engagement can be increased by tapping into students' interests" (Linnenbrink & Pintrich, 2002, p. 319). In the context of risk and crisis, multiple publics are all of those receivers who may be impacted by the potential threat of the circumstances (including those they care about).

Internalization strategies also must be tailored to the intended audience and the risk or crisis type (Sellnow & Sellnow, 2019). To clarify, one might focus on threats to health, safety, welfare, prosperity, happiness, or life to address internalization regardless of the event (Edwards et al., 2020). However, earthquake early warning (EEW) messages might include a countdown that indicates when the intense shaking will begin and a map illustrating where it will take place (Sellnow et al., 2019b). Hurricane forecasts might focus on the CAT level and cone of uncertainty, both of which must be continually updated as the hurricane develops. Instructional messages about food contamination might hone in on symptoms and consequences of eating the tainted product (Sellnow et al., 2017b). Agricultural biosecurity messages might illustrate what happens when a piglet is infected and the potential devastation to farms in terms of animal and economic welfare (Sellnow et al., 2017c). In the case of the novel (new) COVID-19 pandemic, scientists did not know much about it when it first emerged in China, then migrated to Europe, the United States, and other countries around the world. Unfortunately, early messages failed to effectively address internalization for disparate groups. To clarify, early messages sent in the United States claimed that only the elderly and those with compromised immune systems were at-risk. Consequently, young people understood that they would not be affected and even if they did contract the virus, they would likely experience only mild flu-like symptoms. As a result, healthy young adults did not perceive relevance and, thus, large spring break beach parties and other super spreader events continued to occur. By the time scientists realized the potential harm to healthy children and young adults, the disease had spread throughout the United States.

Communication during many crises can be challenging because they not only pose a serious threat but also tend to demand a short response time (Sellnow & Seeger, 2013). To address this challenge effectively, some instructional messages employ exemplars—evocative images, words, and sounds—that function as indexical heuristics that receivers quickly associate with the event (Sellnow & Sellnow, 2019; Sellnow, 2018; Zillman, 2006). For messages intended to improve biosecurity practices among farmers, piles of dead piglets being hauled away in pickup trucks might function as an exemplar to motivate receivers to pay attention. For instance, a sign that includes a red circle with a line through it functions as an exemplar for "do not" or "not allowed" (see figure 4.1). An emergency alert sound can also be used as an exemplar to catch attention; however, since different cultural groups may actually use different sounds for disaster warnings, such messages ought to be tailored accordingly. For instance, the warning sound for earthquakes used in Japan is not the same as the one used in the United States. Similarly, drums are used for mudslide warning alerts in the Bududah District of Uganda (Mushengyezi, 2003). Color may be another exemplar to be used as an indexical heuristic. However, the meanings of the colors chosen must be understood similarly across cultural and co-cultural groups. For example, the color used

Figure 4.1 Symbolic of Most Serious Warnings in Western Cultures. *Source*: This photo by an unknown author is licensed under CC–3BY–SA.

Figure 4.2 Symbolic of Most Dangerous Weather Condition.

for the highest threat level in the United States is red; however, the color black is used for the most dangerous rain storms in Hong Kong (see figure 4.2).

During the 2020 COVID-19 pandemic, masks may have functioned as exemplars. However, because the meaning of wearing a mask became associated with political affiliation in the United States, the mask symbol failed to serve its purpose as an indexical heuristic for containing the spread of the virus. Instead, many equated wearing a mask with supporting/not supporting a certain political party's agenda.

D: Distribution

The question effective instructional risk and crisis messages must address regarding distribution is not about content but, rather, delivery: *Which communication channel(s) and sources will best reach various target public(s)?* Channels range from interpersonal word-of-mouth to legacy media (e.g., newspapers, magazines, radio, TV, brochures and flyers, and billboards) to social media (e.g., Facebook, Twitter, YouTube, Instagram, and TikTok). IMC recognizes the utility and impact of all these channels, including the expanding relevance of social media (Vinhateiro & Cronen, 2016). Sources range from scientific experts to government officials to news media outlets to social media influencers to local opinion leaders.

The abundance of channel choices available today presents both opportunities and challenges. For instance, risk and crisis communicators may send warning message through multiple channels, which should, in turn, reach broad audiences. Challenges stem from accessibility issues and message incongruity across channels (Sellnow & Sellnow, 2019).

Regarding accessibility, not all people and groups have reliable access to all of these channels. For example, spokespersons should not assume a smartphone app is the best way to warn all potential victims of a crisis. According to recent PEW research center statistics, 81 percent of Americans own a smartphone (Anderson, 2019). That means nearly 20 percent do not even own one, let alone use it for such information seeking. Moreover, even those who have smartphones might lose access when phone towers are compromised, as was the case when Hurricane Maria devastated Puerto Rico in 2017 (Gill, 2019). Considering social media, about 70 percent of Americans use some type of social media for news, information sharing, or entertainment. Moreover, only about 70 percent use Facebook daily and far less (20 percent) use Twitter at all (Pew Research Center, 2019).

Not only does accessibility pose a challenge, different publics also seek information from different channels (Sellnow & Sellnow, 2019). Although social media is a common place where many Americans seek information; in Sweden, newspapers remain the most common channel used for seeking information about risk and crisis events (Sellnow et al., 2019a). Television and radio remain popular among many publics in the United States that do engage with other technologies. Thus, spokespersons must utilize multiple communication channels if they want to reach broad and disparate people and publics effectively.

Similarly, the communication channel poses a challenge for reaching various publics when complicated by the source from whom the communication comes (Sellnow & Sellnow, 2019). Different people and publics seek information from sources they perceive as trustworthy. It follows that a source one person or group deems to be credible may not be similarly trusted by another person or group. For example, in the case of natural disasters such as floods, earthquakes, and hurricanes, some people and publics tend to trust local authorities more than government officials or national media. In the case of the 1997 Red River valley floods in North Dakota, local residents tended to rely on the local emergency manager rather than the national reporters covering the crisis (Sellnow & Seeger, 2001). Moreover, people seek convergence among various sources when making risk and crisis decisions (Anthony & Sellnow, 2016). To be most effective, then, various sources need to participate in ongoing communication with one another to ensure that they are sharing a similar message about what is happening, what is being done, and what to do (Sellnow et al., 2019c).

In other words, people typically seek confirmation by consulting multiple sources (Anthony et al., 2013). When they discover convergence (similar messages) across sources, they are more likely to accept the message as true (Anthony & Sellnow, 2016). Conversely, when they discover divergence among various sources, they may not know which one to believe or even discount all of them as misinformed, misleading, or intentionally deceptive (e.g., "fake" news) (Getchell et al., 2018; Tando, Jr. et al., 2018). One emerging line of research to address this challenge suggests implementing communities of practice (CoP) before a risk situation manifests into a crisis event (Edwards et al., 2020; Sellnow et al., 2017a). A CoP is essentially a highly collaborative, diverse group of people who "share a concern, a set of problems, or a passion about a topic, and who deepen their knowledge and expertise in this area by interacting in an ongoing basis" (Wenger et al., 2002, p. 4). One key reason the swine industry was able to bolster agricultural biosecurity practices quickly and efficiently to contain the devastatingly deadly PEDv pandemic in 2014, has been traced to the industry functioning as a CoP before and during the event (Sellnow et al., 2017c). Arguably, in the case of the COVID-19 outbreak in the United States, many lives may have been saved and the spread of the virus contained more quickly had various sources (e.g., federal/state/local governments, public health agencies, medical professionals, scientific communities, and news media) operated as a CoP to examine the novel virus, make decisions, and communicate consistent messages.

In sum, many mistakes were made with regard to the distribution of messages in the United States during the 2020 COVID-19 coronavirus pandemic. Because competing narratives were being sent by health scientists, federal and local government officials, local medical professionals, and social media influencers, unnecessary confusion about the disease and how to manage it ensued (Littlefield, 2020a). Consequently, the disease spread rampantly across the country and many more lives were lost than if a consistent message been agreed upon and communicated from disparate sources. These negative implications could have been reduced or remedied though effective IMC.

E: Explanation

To address explanation, responses to the question—*What is happening and why, as well as, what is being done to address the crisis?*—must be accurate (regarding both what is known and unknown, as well as what is being done to find answers to the unknown) and communicated in such a way as to be understood by the target audience(s). Perhaps most important here is the need to be honest and transparent when sharing both what is known and unknown as the crisis unfolds. The ethic of significant choice research argues that consumers have a right to know what is going on in order to make informed choices

(Nilson, 1974). They are denied the opportunity to do so when information is withheld, misrepresented, or wrong (Ulmer & Sellnow, 1997). Consequences can be particularly devastating when spokespersons do so knowingly and strategically (Sohn & Edwards, 2018). Negative consequences of engaging in strategic ambiguity have been illustrated in contexts ranging from tobacco use to health care to food safety and from banking to politics to CSR (e.g., Carmon, 2013; Eisenberg, 1984; Wexler, 2009). In the case of the coronavirus, for instance, mistakes were made in explaining what was and was not known early on. As a result, people were confused when the nature of the virus, how it spreads, and who is most at risk kept changing. Had early communication acknowledged more directly what was not yet known and what scientists were doing to find out, consumers may have been more open to interpreting changing information as a gradual increase in understanding rather than confusing mixed messages that could not be trusted. From an IMC perspective, acknowledging uncertainty in the sensemaking process gives organizations greater agility in their response as more details are revealed (Fellows, 2016).

In addition to being accurate and transparent, spokespersons must craft messages that translate information intelligibly to disparate publics. It probably goes without saying that language barriers ought to be overcome so people can discern information as presented in a language they are fluent in, which is typically their first language (a.k.a. mother tongue) (Rani, 2016). Nevertheless, too often, crisis spokespersons fail to take this into account by providing explanations in a variety of languages to reach diverse publics most effectively (Fischer et al., 2016). The fact that crises often cross national and international boundaries heightens the need to do so. In the case of COVID-19, for example, explanations were offered in only a few of the 5,000–6,000 languages used globally (Piller et al., 2020). The WHO, for example, provided information in nine languages, with English dominating as the "language of record" ("Coronavirus disease (COVID-19) pandemic," 2020).

Intelligible translation also requires spokespersons to explain information that accounts for disparate literacy and numeracy levels among receivers (Sellnow & Sellnow, 2019). In other words, accurate technical and scientific information must be translated in ways that make sense to and are relevant to members of the target audience(s). Consider, for example, earthquake early warning (EEW) messages. Although accurate science would explain magnitude, intensity, s-waves, as well as probability of aftershocks and swarms, what people need to know is how intense the shaking will be, when it will start, and what they should do for protection (Sellnow & Sellnow, 2019). Providing too much technical information is more likely to confuse folks not schooled in earthquake science and may take more time than is available to take protective action. Moreover, when explanations are offered using numerical relationships rather than simple words or visual exemplars, numeracy levels can further impede chances that people will understand what is happening and what to do (Peters et al., 2006). When messages during the COVID-19 pandemic used terms such as fomite (objects that may carry and transmit the virus), aerosol (transmitted through the air), novel (new), asymptomatic (disease carriers and spreaders that have no symptoms), and PPE or even personal protective equipment (face masks, gowns, and gloves used to protect people from catching COVID-19 when in close contact with others), diverse publics were less likely to understand than had they relied instead on the simple definitions in simple language.

A: Action

To address the action element, effective instructional risk and crisis messages answer the question: *What should I and those I care about do (and NOT do) to ensure safety and well-being, as well as mitigate potential harms?* McKendree (2016) asserts, from an IMC perspective, "The strength of a crisis response relies upon action—in particular, coordinated, although not always agreed upon, action" (p. 132). To be most effective, actions will be described as specific actionable instructions, introduced before the onset of the crisis event as well as during it, and conveyed in ways that rely on multimodal communication (verbal, aural, visual) (Sellnow & Sellnow, 2019).

Before a risk situation manifests into a crisis event, spokespersons generally enjoy the luxury of time to engage in meaningful dialogue about potential threats and actions to take. Just as key stakeholders use this time to establish communities of practice and build trust with stakeholders, so too can this time be used to engage in educational training campaigns preparing them to act quickly in the event of an acute crisis outbreak. For example, the Southern California Earthquake Council (SCEC) conducts what it calls the *Great Shake Out Earthquake Drill* annually in October (Southern California Earthquake Center, 2020). This campaign attracts more than five million participants globally each year. On a specific date and time, a practice alert warning sounds and everyone practices the specific actions steps to "drop, take cover, and hold on" as if an intense earthquake were imminent. This is followed by educational training and discussion designed to prepare people to take the desired actions when an earthquake strikes. In essence, doing so helps develop muscle memory to act quickly when time is of the essence. Similarly, an educational campaign was conducted for crisis preparedness in Sweden. It focused on what to have at hand in your home to be ready for lockdown in a crisis (Sellnow et al., 2020). In the case of the coronavirus pandemic and future pandemics that will inevitably occur, similar campaigns could be developed and implemented to educate people and publics about what to do for self-protection (e.g., second-hand washing, mask wearing, social distancing) and why, as well as how (practice drills to create muscle memory). If pre-crisis educational campaigns are not done or are too late, the urgency created through internalization will still motivate people to act. It just won't be second nature.

Because crisis events typically impose a serious threat and demand action within a short response time, pre-crises educational campaigns are critical. Effective instructional communication during the event needs to motivate people to pay attention and act, inform people in ways that are accurate and intelligible, and provide specific actionable instructions for protection very quickly. In the case of earthquake early warning (EEW) messages, the time allotted may even be ten seconds or less (Sellnow et al., 2019b). Another way to address this challenge is through multimodal communication. In the case of EEW, research reveals that aural alert sounds, verbal intensity level descriptions (rather than numerical), and visual exemplars can serve as heuristic shortcuts to action when time is of the essence (see figure 4.3).

Finally, specific action steps should be created and implemented for those not directly in harm's way. Because families are rarely geographically bound today, it is likely that even when a crisis event does not impact us directly, a loved one may be in harm's way. Moreover, it is human nature to want to help even when we don't have a loved one impacted directly. Most often, people are directed to donate money to a particular charity that will aid relief efforts. This is most certainly one option. However, effective instructional risk and crisis communication research suggests publishing and promoting a *preferred list* of how to help on a website(s) and via social media (see figure 4.4).

In sum, although we have described each element of the IDEA model in isolation, they actually function fluidly together in effective instructional risk and crisis communication. The key is that all need to be addressed. When one is overlooked, research illustrates that negative implications arise. For

Figure 4.3 **Drop, Cover, Hold On Action Step Exemplar.** *Source*: This photo by unknown author is licensed under CC BY.

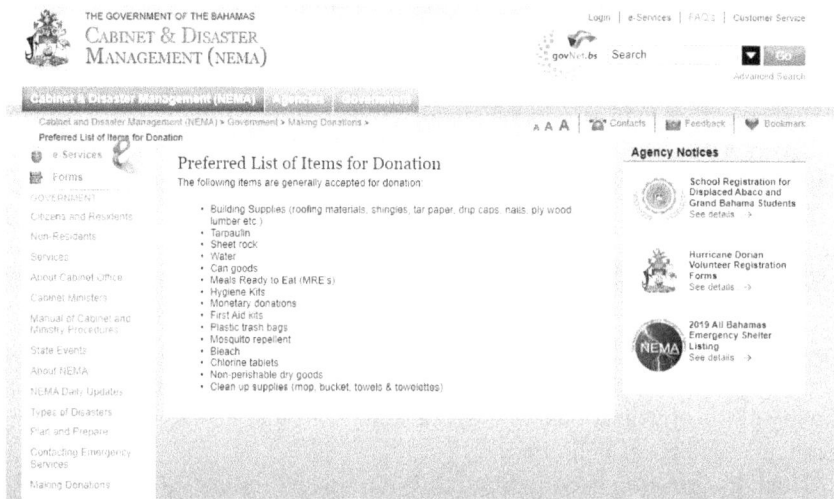

Figure 4.4 How to Help.

example, many such messages privilege explanation at the expense of action or internalization (e.g., Frisby et al., 2014; Sellnow-Richmond et al., 2018). In these cases, messages fail because receivers are left wondering what they are supposed to do/not do to protect themselves and those they care about (action) and why (internalization). Consequently, they usually end up doing nothing at all or precisely doing the wrong thing; and, as a result, heighten negative impact (Seeger, 2006). Even when messages offer specific protective action steps and intelligibly translated accurate explanations but fail to address internalization, receivers are typically not motivated to pay attention or remember or comply (Merrill et al., 2019). Moreover, even when they do enact the desired behaviors, they gradually become complacent and noncompliant as time goes on (Sellnow et al., 2017c). Thus, while it is prudent to describe each element in isolation for cognitive learning, spokespersons will only be successful when all elements are addressed in ways that operate fluidly throughout the communication and thereby achieve affective and behavioral learning.

APPLICATIONS OF THE IDEA MODEL IN IMC ORGANIZATIONS

The IDEA model provides a framework for constructing messages that generate learning on the part of those receiving them. This coincides with what organizations seek to achieve using IMC. Developing consistent and coherent communication strategies is the goal of organizations using IMC because when they present appropriate stimuli to a defined target audience, the intended outcome is the eliciting of a desired set of responses (Kitchen & De Pelsmacker, 2004).

In stage 1 of IMC, the organization combines all of the various tools of the marketing communication mix (e.g., advertising, sales promotion, public relations, personal selling, and direct marketing). These tools vary in their effectiveness. For example, personal selling and direct marketing score high in the ability to deliver a personal message, while advertising, sales promotion, and public relations score low. Similarly, sales promotions and direct marketing provide the decision-makers with more control over the ability to target particular audiences, while traditional public relations scores low in this category. Because stage one is completed without any external input, the ability of the organization to incorporate elements that will be internalized by particular audiences is limited.

If an organization is committed to IMC, stage 2 initiates the gathering of extensive information about potential customers, consumers, and those who may be exposed to the campaign. In this stage, the IMC organization reaches out to sources of data that can provide information about the end-consumers or users of their product (Kitchen & De Pelsmacker, 2004). Some consumers may respond positively to money-based incentives in the form of price reductions that are immediate and easy to obtain. For these individuals, coupons and cash refunds may be preferred. Other potential customers may be motivated with prize-related incentives that provide a chance to win something. These individuals may respond to contests and sweepstakes where they can improve their chances of winning by demonstrating something that the organization uses to attract their attention. In this stage of IMC, the organization is able to find appeals that will aid in the internalization of the message, thereby focusing the attention of the publics on the product; or in the case of a risk or crisis, on the situation that is prompting the message.

Stage 2 also enables the decision-maker to identify audience characteristics that affect how information should be explained. In the marketing of a product, the collection of useful customer information is gathered with the goal of building and maintaining a long-term relationship. Because audiences rely on many different media, knowing their preferences, and to what type of messages are they most likely to be responsive, will enable the decision-makers to construct campaigns with enough information to establish and maintain customer loyalty to the brand. In the explanation step of the IDEA model, the need to present sufficient information to enable the receiver of the message is essential in order for them to understand the benefits of the product (in the case of appealing to the consumer) or to recognize the nature and severity of a pending situation (in the case of a potential risk or crisis event). In stage 2 of IMC, the data collected also aids the distribution step of the IDEA model because how, when, and from whom the message comes will affect the chosen channel and network for conveying the campaign or crisis message.

In stage 3 of IMC, organizations input the information they collect into databases that can be sorted and used to change customer data into customer knowledge. When particular appeals can be tested across different groups, results can be beneficial when suggesting preferred actions on the part of consumers or publics affected by potential risks or crises. Without segmentation, the actions must be suggested for the broader or universal audience (Perelman & Olbrechts-Tyteca, 1958/1971). The universal audience is characterized as being similar with regard to its preference for knowledge and accepted facts. Without knowledge of the particular audiences within the universal, specific appeals may be misdirected or inappropriate. The IDEA model tailors the action step to provide reasonable strategies that can be accomplished to achieve the desired outcome. In IMC, without segmentation through the creation of databases, the organization would be unable to reach the wide variety of its potential audiences (e.g., local community, government/policy-makers, suppliers, distributors, families of employees, and trade unions). Similarly, in risk or crisis situations, without knowledge of the multiple publics within the universal audience, specific strategies for action may be perceived as insensitive or unacceptable.

When an organization reaches stage 4 of IMC, the decision-makers are constantly monitoring the responses to the communication to determine which strategies are working and which are not. The return on investment plays a major role in the process because organizations do not want to communicate ineffectively with their customers or potential consumers. Similarly, in a risk or crisis situation, the decision-makers should be monitoring their communication in real time because as the dynamics of the situation change, the priorities of the decision-maker about how to communicate effectively should be affected (Littlefield, 2020b). At this point, the IDEA model is reliant upon having all of the available information about the particular audiences to adjust the message. If the publics did not internalize the severity of the situation, a different approach may be required. If the explanation was complicated or the examples were not well-selected, the message may need to be refined. In the event that the strategies were not followed, other options must identified to achieve the desired outcome. Finally, if the distribution of the message did not reach the intended publics, a different channel or spokesperson may be identified that will convey the intended message to the affected publics.

THE IDEA MODEL AND CULTURAL APPROACHES

The introduction of different cultural approaches for risk and crisis communication provides an opportunity to consider how the IDEA model functions in different contexts. The CN, CS, and CC approaches are based upon different assumptions and reflect contrasting elements.

The CN approach is designed for the universal audience using the rational world paradigm for information processing. Fisher (2017) explained that the rational world paradigm relies on facts and information from experts in order to make decisions. Arguments are developed with subject matter knowledge and conveyed from the perspective of advocacy. The decision-makers in this context dominate the discussion with the superiority of their rational discourse and make choices based upon what they perceive to be the most compelling arguments. Using the IDEA model in the culture neutral context requires the decision-maker to rely on general information and examples with the potential to appeal to multiple publics simultaneously. The explanation of the situation must use generic language and the decision-maker must rely upon common knowledge in order to reach the greatest number of people. Similarly, the suggested action or strategy to address the situation will lack specificity and be descriptive of what could be done by most individuals. A major challenge for the decision-maker is the inability to alter the distribution of the message based upon resistance from particular groups within the universal audience when internalization is thwarted, explanation is insufficient, or action is limited.

The CS approach allows for some adaptation to the particular audiences selected by the decision-maker as significant enough to warrant special consideration. While the controls held by the decision-makers are similar to those in the CN approach, selected information is used to appeal to those characteristics deemed salient by those who create and disseminate the message. While the rational world paradigm remains at the core of the CS approach, the introduction of narratives from the identified publics provides a greater opportunity to make the connections needed for internalization to occur and for examples to be chosen that are perceived as relevant to the publics. The distribution of the message is likely to focus on those channels identified by the decision-maker as best suited to reach the intended publics.

The CC approach provides for the greatest application of the IDEA model due to the focus on the particular audiences to which the messages are directed. When members of multiple publics are brought into the decision-making process, the ability to identify relevant and meaningful connections enhances their ability to internalize the messages and become vested in the issue at hand. When members of the publics are able to share their stories, the rhetorical choices used to explain the situation are built upon the lived experiences of those who co-create the messages. Because the affected groups have the ability to participate in the process of identifying strategies to respond to a crisis or other situation, the likelihood of the options being accepted and acted upon is greater. Finally, in the CC approach, the collective process of decision-making provides for clarity when deciding how to distribute the message across multiple publics with multiple spokespersons.

SUMMARY

This chapter provided a detailed description of the IDEA model in the context of IMC. The model's elements—internalization, distribution, explanation, and action—help message spokespersons design and distribute messages design to motivate receives to internalize the potential impact of the risk or crisis event, reach disparate target public(s) via appropriate channels, offer a honest and accurate explanation of the event via intelligible translations, and provide specific self-protection action steps to take. The usefulness of the model was demonstrated through a variety of national and international contexts. As the IDEA model is layered upon the workings of organizations utilizing IMC, the relationship of the four elements to the stages of IMC provided insight into how to develop consistent and coherent messaging more effectively. Finally, through a discussion of the cultural approaches identified in this book, the IDEA model revealed how the focus on different audiences could impact how decision-makers crafted and disseminated messages designed to save lives and livelihoods.

In the following chapters, the three approaches—CN, CS, and CC—will be illustrated through a discussion of three recent crises: The Zika mega-crisis affecting the western hemisphere; the Hurricane Dorian crisis affecting the Bahamas and southeastern United States; and ASFv that affected producers in several developed countries, including the United States. Through an examination of each crisis, the cultural approaches taken by the decision-makers disseminating risk and crisis messages will be illustrated to show how the different cultural messages were developed and presented, how the publics responded to the cultural approaches in the messages, how the approaches in the messages facilitated effective communication, and limitations to the cultural approaches that were utilized.

Chapter 5

The Culture-Neutral Approach

Chapter 4 described the IDEA model in the context of IMC. The four elements reinforce an audience-focused perspective through the process of helping recipients internalize the potential impacts they may experience due to risk or crisis events, identifying appropriate channels for distributing the messages, offering an accurate and understandable explanation of the nature of the risk or crisis, and providing specific self-protective actionable instructions for protection. The utility of the model across contexts was illustrated through examples reflecting national and international risk situations and crisis events.

This chapter provides a detailed examination of the first of the three communication approaches that bring a cultural perspective to the process. The CN approach emphasizes the following dimensions: The presence of the managerial/elite perspective; the use of scripted messages; the one-way nature of the message with no feedback; the traditional public relations single-spokesperson model; and the application of the social scientific perspective to the approach. Following this description, the CN approach is discussed with examples from the WHO's messages to the global community about ZIKv to show: (1) When CN communication was used (pre-crisis, crisis, and post-crisis); (2) how CN messages were presented (using best practices); (3) what the responses were to the CN messages; (4) how the CN approach facilitated effective risk communication; and (5) what limitations to the CN approach were evident. Intersecting this analysis is an overlay of the IDEA model to reveal how CN communication is less effective in conveying risk and crisis information and directives to diverse publics. From an IMC perspective, the ineffectiveness of CN messages stems from a lack of agility based on differing audience needs (Fellows, 2016).

THE CULTURE-NEUTRAL APPROACH

When organizations begin utilizing IMC, they enter the first stage where the primary focus is coordinating the internal processes necessary to launch a campaign. The process requires a high degree of interpersonal and cross-functional communication (Kitchen & DePelsmacker, 2004) with the goal of creating consistent and coherent messages designed to attract potential buyers or subscribers to the product or services being promoted. This stage reflects what happens when organizations utilize a CN approach to risk and crisis communication. The organization has an internal focus to produce coherent and consistent messages that will instruct and persuade publics to act in their best interests when confronting a risk or crisis. More specifically, the CN approach is essentially a managerial/elite perspective that directs a single spokesperson to use scripted messages without soliciting feedback to instruct or persuade a universal audience to take the desired action.

Managerial/Elite Perspective

The CN approach originates in the belief that messages should be designed for the universal audience (Perelman & Olbrechts-Tyteca, 1958/1971). This affinity between the manager and the universal audience is based on an assumption that both represent reasonable and rational individuals. The structures in place at government or institutional levels place the decision-makers in an elite position of being able to prioritize all aspects of message preparation and dissemination. The decision-makers have been privileged with education, financial and material resources, and legitimacy within the organization, to name a few. The decision-maker's ethnocentricity is expressed in the message because it reflects the outer limits of what should be known or acted upon in a situation. The perceived positive intent of the decision-maker to provide instructional content may be helpful, but the decision-maker's interest in developing a relationship with publics is not a priority. Once the information is conveyed, the decision-maker leaves it up to the publics to act. In essence, "We tell them what should happen if they follow our directives; the choice to act is up to them." The decision to transfer responsibility for action to those receiving the universal message represents a managerial perspective. As a result, the vertical integration of IMC carries this ethnocentricity to all levels of the organization as it conveys the position of the top decision-makers to those producing what should be consistent and coherent messages.

Scripted Message

CN messages are designed to be objective and free from cultural content. The objectivity of CN messages is valued because it presents the facts and expects the weight of evidence to support the conclusions being drawn and the preventive strategies offered. The reliance on objective information reflects what the sender regards as credible information; thus, scripted messages are prepared with no intention to modify them (Rykiel, 2001). Scripted messages are preplanned communication. Moreover, CN communication is not designed to be interactive. The decision-maker anticipates what should be included based on preferred models of interaction and prepares the message in advance. Feedback is not expected from the universal audience, nor would the sender of the message expect to modify preplanned communication because it is objective and if followed, will achieve intended results. The role of the audience is passively to accept the message.

One-Way with No Feedback

Because CN messages are directed to the universal audience, they tend to be created in such a way that the content stands for itself. The speaker's view of the audience dominates and because decision-makers view facts as indisputable, the message is created without audience involvement or interaction. In contrast to the circular communication model where sender and receiver communicate in a loop whereby feedback influences message modification, the CN approach is one-way. The message is transmitted, and feedback is irrelevant. The decision-makers use available material from what they deem to be credible sources to construct messages they expect will be universally accepted. Once the message is sent, their purpose has been achieved. Within the context of IMC, CN communication emanates from stage 1 practices that foster the creation of coherent messages reflecting standard practices accepted by those sharing the ethnocentric perspectives of the decision-makers.

Traditional Public Relations Single-Spokesperson Model

The single-spokesperson model is predicated on the belief that if the presentation of the message is centralized to one person or a single source, the consistency of the person or source will add credibility to the message being presented to the universal audience. Drawing from what Klopf (1991) described as projective cognitive similarity, or the belief that "the person with whom we are talking perceives, judges, thinks, and reasons the same way we do" (p. 223), CN communication appears logical and well-suited to the universal audience. When organizations use the CN approach, they select spokespeople who appear and sound like the decision-makers who chose them. This ethnocentric perspective is reinforced by vertical integration in IMC stage 1 that prioritizes using spokespeople who share the characteristics of the decision-maker.

Social Scientific Perspective

CN communication views problems from a macro-perspective. The focus is on description and prediction. The social scientific focus looks, "beyond the surface in examination of the phenomenon involved, the institution, or whatever is the focus of study, to see what is in fact functionally imperative" (Randar, 1973, p. 84). Social scientists describe, define, and predict behavior. They collect and manipulate data into categories that can be compared to determine strategies based on their predicted effectiveness. They view their role as helping society understand how to function, and in the case of risk or crisis, what to do to save lives and livelihoods. When decision-makers follow this social scientific paradigm, they create and disseminate messages that rely on probability and past actions to help society move forward. CN messages focus on the universal thereby prioritizing objective and factual content for the *general public*. This motivation devalues subjectivity because it does not serve the greater good and prioritizes the needs at the potential expense of the universal audience.

APPLYING THE IDEA MODEL TO CN COMMUNICATION

When examining CN communication through the lens of the IDEA model, the limitations of this approach become clear. According to Sellnow and Sellnow (2014), three key elements affect message compliance: internalization, explanation, and action. According to the model, messages are designed to capture the interest of their intended audiences in such a way that they are internalized. To be explanatory, messages need to provide sufficient information (e.g., what is happening, why, and what is being done to reduce risk) in intelligible terms that audiences understand. Finally, messages need to provide actionable steps audiences should take to protect themselves, their families, and their community. These three elements function best when distributed through appropriate communication channels that are accessible to the intended audiences.

Messages disseminated via CN are designed for the universal audience. Thus, when considering what elements of the message would be perceived as most relevant to particular groups, the absence of cultural content limits the internalization that invites marginalized publics to pay attention to the message. Since the content is designed with objectivity as a goal, facts and examples include and mirror scientific and technical terminology and concepts that the decision-maker considers to be relevant and necessary to portray the need for compliant behavior. Because the explanation suggested in the IDEA Model provides sufficient information for audiences to know what is happening or about to happen, the use of CN language, terminology, and examples that are not in the lexicon or experiences of marginalized publics receiving the messages may overwhelm or confuse them. Without internalizing the need to act or understand the imperative content describing the context of the crisis situation, the suggested action steps intended to save lives or mitigate a crisis are unlikely to produce the intended outcomes. Finally, the CN approach uses the traditional media channels most accessible to the decision-makers—rather than the receivers—to disseminate the messages. With the IDEA approach, decision-makers use modes of distribution that are most accessible to the audiences who will receive the messages.

EXAMPLE OF CN COMMUNICATION

What follows is an example of how CN communication was used by the WHO decision-makers to communicate about ZIKv, how the universal and particular publics responded to CN messages, how the media and publics evaluated the effectiveness of those CN messages, and limitations to the CN approach from the perspective of best practices and IMC.

The Crisis: Zika Virus and the World Health Organization

The selected crisis—ZIKv and its effect on humans, and especially pregnant women—provides the backdrop for revealing the CN approach to message creation used by the WHO between October 2015 and February 2016. Contextual background was drawn from a *Lexis-Nexis* search of several hundred newspapers, magazines, and other online sources, beginning when the virus was first detected in the Americas until February 2016 when a state of crisis was declared in several Latin American countries, as well as in several of the United States of America. A total of 136 news articles were selected by removing duplicates and including only sources that specifically included information pertinent to the emerging 2016 ZIKv on the American continents.

The WHO messages were drawn from *Disease Outbreak News*, which is posted on the WHO website (WHO, 2020). These messages represent the official public communication issued by the WHO as ZIKv emerged in the Americas as a major health crisis from October 2015 to February 2016. Twenty-four of these *Disease Outbreak News* items were collected, ranging in length from two to sixteen paragraphs (M=six paragraphs per message). These messages revealed the tendency to cluster around content themes prioritized by the WHO as it disseminated information about ZIKv. More specifically, these themes were: To release information in a timely manner about the virus; to provide certainty about the virus information being released; to focus on who was responsible for taking action to prevent the spread of the virus; and to provide enough information so publics would know how to prevent the spread of the virus (Littlefield, 2020b).

Timing of CN Communication

ZIKv gained attention from the international community in May of 2015 when the WHO issued an epidemiological alert after incidents of the virus were peaking during the first half of 2016. After five years, the status of ZIKv is reported as "transmission persists at low levels . . . and is not uniformly distributed within countries" (WHO, 2020).

Pre-Crisis

The pre-crisis period for ZIKv in the Americas went from October 2015 through January 2016. The CN communication messages during this period were official reports of detection and constituted general warnings or suggested prevention strategies. Initially, the message content focused on Aedes aegypti mosquito as the carrier of the virus and what steps could be taken to control the mosquito population around where people lived. When microcephaly among babies whose mothers had contracted the virus and neurological syndromes associated with Guillain-Barré were detected, the focus of content expanded to include warnings about sexual transmission as another way to contract the virus, and the prevention strategies shifted to include suggestions about how to avoid contracting the virus sexually.

Crisis

The crisis became official on February 1, 2016, when the director-general of the WHO explicitly reported ZIKv as an International Public Health Emergency based on information linking microcephaly and other neurological disorders to ZIKv provided by Brazil, France, the United States, and El Salvador (WHO, 2016d). This was only the fourth time such a declaration had been made (previous alerts were for Ebola, Swine Flu, and Polio), and the first time for a mosquito-borne illness (Vickery, 2016). This worldwide announcement resulted in more explicit and directive messages to reduce infection with ZIKv, including precautionary measures, longer-term measures to develop therapeutics and diagnostics, travel measures and restrictions, and data-sharing recommendations (WHO, 2016d).

Post-Crisis

The post-crisis period began in March 2016 and continues to present, as the WHO persists with what are pre-crisis communication warning about what steps are necessary to avoid a future "emergence, re-emergence, and global spread of Zika and its complications" (WHO, 2019). During the post-crisis period, content reflecting organizational learning have focused on strategies to strengthen public health systems for early detection and response, and the need to work with regional and national health authorities to secure accurate epidemiologic data on ZIKv. The WHO continues to address the threat of ZIKv transmission, as well as to other mosquito-borne viruses that may emerge or re-emerge (WHO, 2019).

Use of CN Messages

The CN messages about the ZIKv are based on a managerial perspective toward governmental and public health entities and directed to the universal audience. They are scripted and objectively broad in scope, designed for educated publics using the rational world paradigm as a basis for evaluating the messages. The messages were scientific, fact-based, and consistent, and the WHO controlled the narrative through its one-way distribution through the posting of *Disease Outbreak News* on its website. The WHO served as the spokesperson and directed its messages to other agencies, including the CDC and regional and national public health agencies. With a goal to save lives and prevent health complications, the WHO described, defined, and forecasted ZIKv from a social scientific outlook.

Appeals to Rational World Paradigm

Appealing to the rational world paradigm of information processing reflected how the WHO presented its CN messages. The rational world paradigm presupposes that humans are rational beings who rely on argument as the paradigmatic mode of decision-making and communication. Logical arguments based upon verifiable, relevant facts from credible sources are the basis of proof (Fisher, 1978), and rationality is determined by subject matter knowledge and the ability to use argumentation skills appropriate to the situations or context—in this case, global public health.

Initially, the credibility of the WHO was demonstrated through its preeminence as the leading global agency responsible for overseeing the detection and prevention of ZIKv. All twenty-four of the messages analyzed here included paragraphs with WHO pronouncements, protocol, plans, or other recommendations. The WHO controlled the narrative by being the agency receiving public health reports identifying the detection of the virus. The use of the phrase, "WHO recommends . . ." in more than half of the messages is an example of the control WHO exercised regarding its communication.

A second reason for the CN approach in the WHO messages was their timing of message publication in relation to the date when a case of ZIKv was detected.

Specifically, the date when a case of ZIKv was detected always was prioritized in the first or second paragraphs of the selected news reports. For example, "On 24 November, the National IHR Focal Point of El Salvador notified PAHO/WHO of 3 laboratory confirmed autochthonous cases of Zika Virus infection" (WHO, 2015b). The lag between the date of detection (November 24) and the date of publication (November 27) was three days. Littlefield (2020b) found that in 83.33 percent of the twenty-four articles, the difference between the identification date of the virus and its reporting date was within nine days.

A third way the WHO messages fit the rational world paradigm stemmed from a reliance on scientific certainty of the facts. In all twenty-four of the messages, indicators of certainty were present to provide credibility to the identification of the virus. In nineteen articles (70.16%), laboratory confirmation of ZIKv was prioritized in the first paragraph and an additional ten messages provided confirmation in paragraph two (Littlefield, 2020b). Finally, as would be expected, sixteen of the articles included content in one or more paragraphs about ZIKv and ways to prevent exposure. In contrast, eight provided no background information, narratives about the virus, or mitigation strategies that would be expected if messages were developed for particular cultural audiences (Littlefield, 2020b).

In summary, the WHO was characterized as using a CN approach based upon its control of the narrative as the global leader in public health, the immediacy of its reporting of cases, the certainty provided by its verification of the cases, and the presentation of content about ZIKv and how to avoid contracting the virus.

Application of Best Practices

When reviewing the CN messages disseminated by the WHO about ZIKv, best practices involving the universal audience were identified. Because the reports were in the form of scripted, one-way messages designed for transmission without feedback, they represented the perspective of the WHO and served to present the relevant information to be acted upon by other entities, including governmental entities and communities (WHO, 2016c).

Strategic Planning Best Practices

Advanced planning to guarantee a prompt response to ZIKv and the establishment of a crisis communication network was reflected in the WHO advice directed at Member States of PAHO/WHO where ZIKv was detected:

> Establish and maintain the capacity to detect and confirm cases of Zika virus infection, prepare . . . health services for a potential additional burden at all levels of health care, and implement an effective public communications strategy to reduce the mosquitoes that transmit this disease. (WHO, 2015a)

The existence of the WHO and media platforms designed to provide information pertinent to the well-being of the global public reflected the best practices associated with strategic planning (Veil et al., 2020).

Inclusive Approach Best Practices

Within the twenty-four messages analyzed during this period, the best practices reflecting inclusive approach were limited to those reflecting the focus of interest as being on the victims of ZIKv. There was no indication that specific public concerns were directly influencing how the WHO reported about the virus. However, in twenty-three of the messages, the content prioritized the focus of interest on potential victims of ZIKv. As ZIKv spread and its effects were identified, the messages became more specific about those who should be concerned about contracting the virus, particularly "people traveling to high risk areas, especially pregnant women," young children, and the elderly (WHO, 2016d). The WHO messages were posted in English and cultural differences associated with affected groups were not reflected in the messages, beyond economic differences associated with warnings to those people living outside of the region with the resources to travel.

The immediacy and regularity of reporting confirmed cases of ZIKv through the WHO website provided for the best practice of being accessible to the media in gaining access to the scientific facts associated with the megacrisis. The mention of the WHO in nearly every publication referencing ZIKv demonstrated how ubiquitous the WHO reports were and how much authority that the WHO had in providing global public health information. However, it was not until the WHO's director-general's declaration of the international public health alert on February 1 that WHO officials interacted directly with representatives of the media about the crisis (WHO, 2016d).

Within the messages, the WHO expressed collaboration with other multinational entities, including the PAHO, the United States Centers for Disease Control and Prevention (CDC), and Caribbean Public Health Agency (CARPHA). The WHO justified this coordination: "Because the science, and therefore the risk, is not well-understood, the global response needs to be coordinated and adequately-resourced with rapid investigations to understand and then mitigate the impact of Zika virus disease" (WHO, 2016e). The media reported about the WHO's collaboration with credible sources and partners as it covered ZIKv, thereby enhancing confidence in the quality of the information being disseminated. These partners included international partners such as the European Centre for Disease Surveillance and Control (MacCormaic, 2016), and Canadian Blood Services (Keaton & Cheng, 2016); national partners like the National Health Information Center ("Washington: Zika virus," 2016) and American Red Cross (Sun, Dennis, & Cha, 2016); political entities, like The White House ("Officials study virus," 2016) and the Obama administration ("Barack Obama seeks," 2016); and numerous health entities such as California Department of Public Health (Abram, 2016), American College of Obstetricians and Gynecologists (Washington: Zika virus, 2016), and Oswaldo Cruz Foundation in Brazil (Bevins, 2016).

Responsible Communication Best Practices

Among the best practices identified in this category by Veil et al. (2020), several were reflected in the CN messages of the WHO. For example, although all twenty-four messages included indicators of certainty by mentioning laboratory-confirmed or -unconfirmed cases of ZIKv, because of its reliance on scientific verification for the facts, the WHO repeatedly rejected certainty. This was particularly true when pressed to draw a causal relationship between ZIKv and birth defects and neurological syndromes. For example, the WHO often used language, such as: "Despite reports of a potential association between Zika virus and microcephaly . . . and other neurological disorders, a causal relationship between these events has not yet been confirmed" (WHO, 2016d); and "a causal relationship has not been established, but is strongly suspected" (WHO, 2016a).

Sixteen of the messages included some amount of content in one or more of the paragraphs about ZIKv and ways to prevent exposure. The suggestions focused on "reducing the breeding of mosquitoes through source reduction (removal and modification of breeding sites) and reducing contact between mosquitoes and people" (WHO, 2015c). The best practice of being candid, open, and honest in messages about ZIKv—to the point of being devoid of speculation—was characteristic of how the WHO identified confirmed cases, reported background and factual information about the virus and proposed mitigation strategies.

Due to the official nature of the communication, messages were not tailored to diverse audiences and generally were not shown to express compassion, concern, or empathy (Littlefield, 2020b). Ten of the messages did not provide any mention of vulnerable groups, use language choices reflecting cultural sensitivity, or prioritize victims affected by ZIKv. After this initial period, the messages included varying levels of reference to vulnerable groups (especially pregnant women, children, and the elderly), areas of high risk (Central and South America), language sensitivity, and victim support. It should be noted that these references were not specific but used to represent the universal (e.g., all pregnant women in contrast with specific groups or individual women experiencing the virus). In addition, these references came in the last one or two paragraphs of the report, demonstrating a lack of prioritization by the decision-makers in the creation of the messages (Littlefield, 2020b).

Corrective Action Best Practices

As time progressed, the WHO demonstrated the best practice of continuously evaluating and updating its crisis plans and recommendations; in particular, as the effects of the virus on pregnant women were confirmed. Initially, in the pre-crisis state, strategic communication responses were preventive. For example, following the WHO's prioritization, pre-crisis messages came in the form of general warnings or suggested preventive strategies and the transmission of ZIKv was linked to the bite of an infected mosquito ("Washington: Interim guidelines," 2016). In response, the WHO provided proven public health strategies to protect people from getting infected, such as "using barriers such as insect screens, closed doors and windows, long clothing and repellents" (WHO, 2016b). When the transmission of ZIKv was detected through sexual transmission, when scientists were less certain, the WHO initially provided a risk assessment reflecting uncertainty: "The risk of disease spread through sexual activity is very limited" (WHO, 2016f). Later, as sexual transmission was confirmed with certainty, the WHO issued more specific guidelines to control transmission that involved "correct and consistent use of condoms or abstinence to prevent sexual transmission of Zika virus" (WHO, 2016g).

Overall, the WHO CN messages followed best practices in strategic planning, inclusivity, responsible communication, and corrective actions. However, the development of the content was directed toward the universal audience, and even references to groups, were generic and lacking cultural specificity.

Responses to CN Messages

The responses to the CN messages of the WHO varied depending upon the choices available to those involved. For those who were geographically bound to the region most affected by ZIKv, panic and fear was high; and those with the personal resources to choose whether or not to travel to the region had the agency to change their plans. Responses from the business and religious leaders reflected a lack of input prior to the release of the messages, as the business leaders sought to promote the safety of the Summer Olympic Games in contrast to warnings to stay away; and the Catholic Church and its followers found the WHO messages to be in conflict with their fundamental religious beliefs about contraception.

As the connection between ZIKv and microcephaly became clearer, pregnant women and women planning to conceive that lived in the affected region became more anxious: "All of the women I see at the hospital or in my office who are pregnant or wanting to get pregnant are very alarmed, almost panicky" ("Brazil fears birth," 2016); "Many pregnant women across Brazil are in a panic," and, "The situation is incredibly frightening" (Romero, 2016). Based on these reactions, the Brazilian government urged women to take precautions to wear long pants and apply insect repellent to avoid mosquito bites.

For those with the agency to determine whether to travel to the region, the WHO messages prompted women to reconsider travel plans. For example, in one report, Russell Smith and his pregnant wife, Rosemary Saponaro of Merrick, were supposed to travel on a Norwegian Cruise Line ship to visit eight ports in Zika-endemic countries. The couple canceled the trip even though the company would not refund the tickets (Ricks & Chayas, 2016). Lauren Machowsky, a travel advisor at New York-based Smartflyer, told reporters: "There's been a lot of cancellations. Some people are freaked out." Parenting website babycenter.com asked pregnant readers with plans to travel to Zika-affected areas if they would change course: "About half of 1,118 respondents said they planned to cancel, and 27% said they were keeping their plans. The rest were undecided" ("Health Ministry issues," 2016). The news of ZIKv had an impact on tourism in Puerto Rico, with some tourist groups canceling reservations, particularly weddings in hotels on the Caribbean island ("Puerto Rico declares," 2016).

For businesses and government, the WHO reports of a spreading virus threatened the Summer Olympic Games and the economic welfare of Brazil: "There were fears this summer's Olympic Games in Rio could be a multibillion pound flop as athletes and fans may stay away from Brazil, where the virus has been linked to thousands of babies being born with microcephaly, or small heads" (White, 2016). Some officials took issue with the CDS's warning. For example, Henrique Alves, Brazil's tourism minister, argued that the Brazilian authorities were adopting measures to prevent Zika from intensifying in the country. Philip Wilkinson, a spokesperson for the committee organizing the Olympics stressed: "Rio 2016 will continue to monitor the issue closely and follow guidance from the Brazilian Ministry of Health. Authorities in Brazil insist that they are taking steps to fight Zika, including vaccine research" (Romero, 2016). The organizers of the Summer Olympics in Brazil said they'll be on high alert to prevent Zika and would daily seek out stagnant water where Zika-spreading mosquitoes could breed ("Washington: Zika virus," 2016).

Another group that was caught off guard by the CN approach was the Catholic Church. When ZIKv was tied to infected mosquitoes, the message posed no direct threat to the region's faith communities where a major portion of the population is Roman Catholic. However, when ZIKv was found to be sexually transmitted, and the WHO issued a recommended strategy that involved the use of condoms and abstinence, the CN response produced a strong reaction from the church leaders. This message and implicit endorsement of birth control was in opposition to the church that has long condemned contraception. The Rev. Hector Figueroa, a priest in charge of health issues in the San Salvador Archdiocese, said that the WHO pregnancy alert appeared in the Salvadoran news media Friday morning and that the archbishop had not had time to formulate an official response: "Morality says that people shouldn't have that control over procreation. But the church also isn't going to say something that runs contrary to life and health. This is a very delicate issue" (Partlow, 2016). In addition to contraception, ZIKv also prompted debate on whether abortion should be used to stop pregnancies with babies having microcephaly: "The virus has also prompted debate on abortion in largely Catholic Latin America and the Caribbean. Calls to ease laws that restrict abortions have gained momentum but are being resisted by conservative religious authorities, causing an increase in the rate of illegal abortions in Brazil" ("Zika spurs global," 2016).

In short, responses to the WHO messages varied. Individuals who were bound to the region most affected by the virus experienced panic because the risk of contracting the virus was great and the options to relocate were limited. For those with the agency to control their travel plans, the warnings were effective and resulted in travel options to reduce the risk. Because of the nature of CN messages, the WHO developed them for a universal audience. In so doing, economic and religious entities were put into the position of confronting the WHO messages either by suggesting that they were reducing the risk (as in the case of the Summer Olympics) or by opposing the strategy (as in the case of contraception).

Effectiveness of CN Messages

When examining the effectiveness of the CN messages pertaining to the ZIKv, the IDEA model of instructional communication provides insight. The internalization of the crisis as being relevant to the individual must be realized to compel individuals to take necessary action to avoid contracting the virus. In the WHO messages, the messages were not designed to have that result. Rather than to bring the crisis into the inner-most sphere of ethnocentricity for the individual, the crisis was introduced at the national or global sphere. Thus, for those individuals who became aware of the crisis, the explanation phase of the model provided scientific facts, information about the Aeges mosquito and how to destroy its environment. Later, when certainty about the sexual transmission of the virus was established, the danger for pregnant women was more immediate because contracting the virus was drawn into the personal sphere. The action steps in the CN messages suggested universal ways to be protected from being bitten. The channel for distributing the CN message was not directed toward the publics but rather to the scientific community and governmental partners, as well as to the media. The absence of direct communication with the affected publics was another reason limiting the effectiveness of the WHO's messages.

The lack of recognition of how the CN message would be perceived by economic and religious entities resulted in these groups having to respond in a way that countered the recommendations and suggested an alternative worldview. While travel agencies and promoters of the Summer Olympic Games assured patrons that they would receive refunds if they changed their plans, they issued messages that minimized the risk and assured potential visitors that the crisis was being managed. For the leaders in the Catholic Church, messages pertaining to cultural beliefs, particularly about sexual transmission of the virus were less effective because there was no cultural sensitivity shown toward those who may oppose conception and who may not be willing to sacrifice the opportunity to conceive a child in order to avoid contracting the virus. Salina Velasquez Cortez who had been trying to conceive for the past two years, said there was no way she would stop trying despite the health warning: "After so much time wanting to be a mother, I'm not going to give up now . . . I think it's absurd" (Partlow, 2016). The CN messages did not recognize the need to work with those who may be adversely affected by suggested strategies to confront ZIKv. Rather, the CN message about discouraging tourist travel and using contraceptives was issued in the same way as the scientific information about the mosquito.

Limitations of CN Approach

Even though the CN approach has limitations, several reasons explain why the WHO may have used this approach when responding to ZIKv, including the role of the WHO as a leading organization promoting global public health; the nature of the WHO message content; and the basis for the reasoning used by the WHO audiences. First, the *global role* played by the WHO as a leader in the promotion of public health is well-established, having grown out of the International Sanitary Conferences held between 1851 and 1938 to combat major diseases such as cholera, yellow fever, and the bubonic plague. As an agency of the United Nations, the WHO was created on April 7, 1948, following World War II. As Beech (2020) described, the WHO plays many roles, including "advocating for universal healthcare, monitoring public health risks, setting health standards and guidelines, coordinating international responses to health emergencies, fighting infectious diseases like HIV and tuberculosis, and promoting better nutrition, housing and sanitation in the name of overall well-being." Because of its role as the premiere global agency with the mission to provide "all peoples of the highest possible level of health" (Beech, 2020), the WHO is regarded as the gold standard by which other agencies base their decision-making.

A second reason CN was used by the WHO may stem from *the nature or content* of its messages. Because the WHO carries the global authority of the United Nations and the world's public health community, its messages must be compelling and directed toward the universal audience. Within this audience are agencies and governmental entities—similar in function and purpose to the WHO—that enact guidelines and strategies to reduce the threat of a worldwide crisis or pandemic. Perelman and Olbrechts-Tyteca (1958/1971) addressed the need for such broad messages when speaking to the universal audience: "Argumentation addressed to a universal audience must convince . . . that the reasons adduced are of a compelling character, that they are self-evident, and possess an absolute and timeless validity, independent of local or historical contingencies." In other words, to appeal to the universal audience, there must be certitude, or the complete belief that excludes all doubt, "employing nothing but logical proof" (p. 32). The objective, fact-based, impersonal, transparent messages of the WHO did not include information aimed at particular audiences because what might appeal to one group may be unacceptable to others. Thus, the content of the WHO ZIKv messages was meant to leave little doubt that the information being provided was "real, true, and objectively valid" (p. 33).

Finally, the CN approach may have been used by the WHO because the audience expected such messages from the WHO (Fisher, 2017). In contrast to the rational world paradigm, Fisher (2017) presents the narrative paradigm whereby humans are essentially storytellers and the rationality of their narratives is determined by their probability and fidelity. If a story rings true with what the listeners know to be true in their lives, even what is known to be factual can be discounted (Hardy et al., 2019). Because the WHO's audience would expect information consistent with the conventions of logical proof in the context of global public health, the absence of narratives reflective of that would communicate matters of "history, biography, culture, and character" were in character (Fisher, 2017, p. 269).

SUMMARY

This chapter provided an expanded description of the CN approach to risk and crisis communication through the dimensions of a managerial/elite perspective, scripted messages, one-way communication, traditional single-spokesperson model, and the lens of social science. Critiquing this approach using the IDEA model, culture-neutral communication excludes cultural content to promote internalization, provides terminology and scientific information that may confuse or overwhelm audiences, and suggests actions that may not be within the capacity or worldview of the audience to execute. Through the example of the ZIKv mega-crisis, the CN approach showed when CN communication was used (pre-crisis, crisis, post-crisis); how CN messages were presented (using best practices); what the responses to the CN messages were; how the CN approach facilitated effective risk communication;

and limitations to the CN approach. In the next chapter, the advantages of using a CS variation of source-controlled risk and crisis communication is shown in the context of Hurricane Dorian, a Category 5 Atlantic hurricane that struck the Bahamas and is regarded as the worst natural disaster in the country's history.

Chapter 6

The Culturally Sensitive Approach

Chapter 5 provided a detailed examination of the CN approach to risk and crisis communication within the context of IMC, emphasizing its managerial/elite single-spokesperson perspective, scripted message, one-way dissemination, and social scientific orientation. The ZIKv mega-crisis was used to reveal when CN communication was used (pre-crisis, crisis, and post-crisis); how CN messages were presented (using best practices as a tool for evaluation of effectiveness); what responses from publics resulted from the CN messages; how the CN approach facilitated risk communication; and the limitations of the CN approach. Intersecting this analysis is the overlay of the IDEA model to reveal how CN communication is less effective in conveying risk and crisis information and directives. In chapter 6, the CS approach is illustrated within the context of IMC, with the emphasis on the following dimensions: managerial/elite perspective; scripted message; one-way limited feedback; multiple-spokesperson model; cultural adaptation (e.g., learning styles and communication perspectives); and the interpretive perspective. This approach is illustrated with the example of Hurricane Dorian that devastated the Bahamas and surrounding islands and Florida to show: (1) when CS communication was used (pre-crisis, crisis, post-crisis); (2) how CS messages were presented (using best practices); (3) what responses resulted from the CS messages; (4) how the CS approach facilitated effective risk communication; and (5) what limitations to the CS approach were evident.

THE CULTURALLY SENSITIVE APPROACH

The CS approach begins to take shape in stage 2 of IMC. In this stage, the organization has committed resources, time, and money to understand its consumers, customers, and potential publics. In stage 2, an attempt is made to learn what customers and consumers want to hear, when they want the information, where they want to get the information, and which media they prefer. This represents "outside-in marketing" (Kitchen & De Pelsmacker, 2004, p. 26) and requires external integration with entities outside of the organization to acquire information about customer preferences.

The IMC process of learning about the consumer reflects the process used by those employing the CS approach to risk and crisis communication. To determine the strategies to include in messages designed for vulnerable publics, communicators must choose from among many cultural categories. Abramson and Moran (2018) offered ten broad categories to understand cultural groups and how they respond to messages, including a sense of self and space; communication and language; dress and appearance; food and feeding habits; time and time consciousness; relationships; values and norms; beliefs and attitudes; mental process and learning; and work habits and practices. To illustrate how these categories of culture affect communication, one might consider how the variable of time and time consciousness affects the publics' response times when notified of an impending risk or crisis. Similarly, how cultures view human relationships may influence whether men will take advice from women as spokespersons. If publics are influenced by religious traditions, they may not be willing to act while engaging in religious practices or during religious observances.

Managerial/Elite Perspective

The CS approach holds the perspective that to reach groups that are targeted as vulnerable or in danger, messages should be designed for the particular audience (Perelman & Olbrechts-Tyteca (1958/1971)). This perspective stands in direct contrast to the universal audience of the CN approach. Particular audiences have cultural characteristics that are identifiable by a decision-maker in an organization seeking to disseminate a message. Based upon how much time and energy has been invested in studying these characteristics, the decision-maker is in the position to determine which characteristics will be addressed in message preparation and dissemination. The decision-makers have access to the data available and create a message that aligns with what they consider to be the most effective ways to reach the target audience. If the publics include Spanish speaking people, the decision-makers may decide to disseminate the message in Spanish. In doing so, the decision-makers believe they are showing cultural sensitivity toward the Spanish-speakers in the audience. If the publics include individuals with strong spiritual beliefs, decision-makers may decide to avoid suggesting controversial communication strategies. For example, decision-makers may decide to avoid suggesting the use of contraceptives to devout Catholics following their contraction of ZIKv to avoid the risk of microcephaly in unborn children. Rather, strategies focused on eliminating standing water and wearing long-sleeves and pants may be better suited to the Catholic audience. The decision-makers also may choose to use the vernacular of the targeted publics because common words and phrases are more likely to be understood. By using appeals that the CS decision-maker believes will be received positively by the intended audiences, they view their intent as helpful. CS communicators exhibit an awareness of primary cultural norms and values in CS messages, even if they personally do not accept them. However, the worldview of the decision-maker remains in the elite position by making the choices about what appeals are used, when they are used, and how they are communicated to the intended publics. Once the CS messages are created and disseminated, the decision-maker expects that the publics will respond favorably and recognize the effort made to appeal to their observable cultural characteristics and preferences. But cultural sensitivity cannot be generalized beyond the particular cultural group so there is no guarantee that sensitivity will be met with receptivity by the vulnerable publics. The source of the CS message is the sender and the responsibility for action remains with the publics receiving the messages. By modifying the CN messages to include CS content, decision-makers can indicate their efforts as being other-focused, even though they control the choice of cultural content to achieve their self-focused objective of message dissemination in a crisis situation.

Scripted Message

SC messages give the appearance of being subjective because cultural content is included by the decision-makers. However, just as in CN messages, facts and evidence to support the conclusions being drawn by decision-makers provide the substance of the risk and crisis messages. The decision-makers have not changed the content of the messages; rather, they have decorated their messages with cultural markers that may have some appeal to particular audiences. The CS message reflects even greater preplanning because the organization has gathered data from intended publics to learn more about them. This data has been horizontally integrated within the IMC organization, so all departments are aware of the dominant cultural characteristics. As the decision-makers take the data collected from stage 2 IMC and craft risk or crisis messages, the only feedback expected from publics is compliance and the acknowledgment that the messages had recognizable cultural identification (e.g., language, values, and worldview). The role of the audience is acceptance and acknowledgment, and the sender controls the process.

One-Way with Limited Feedback

Just as in CN messages, the CS approach is one-way with the sender disseminating the message to the universal audience while acknowledging the presence of particular audiences within that larger body who are identified through language and other cultural markers. The difference with CS communication comes from the efforts of the organization to move from stage 1 to stage 2 in IMC. Without data collection and analysis of potential publics in stage 2, CS communication cannot occur. The data collection process is ongoing, and organizations can discern public response to the messages as they are being disseminated. If vulnerable publics respond to the CS messages by complying with instructional or persuasive risk and crisis messages, decision-makers may determine the characteristics they sought to appeal to were, in fact, influential. In that case, they may continue using the cultural strategies in future messages. In contrast, if vulnerable publics do not respond as the decision-makers hoped, through data collection and sharing of that information throughout the organization, different cultural markers may be chosen in hopes they will be more appealing to the publics and internalized. In either case, the decision-makers create the messages without the involvement of the publics in the process.

Multiple-Spokesperson Model

The multiple-spokesperson model is used by organizations when they determine that having someone from the cultural groups being targeted in the message will be helpful in gaining compliance from the intended audiences. In these cases, the decision-maker has gathered data and determined that the risk or crisis message will be perceived as more credible and culturally sensitive if a spokesperson from each intended public is used to convey it. We know that the existence of the universal audience implies the presence of multiple particular audiences within it (Perelman & Olbrechts-Tyteca, 1958/1971). Thus, each of these particular audiences may represent a different cultural perspective, necessitating the need for multiple spokespersons to convey the scripted message. The control of the managers or decision-makers in the process remains evident because these elites select the individuals who they believe will be the most credible as spokespeople. An additional benefit of the multiple-spokesperson model is the opportunity for limited feedback because as the spokesperson presents the risk or crisis message to the intended audience, the opportunity for interaction exists.

Cultural Adaptation

Risk and crisis messages are designed to instruct and motivate people to take the necessary steps to save their lives and livelihoods. However, to gain compliance of affected publics in a crisis, decision-makers must prepare for resistance based on conflicting values, history with external agencies, and social habits of the group. As Littlefield (2015) noted: "depending upon one's ethnicity, country of origin, economic status, education level, access to information, literacy, and social standing, the receiver of a message may be more or less likely to respond according to cultural beliefs and values than directly to the content of the message" (p. 3). Thus, to gain compliance, CS decision-makers must realize what publics may give up if they comply. Rogers (2003) suggested that when ideas are diffused into social systems, the process involves five steps: knowledge; persuasion, decision, implementation, and confirmation. Individuals need to understand what is happening, be persuaded that some action should be taken, make the commitment to do what is requested, actually take the necessary steps to act, and then determine that it was the right thing to do. Suggesting that what decision-makers regard as the right thing to do may not be viewed similarly by the affected publics reflects the managerial perspective of the elites who believe they know what is best. Decision-makers using CS communication believe they will face less resistance from publics as cultural adaptation occurs within the particular audiences who receive risk and crisis messages.

Interpretive Perspective

Like social scientists, interpretive scholars describe what they observe, but because the contexts affect how they view a phenomenon, they are unwilling to generalize or predict what their observations mean in the larger context. This characteristic is relevant when considering CS communication because an effort is made by decision-makers to single out cultural categories to enhance the receptivity of the audience to the risk and crisis messages. From the IMC perspective, the data collected in stage 2 may is mostly descriptive in nature. The demographics identify the size of the cultural group, the gender breakdown of its members, literacy levels, religious or spiritual orientation, employment, and education levels of the cultural group, to name a few. How these data are interpreted by the decision-makers determines what demographics are prioritized in the content to encourage the publics to pay attention to the message, explain what is happening, and encourage specific action for self-protection and mitigation of harmful crisis effects.

The interpretive perspective recognizes that members of cultural groups create shared meanings and communicate with each other in unique ways. How meanings are created and conveyed is limited to the cultural groups in which they exist, and they cannot be universally applied. Thus, if decision-makers want to effectively disseminate a risk or crisis message, they must understand the uniqueness of each particular audience and how that audience must receive the message in order to achieve the intended outcome. The ethnocentricity of the decision-makers must be modified with alternative ways of presenting the messages based upon how they interpret what will be meaningful and positively received by the publics.

APPLYING THE IDEA MODEL TO CS COMMUNICATION

As CS communication is examined through the application of the IDEA Model, all elements become part of the decision-maker's toolkit when crafting risk and crisis messages. As Sellnow and Sellnow (2014) noted, messages must contain internalization, explanation, and action, and be distributed through the appropriate channels to gain compliance. Elements of culture can be part of or influence each part of the model. To begin, internalization occurs when the intended audience sees, hears, or experiences something that captures their attention and compels them to focus on the message. For example, if decision-makers wanted to reach an audience who supported human rights and abhorred racism, they might use a digital recording of a White police officer kneeling on the neck of a Black man to commands attention and focuses the observer on racist police practices. The internalization caused by the selected image would be culturally sensitive because the video was selected for its appeal to an audience that is receptive to the crisis being addressed by the decision-makers.

When explaining the crisis, the literacy levels of the particular audience members influence the CS decision-makers to use commonly understood language and examples that have meaning within the cultural group. Using real examples of how similar crises have affected other groups and will affect the intended audience provides the CS communicator with sufficient information to convey the message without overwhelming the publics who need to know what is happening. Understanding cultural characteristics will help decision-makers to determine the timing and use of appropriate action steps that the publics need to take to protect themselves and their livelihoods. Knowing when to provide the information based upon religious or spiritual observances, understanding the dynamics of family relationships, and taking into account the agency of the publics based upon their worldviews provides the decision-makers using CS communication with the ability to select content that will most effectively convey their intended risk and crisis messages. Sensitivity to such questions of timing is a long-standing dimension of effectively practices IMC (Persuit, 2016).

Finally, once the CS decision-makers have used cultural elements to capture their audience members' attention, incorporated explanation in a way that is understood within the cultural group, and suggested strategies that are compatible with cultural practices and norms, the final element of the IDEA model calls for the distribution of the message using the appropriate means of conveyance. The decision-makers in IMC will have collected data indicating the publics' preferences for how to receive information. This descriptive data will inform the process and enable decision-makers to structure the release of their risk and crisis messages in ways that are most appropriate for the multiple publics who will need to receive them.

EXAMPLE OF CS COMMUNICATION: HURRICANE DORIAN CRISIS

This section illustrates how CS communication was used by decision-makers at the National Hurricane Center, how the tourists and residents responded to CS messages, how the media and publics evaluated the effectiveness of CS messages, and limitations to the CN approach from the perspective of best practices and IMC.

The Crisis: Hurricane Dorian and the National Hurricane Center

The selected crisis—Hurricane Dorian—and its effects on communities provides the context for illustrating the CS approach to message creation used by the NHC between August 24 and September 10, 2019. Data for this analysis were drawn from the Hurricane Dorian Advisory Archive from August 24 to September 9, 2019. The NHC posted 64 forecast advisories, 64 public advisories with 140 updates, 64 discussions, and 64 wind speed probabilities during this time frame (National Oceanic and Atmospheric Administration, 2019). The forecast advisories, discussions, and wind speed probabilities were culture-neutral due to their heavily scientific nature of information. The 204 public advisories and updates were designed for publics who were in the path of the hurricane and came in the form of numbered bulletins originating at the National Weather Service NHC in Miami, Florida. A random sample of sixteen (one from each day that bulletins were posted) was analyzed. Each bulletin included a summary of information pertinent to the hurricane: Present location; maximum sustained winds; present movement; and minimum central pressure. This is followed by watches and warnings associated with the current advisory; discussion and outlook for the short term; and hazards affecting land.

Hurricane Dorian was selected because it represents a crisis that was originally forecast to impact Florida most directly and then shifted to instead devastate the Bahamas most dramatically, as well as other states along the entire eastern coasts of the United States and Canada (see table 6.1). As such, to be successful, the NHC would need to design and deliver messages that were sensitive to the norms and values of distinctly different cultural groups. Specifically modifying the messages to include geographic areas to be next impacted by Hurricane Dorian was a CS decision-made by NHC.

Timeline of Crisis Phases

As is the case with any tropical disturbance that develops in the Atlantic Ocean, the NHC monitors wind and rotation speeds as they create forecasts for people living in places where these storms may potentially strike. Ultimately, when

Table 6.1 Location of Land Areas Directly Affected by Hurricane Dorian

Date	Bulletin #	Land Areas Directly Affected
August 24	1	No specific land areas identified
August 25	4	Barbados
August 26	7A	Barbados
		St. Lucia
August 27	11A	St. Lucia
August 28	15A	Puerto Rico
August 29	20	San Juan, Puerto Rico
		Southeastern Bahamas
August 30	26	Northwest Bahamas
		West Palm Beach, Florida
August 31	27A	Northwest Bahamas
		West Palm Beach, Florida
September 1	31A	Great Abaco Island
		West Palm Beach, Florida
September 2	35A	Grand Bahama Island
September 3	41	Freeport, Grand Bahama Island
		Fort Pierce, Florida
		South Santee River, South Carolina
		Cape Lookout, North Carolina
September 4	44	Daytona Beach, Florida
September 5	47A	Southeastern and Mid-Atlantic Coasts
		South Carolina
		North Carolina
September 6	51A	Eastern North Carolina
September 7	56	New England
		Southeast Massachusetts
		Nova Scotia
		Newfoundland
		Lower North Short Quebec
September 8	60A	Atlantic Canada
September 10		Dissipated near Greenland

Source: National Oceanic and Atmospheric Administration, 2019.

speeds and rotation warrant, these disturbances are named. Hurricane Dorian, literally the most powerful Atlantic hurricane up to that time, was named a tropical wave on August 24 while it was still located in the middle of the Atlantic. The NHC redefined it as a hurricane on August 28. The first hurricane warning was issued on August 30. For these reasons, we surmise that the pre-crisis phase began August 24 and remained in pre-crisis for the Bahamas until it reached its peak as a Category 5 hurricane by September 1. At that point, it became a crisis as it made landfall and remained stationary there until it began moving to the northwest on September 3, parallel to the east coast of Florida (Weather.gov, 2019).

As the hurricane traveled up the eastern seaboard, new geographic locations moved from pre-crisis to crisis phase as warnings shifted to focus on them. Once the hurricane trajectory moved out a given location, communities in that area moved into the post-crisis phase. Finally, all communities were in post-crisis by the time the hurricane dissipated on September 10 somewhere in the Atlantic near Greenland. Thus, for a slow-moving crisis such as Hurricane Dorian, the shifts from pre-crisis to crisis and then to post-crisis were fluid, in that they advanced with the storm as it proceeded along its path. With this context in mind, the following sections describe messages offered in the NHC Bulletins that used elements of the IDEA model for effective instructional risk and crisis communication messages generally, and CS components specifically related to each element.

Use of CS Messages as Illustrated via the IDEA Model

This section provides examples of CS messages used by the NHC through the lens of the IDEA model for effective instructional risk and crisis communication described in chapter 4. In doing so, both strengths and limitations of the messages are clarified in terms of how well they illustrate cultural sensitivity and how they demonstrate each element of the model.

Internalization

To be effective, instructional risk and crisis messages must motivate receivers to take notice and pay attention to what is being communicated to them. This can be achieved by highlighting personal relevance and potential impact (i.e., Will it impact me and/or those I care about, and how?). Some strategies for compelling receivers to pay attention generally include establishing immediacy through compassion and empathy, clarifying proximity and timeline for the events, and using exemplars that appeal to emotions when illustrating potential impact (Sellnow & Sellnow, 2019).

As depicted in figure 6.1, the NHC Bulletins demonstrated cultural sensitivity as they appealed to internalization by clearly identifying specific

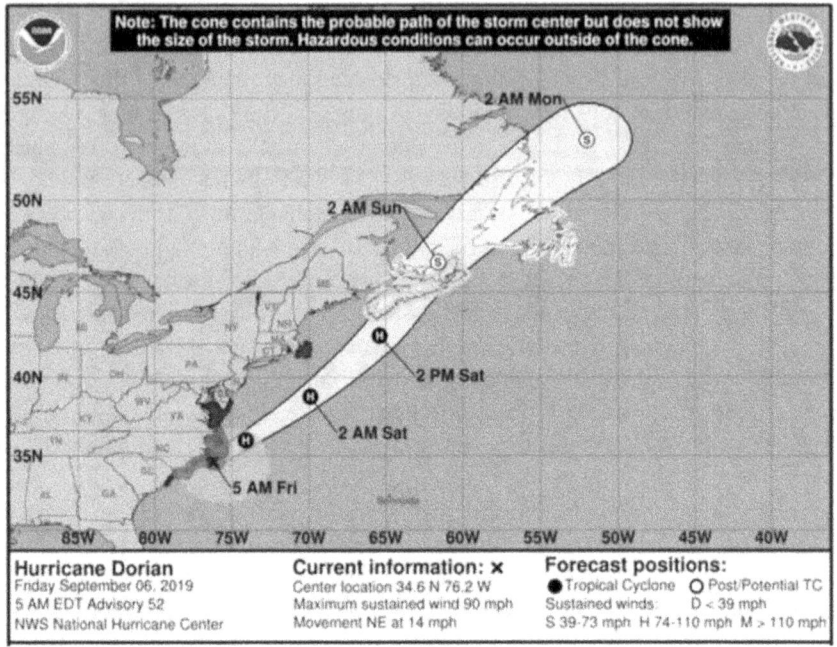

Figure 6.1 Hurricane Dorian Probable Path of the Storm. *Source*: https://search.creativecommons.org/search?q=hurricane%20path.

geographic locations to be impacted, probable storm intensity, and when to expect the storm to actually strike that area. In addition, maps were used to clarify meaning (Lester, 2013). Figure 6.1 shows an example of one such map.

Moreover, previous research confirms that respondents want to see a map to understand fully where the disaster is to occur (Sellnow et al., 2019b). The NHC Bulletins also demonstrated cultural sensitivity as they appealed to internalization by directing the publics to the local weather and meteorologists for up-to-the minute information. Within every Bulletin was a reference to "your local weather service or office," "your national meteorological service," or "your local National Weather Service." In the areas affected by hurricanes, local residents often shelter in place rather than leave their homes. Understanding this, by providing the reinforcement to consult the local authorities in their area, the NHC was demonstrating sensitivity to the tendency of some to resist authority, in spite of the danger. The consistent reference to the "your" pronoun fostered immediacy (Richmond et al., 2018) and rapport (Frisby & Buckner, 2018).

Finally, messages addressed internalization in a CS way by appealing to emotions through the use of exemplars. Exemplars are simply words, phrases, visual images, or sounds that motivate receivers to attend to and remember because they appeal to emotions (Zillmann, 2006). In the sampled Bulletins, the term "life-threatening" was used thirty-three times to describe surf and rip current conditions, storm surge, and flash floods. "Large," "destructive," "powerful," and "dangerous" or "dangerously" were used to describe the hurricane and its effects. These emotive words signaling harmful effects were culturally sensitive because they targeted publics who were either visiting as tourists or living in the region where hurricanes are an annual experience. Table 6.2 provides a listing of the emotive words used in the sixteen sampled messages.

Regarding internalization, the messages offered in the NHC Bulletins seemed to achieve the intended goals of motivating target audiences to take notice of and pay attention to the messages. This was accomplished by illustrating personal relevance and impact in CS ways.

Distribution

To be most effective, instructional risk and crisis messages must be offered regularly as the crisis evolves, provided by a variety of credible sources, and delivered through multiple communication channels that are accessible target populations (Sellnow & Sellnow, 2019). When these strategies are employed, information-seeking produces a congruent narrative that is likely to be trusted by disparate publics (Sellnow et al., 2019a). Challenges include drawing from sources that the targeted publics deem as trustworthy using communication channels that are accessible to those the messages are intended to reach (Sellnow & Sellnow, 2019). For example, not all people have access to computers or internet or choose to seek information from those sources. Moreover, the technology may fail during the disaster as was the cases of

Table 6.2 Examples of Emotive Language Used by NHC

Emotive Word Choices	Frequency of Mention in Sample
"Life-threatening surf and rip current conditions"	15
"Life-threatening storm surge"	9
"Life-threatening flash floods"	9
"Large and destructive waves"	6
"Powerful"	4
"Dangerously close to Florida"	3
"Extremely dangerous"	3
"Dangerous hurricane force winds"	3
"Sustained/strong winds"	2
"Catastrophic"	1
"Large swells"	1
"Dangerous"	1
"Swells could be life-threatening"	1
"Gradually strengthening"	1
"Tropical storm"	1

9/11 terrorist attacks in New York in 2001 and Hurricane Katrina in New Orleans in 2005 (Simon & Teperman, 2001; Spence et al., 2008). Thus, some publics are more likely to rely on legacy media (e.g., print, radio, and TV) than digital media (e.g., smart phones, computers, and internet).

To be culturally sensitive, the selected sources should be perceived as credible by a target audience. These trusted sources may differ for the varied cultural and co-cultural groups (e.g., governmental agencies, local authorities, opinion leaders, media influencers) (Sellnow et al., 2019a). These sources also may differ based on the specific risk situation or crisis event. For example, people may seek information from a health organization or medical professional during a pandemic, the U.S. Department of Agriculture (USDA) or U.S. Food and Drug Administration (USFDA or FDA) regarding food security, and the national or local weather service during a storm. In the sample of NHC Bulletins examined, messages were offered regularly by both local and national authorities. The NHC was also culturally sensitive in the way it directed the publics to the local weather and meteorologists for up to the minute information with references to "your local weather service or office."

Explanation

In addition to the aforementioned strategies related to internalization and distribution, effective instructional risk and crisis messages need to provide accurate information that is explained in ways will be understood by the target audiences (Sellnow & Sellnow, 2019). One challenge to overcome regarding explanation involved making sure that messages were offered in the native language of the audiences (Ravazzani, 2016). Another factor for decision-makers to consider was how to provide clarity about both what is known and unknown as the crisis developed, particularly when it may not have been previously experienced, as in the case of emerging diseases and novel viruses, such as H1N1, SARS, and COVID-19 (Bi et al., 2010; Lipsitch et al., 2020). Finally, translating scientific information accurately and intelligibly to disparate publics who may not be experts in the particular field was essential (Fischer et al., 2016). In fact, the consequences of failing to overcome these challenges in the face of a hurricane would most certainly result in unnecessary harms and deaths (Sellnow et al., 2017a).

The NHC Bulletin messages employed explanation strategies to overcome these barriers in a number of CS ways. For instance, the NHC decision-makers offered messages not only in English but also in Spanish to address the large Hispanic population affected by Hurricane Dorian. In communication distributed by the Department of Public Safety and Homeland Security, useful and necessary information needed such as 911 services, wireless services available, and cable systems were provided in English and Spanish (Public Safety and

Homeland Security, 2019). Most of the information was provided online, which may not be culturally sensitive to those without access to the internet. However, the decision to provide multilingual messages reflected cultural sensitivity.

To address the challenge of addressing what is known and unknown, the NHC was faced with having to deal with probabilities, not predictions. Thus, as the slow-moving storm progressed, it shifted direction and altered the cone of uncertainty. Most hurricanes are prone to dramatic changes in rotation, wind speed, and intensity of impact (Ferro, 2013), as was the case with Hurricane Dorian. To show the publics where the storm was headed, scientists relied on spaghetti plots generated from different computer simulators that were not to be in close agreement with one another. These seemingly contradictory computer-simulated messages, though based on scientific data modeling, contributed to confusion when people attempt to make decisions about preparing to evacuate or stay and shelter in place. However, the use of mapping was a CS decision made for those who may respond to visual rather than aural explanations. Figure 6.2 illustrates the forecast modeling images of Hurricane Dorian that suggested it would most likely hit land in Florida near Cocoa Beach and travel directly through the Orlando area. However, after it stalled in the Bahamas, it ultimately turned out to sea and instead followed the Atlantic seaboard northward. Because forecasting is based on probabilities, it is not predictive. Unfortunately, these changing forecasts—although accurate based on what was known at the time—may have confused and frustrated intended target audiences.

To respond to the needs of the publics for a clear explanation of what to expect, the NHC consistently explained scientific terminology in common

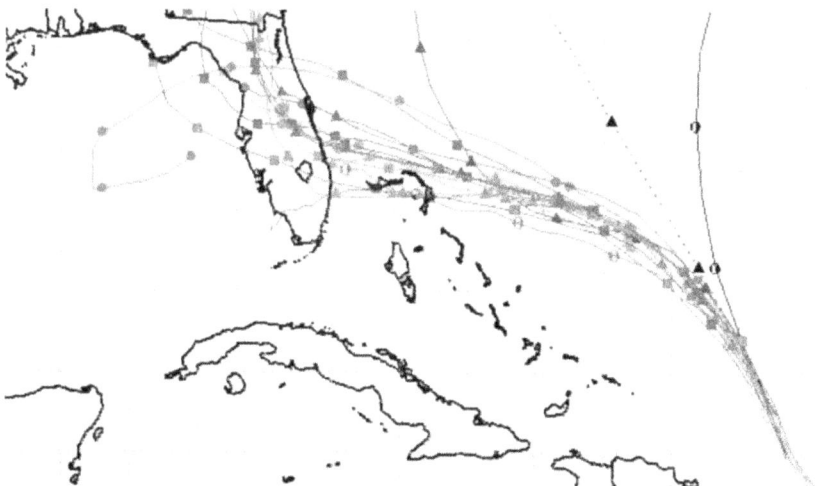

Figure 6.2 Hurricane Dorian Spaghetti Model. *Source*: McBride (2019, September 1). https://heavy.com/news/2019/08/dorian-spaghetti-models/.

terms whenever they used it. To clarify, specific weather terminology was used in fourteen of the sixteen Bulletins examined for this case. In every instance, these accurate and precise terms were defined simply the first time they were used. Following every watch or warning, the NHC used the phrase, "An 'X' watch or warning means . . ." to lead the publics to the meaning of the warning. Table 6.3 provides a listing of weather warning terminology and their meanings as defined in the NHC Bulletins.

Action

Finally, effective instructional risk and crisis messages provide specific actionable directions for protection of oneself and their loved ones, as well as for those not impacted that want to help (Sellnow & Sellnow, 2019). In fact, during crises people want to do something to protect themselves and help others. Previous research confirms that when such directions are missing, people still do something. However, it often is precisely the wrong thing (Sellnow et al., 2017a).

Some challenges to be overcome include being specific in terms of preparing for and responding to the crisis event, particularly when the desired actions change with the evolving crisis. Another is conveying the instructions in ways that are understood and implemented correctly. For example, during

Table 6.3 Weather Warnings Included in NHC Bulletins and Their Meanings

Weather Warning	Explanation of Meaning Provided
Tropical Storm Watch	Tropical storm conditions are possible within the watch area, generally within 48 hours.
Tropical Storm Warning	Tropical storm conditions are expected within the warning area within 36 hours.
Hurricane Watch	Hurricane conditions are possible within the watch area. A watch is typically issued 48 hours before the anticipated first occurrence of tropical-storm-force winds, conditions that make outside preparations difficult or dangerous.
Hurricane Warning	Hurricane conditions are expected somewhere within the warning area. Preparations to protect life and property should be rushed to completion.
Storm Surge Watch	There is a possibility of life-threatening inundation, from rising water moving inland from the coastline, in the indicated locations during the next 48 hours.
Storm Surge Warning	There is a danger of life-threatening inundation, from rising water moving inland from the coastline, during the next 36 hours in the indicated locations. This is a life-threatening situation. People located within these areas should take all necessary actions to protect life and property from rising water and the potential for other dangerous conditions. Promptly follow evacuation and other instructions from local officials.

the COVID-19 crisis, people needed to be instructed in ways that would result in them washing their hands frequently for at least twenty seconds each time (Cavanagh & Wambier, 2020) and wearing masks properly (Feng et al., 2020). To be culturally sensitive, these actionable instructions also need to honor the cultural norms of the target audience. For example, when the WHO offered instructions not to kiss the bodies of those that died from Ebola, they did not honor cultural norms. As a result, the target audiences did not implement the desired protective actions (Cénat et al., 2020; Hewlett & Hewlett, 2007).

Regarding Hurricane Dorian, one challenge to overcome in the action strategy was rooted in the fact that hurricane forecasts changed as the storm progressed. For example, because storm surge predictions may increase dramatically as a hurricane nears land, O'Neil (2014) notes that by the time evacuation is considered a necessary action, it may be too late for residents to leave. National Weather Service Meteorologist John Quagliariello agreed:

> If you live along the coast and haven't prepared yet because you feel Dorian won't be a threat because the center is forecast to pass offshore, you're making a mistake. If you wait until the last minute to leave on Wednesday, you may not be able to because some of those low-lying post roadways may already be flooded from the morning high tide and stay high through the day. (Phillips, 2019)

Summary. The IDEA model of instructional risk and crisis communication offered a lens to discuss the CS approach taken by the NHC as it presented public messages to those visiting and living in the path of Hurricane Dorian. The decisions made by NHC about the content and delivery of content about the path and impact of the hurricane were culturally sensitive but reflected the perspective of NHC about what was important and relevant to share with multiple publics.

Responses to CS Messages

As the local authorities prepared for the hurricane to make landfall, their messages encouraged those in the path of the storm to seek safety. Governor Roy Cooper of North Carolina expressed it as such:

> We are hoping for the best, but preparing for the worst . . . . We know how powerful these storms can be. And so, we have ordered evacuations, because we want them to get to safety. And we are encouraging them—do not ride out this storm. Not only do you put your life at risk but you also put the lives of first responders at risk who would have to go in and rescue you. (Blitzer et al., 2019)

The publics responded in different ways to the NHC messages. For the most part, visitors to the region were following orders. For example, Brevard County issued the evacuation order for Sunday, and John Anderson, a National Guard official, said during a news conference that authorities were experiencing very little resistance to the evacuation orders (Forney & Torres, 2019).

While some were unable to evacuate ahead of the storm, many did find their way to shelters and other places of safety as a result of the messages. Joanne Magley, director of Community Information, Volusia County, described the situation:

> Well, we're definitely prepared for . . . what could be the worst part of the storm if it were to come in a little more on the west, but we feel that people have been heeding the evacuation orders, we have more than 1,000 people in our shelters. And we were out a little earlier today and the streets are pretty bare, so we do feel that people are sheltering in place, those that did not need to evacuate the area. (Church et al., 2019)

Ultimately, state leaders understood that some 830,000 people, many of whom would be evacuating for the fourth time in four years, wouldn't be happy to leave their homes. But, as Governor Henry McMaster of South Carolina noted, "We believe we can keep everyone alive" (Cox Media Group, 2019).

Effectiveness of CS Messages

While the NHC's objective was to warn the publics about the path of the storm and the need to evacuate, the question remains: How well did people respond? The NHC provided geographic references to alert the publics about the path of the hurricane, as well as the impact of its watches and warnings for storm surges, tropical storms, and hurricanes. Because of the storm's unpredictability, for some residents, the messages were about as effective as they could be. Derek Van Dam, a resident of Jensen Beach in South Carolina, described how some felt about the messages' effectiveness:

> You got to consider what they've gone through over the past four or five days. They had a Category 5, or Category 4 hurricane, expected to make landfall on the east coast of their shores. That didn't happen, it's scraping along the coast. They had mandatory evacuations. Those were rescinded, and then, brought back again. So, this flip-flopping is not only a headache for the residents that live here, but also for the county officials that make those important decisions. Of course, people took them seriously when the evacuations were firmed up once again as the models edged closer to the shore. (Church et al., 2019)

Thus, the need to constantly change the message produced less urgency, complicating efforts to encourage residents to evacuate.

The willingness of the residents to comply with the evacuation orders also varied. According to Florida's Division of Emergency Management, more than 9,500 people went to one of its 121 shelters. One of them was thirty-year-old Stefanie Passieux, who took shelter along with her two children and mother. She explained how even within her own family, the evacuation message was perceived differently: "I came yesterday, as soon as it opened. They said we were in a state of emergency so I came. My dad is staying with the cats, but we left. He never leaves. He doesn't do shelters" (Stickings, 2019).

Limitations of CS Approach

Even with reasonable action steps provided in a CS way to mitigate the effects of a crisis or to save lives, decision-makers constructing messages may fail to offer what are considered to be desired actions because residents in a given community have become complacent about the impact of an impending disaster. These disaster subcultures may choose to stay home regardless of the forecast advised actions (Bankoff, 2017). Governor Roy Cooper of North Carolina concurred: "We know what the storms can do. I don't sense any complacency. I do know how difficult and frustrating and sometimes costly that evacuations can be. So, some people, you're just not going to be able to move out. They just refuse to go, understanding the risks that they take" (Blitzer et al., 2019).

SUMMARY

This chapter provided an expanded description of the CS approach to risk and crisis communication through the dimensions of a managerial/elite perspective, scripted messages, one-way communication with limited feedback, the multiple-spokesperson model, cultural adaptation, and the interpretive lens. Critiquing this approach using the IDEA model, CS communication includes cultural content selected by decision-makers based upon their analysis of external publics to promote internalization and focused attention, uses language and examples that relate to intended audiences, and suggests actions that are sensitive to cultural practices and worldviews. The distribution of the message is guided by the decision-makers' understanding of audience preferences based upon data gathered by the organization. Through the example of Hurricane Dorian, the CS approach showed when CS communication was used (pre-crisis, crisis, and post-crisis); how CS messages were presented (using best practices as a means for analyzing effectiveness); what the responses to the CS messages from the particular audiences were; how the CS approach facilitated effective risk and crisis communication; and limitations to the CS approach. The next chapter explains the CC approach using ASFv to demonstrate how decision-makers communicated to control the spread of the virus.

Chapter 7

The Culture-Centered Approach

Chapter 6 described the CS approach within the context of IMC, with an emphasis placed on how the approach reflected the managerial/elite perspective, relied on scripted messages, utilized one-way communication with limited feedback, while involving the multiple spokesperson model, demonstrating cultural adaptation (e.g., learning styles and communication perspectives), and reflecting an interpretive perspective. This approach was illustrated with the example of Hurricane Dorian that devastated the Bahamas and surrounding islands and Florida to show when CS communication was used (pre-crisis, crisis, and post-crisis); how CS messages were presented (using best practices); what responses resulted from the CS messages; how the CS approach facilitated effective risk communication; and what limitations to the CS approach were evident.

In this chapter, the CC approach is explained using the following similar dimensions: audience perspective, developed message, two-way unlimited feedback, multiple spokesperson model, and critical perspective. The IDEA model elucidates how the CC approach results in more effective messaging. Then, ASFv is described as an example to show when CC communication was used (pre-crisis, crisis, and post-crisis); how CC messages were presented (using best practices); what the responses were to the CC messages; how the CC approach facilitated effective risk communication; and what limitations to the CC approach were evident.

THE CULTURE-CENTERED APPROACH

The CC approach differs from the approaches described in chapters 5 and 6 since it includes participants from the affected publics as part of the team creating and transmitting the messages. In his discussion of culture-centered health communication, Dutta (2008) suggested:

> The culture centered approach foregrounds the active participation of community members in the construction of shared meanings and experiences; culture is constituted through this act of participation and therefore is actively constructed by its members. (p. 55)

This perspective has relevance when discussing risk and crisis communication because to gain the advantage of using a cultural perspective, the community members involved must actively participate in the process of developing and disseminating the messages.

The involvement of community members as co-participants in the decision-making process evolved from research focusing on community participation (Lasker & Weiss, 2003; Lasker, Weiss, & Miller, 2001). In community-based research, individuals familiar with local culture collaborate with decision-makers as co-researchers to craft messages. The basis for the co-participant collaboration between decision-maker(s) and community member(s) stems from relationship building during the pre-crisis stage when networks and infrastructure has been initiated or is in place that can bring the team together quickly. Once a crisis erupts, response time is shortened. Thus, messages must be created quickly and then transmitted in a form that is accessible and appropriate for the intended publics. Prior research suggests that when decision-makers align messages with how the publics prefer to receive the information, publics are more likely to respond in the desired manner (Littlefield et al., 2014).

The CC approach provides an opening for decision-makers to challenge the conventional methods for creating and disseminating risk and crisis messages. Agency, which is controlled by the decision-maker with limited to no input from intended audiences in both CN and CS approaches, is shared with community members in the CC approach. The power to shape all aspects of the communication process no longer resides with the decision-maker; rather, community members are valued for their knowledge and the convergence of cultural and expert knowledge creates messages that are positively received and acted upon.

The application of a CC approach to gain participation from community members in the decision-making process is revealed when an IMC organization moves into stage 3 where data can be analyzed and integrated into communication planning and implementation at all levels. This collection of information about potential customers or current consumers provides the decision-maker with the information needed to make decisions about to appeal to the preferences and behaviors of those who are loyal to the product or services provided by the organization. The decisions made in stage 3 are more reflective of what would happen in a CS approach, but when organizational leaders move into stage 4 of IMC, they are more constantly monitoring performance levels from a return on investment perspective and link knowledge into an ongoing evaluation of each served segment of the population. The most effective evaluation involves the publics in the process. At this stage, an IMC organization comes closest to the CC approach to risk and crisis communication. While the focus is fully on how the publics receive and respond to the message, through the evaluation of the message creation, dissemination, and reception of the intended messages, the organization can involve affected publics.

Audience Perspective

The CC approach is predicated on the assumption that all aspects of communication emanate from the perspective of the audience. This poses a challenge for communicators because vulnerable publics respond differently to risks. Hence, one message cannot serve all groups with equal effectiveness. In contrast to the CN and CS perspectives where decision-makers plan the communication approach and manage responses during all stages of a crisis (Coombs, 1998, 1999, 2019; Lindell & Perry, 2004; Rowan, 1991; Slovic, 1986; Tierney, 1999), the audience perspective in the CC approach includes the cultural variables unique to each audience (e.g., ethnicity, economic status, education, family size and status, household structure, information retrieval, language mastery, neighborhood, and technology). The CC approach is best represented when members of the affected audiences are included in the construction and transmission of risk or crisis messages from the start.

The audience perspective also recognizes the need for the sender to establish a relationship with the receivers of the message. As Kitchen and De Pelsmacker (2004) suggested, "The IMC process starts with the customer or prospect and then works back to determine and define the forms and methods through which persuasive communications methods should be developed" (p. 7). If an organization has as its goal the retention of a customer or consumer, a relationship must be developed that can sustain occasional challenges from competing interests. This is also the case with risk and crisis communication. For vulnerable publics to respond to risk and crisis messages as decision-makers want, a relationship must be cultivated that reflects the intent of the decision-maker to be helpful, not hurtful; and to be other-focused rather than self-focused.

Developed Message

When a message is developed, the parties involved in the communication process work together to construct it. Essentially, the decision-makers and publics determine together the appropriate language and content, as well as how the message is presented and disseminated to their constituencies. There are several ways that developed messages differ from scripted messages reflective of CN and CS approaches. Initially, scripted messages reflect the perspective of an individual or small group of decision-makers representing an elite view of what should be communicated and how the message should be disseminated to the publics. In contrast, developed messages involve multiple bodies of knowledge coming from multiple audiences that converge in a shared framework of decision-making. The multiple perspectives involved in a developed message reflect the needs of the publics affected by the risk or crisis. Similarly, whereas scripted messages are created and disseminated without opportunity for feedback, developed messages allow for feedback and modification at any stage in the communication process. Feedback reflects competing perspectives and allows for convergence as an agreement is reached.

Israel et al. (2001) suggested that through the process of developing messages, "Partners contribute their expertise and share responsibilities and ownership to increase understanding of a given phenomenon" (p. 184). They identified the advantages of developed messages as "enhancing relevance"; "addressing complex problems" by drawing from the "diverse skills, knowledge, and expertise" of the participants; using "local knowledge"; building trust among the publics who have "historically been 'subjects' of such research"; bridging "the cultural differences that may exist between the partners involved"; and providing "resources for communities involved" (p. 185).

Two-Way Unlimited Feedback

In CC communication, senders and receivers work together to provide two-way unlimited feedback. Figure 7.1 depicts the communication process where unlimited feedback is enabled.

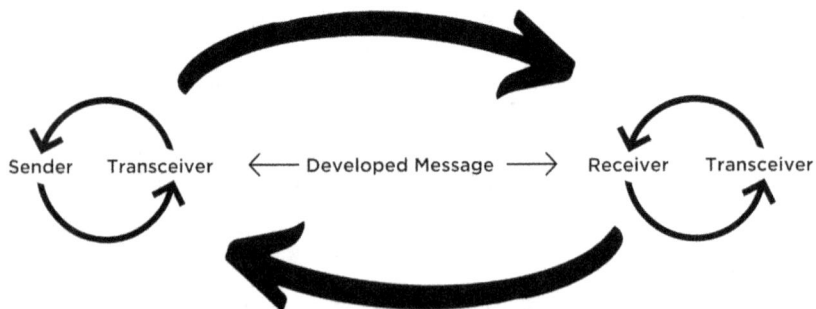

Figure 7.1 Culture-Centered Unlimited Feedback Model.

In the traditional communication model, the sender develops a message, encodes the message in such a way that it can be transmitted to a receiver, who decodes the message in order to understand, and sends feedback to sender of the message. In the CC approach, the senders and receivers become transceivers; that is, they become capable of both sending and receiving messages simultaneously in order to develop a message that reflects their shared perspective, or similar to what Sellnow et al. (2009) described as convergence.

As the figure suggests, the receiver begins sending feedback before the sender has completed the original transmission of a message. Once the sender perceives a response from the receiver that the message is being decoded, the opportunity to modify the original message becomes possible. The transceivers co-create the message in this dynamic communication process. This two-way unlimited feedback is central to the development of the message. The interactive flow of communication from spokesperson to a specific public allows for all participants to add their perspectives to the discussion while the message is being developed. The process is nonlinear in that the dialogic nature of the process encourages individuals to engage through a community-based participatory process.

Multiple Spokesperson Model

When the CC approach is used, all members of the decision-making team become spokespersons for their cultural perspectives. The CC multiple spokesperson model of crisis communication (Sellnow et al., 2009) describes how multiple spokespersons are involved in the process of developing messages for specific publics.

In figure 7.2, during the pre-crisis stage, the decision-maker and cultural agents develop a relationship that enables them to come together to develop a message when a risk or crisis response is needed. The decision-maker likely remains as a contact person with the organization for the cultural agents (or co-decision-makers) who ultimately are responsible for presenting the developed message in a meaningful way to their respective publics.

Critical Perspective

When applying the CC approach to risk and crisis communication, the critical perspective views the reality of the situation as subjective and focuses on the importance of studying the context in which communication occurs. The critical perspective allows for the comparison of different attitudes from those involved toward the risk or crisis situation and explores the impact of power differentiation within a culture as a means for understanding why

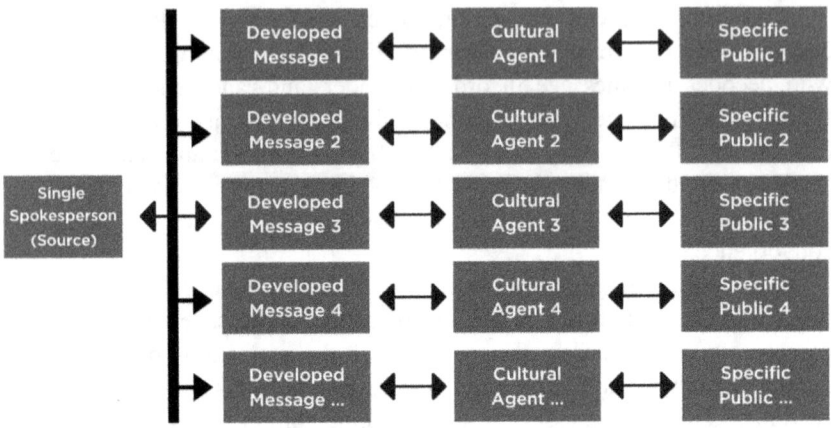

Figure 7.2 Culture-Centered Multiple Spokesperson Model of Crisis Communication.

vulnerable publics may not respond to messages as the decision-makers intended.

The critical perspective is useful in stage 4 of IMC because decision-makers may focus not only on studying human behavior across cultures, but also in affecting change in society. From the CC perspective, if IMC decision-makers consider the role of power as they involve members from their intended audiences in the process, they can assist people in opposing what may be oppressive forces in society. Those people who take the critical perspective seek to deconstruct assumptions about reality to challenge social realities that reinforce the exploitation of some groups within society (Flammia & Sadri, 2011).

In most crisis situations, communication power is not distributed equally between the decision-makers and those who receive the messages. The CC approach enables IMCs to conduct analyses of media and other aspects of popular culture with the involvement of those impacted by the messages. For example, decision-makers seeking to use social media to disseminate risk or crisis messages must consider issues of use that may influence how particular publics will access the messages (Clark et al., 2004). Thus, the IMC decision-maker using a CC approach involves community members in shaping the response of particular audiences to messages disseminated over social media.

APPLYING THE IDEA MODEL TO CC COMMUNICATION

The IDEA Model is most effectively revealed when using the CC approach to risk and crisis communication. As Sellnow and Sellnow (2014) suggest, the integration of internalization, explanation, action, and distribution of risk and crisis messages provides for the most effective communication. When a community-based participatory model is used, decision-makers create a decision-making team with the agency to bring their collective knowledge and experience into the process to satisfy each element of the IDEA Model.

First, when messages include elements that capture the attention of the audience, internalization occurs and compels those who receive the message to pay attention and want to know more about what is happening and why. Having members of the affected publics as part of the decision-making team that is deciding on the most meaningful elements to include in the message will increase the likelihood that the risk and crisis message will be internalized by the publics. These elements may include well-known people, cultural and contextual artifacts, symbols, or other identifiers that have meaning to the publics; and come from knowing and accepting the values and norms of the publics being addressed.

Next, by having members of the publics involved in selecting examples and content that relates to them, decision-makers are increasing the relatability of the information and providing audiences with what they need to know what is happening. Messages must provide the details in such a way that publics are not overwhelmed but feel sufficiently informed about what is going on. Attention to the language used by the cultural group and the levels of literacy and education levels of the publics also will help CC communicators convey messages that will be received and understood by audiences.

Because the decision-makers have integrated members of the affected publics into their leadership circle, the actions that are recommended to save the public from harm or mitigate the crisis will be inherently more credible and realistic. Awareness of how the publics view the nature and purpose of their lives, as well as their place in the cosmos, can help communicators to tailor actions that are compatible with their worldviews. The culture centeredness of the message positions it as doable with those who are asked to comply; and because the affected publics see and know those who are involved in the creation and dissemination of the messages, the distribution of the message is met with greater receptivity.

EXAMPLE OF CC COMMUNICATION: AFRICAN SWINE FEVER VIRUS

In this section, ASFv is used to demonstrate how the National Pork Board used CC communication, how the universal and particular publics responded to CC messages, how the media and publics evaluated the effectiveness of

CC messages, and what were the limitations to the CC approach from the perspective of best practices and IMC.

The Crisis: African Swine Fever Virus and the National Pork Board

We selected ASFv as a case to represent the CC approach because the crisis communication response, coordinated largely by the National Pork Board, features a highly inclusive focus on the audience. To understand the ASFv response, we explain how the lessons of effective crisis communication and biosecurity practices learned from responding to another disease, PEDv, have directly influenced the response to ASFv. These lessons clearly reflect the essential elements of a CC approach. Specifically, all stakeholders involved in the ASFv response are included in a comprehensive network sharing messages about effective biosecurity measures, stories collected from workers on the front lines practicing biosecurity help to form the messages, and ample opportunity has been given for stakeholders to share their feedback. Moreover, multiple spokespersons are used to disseminate the messages from a critical perspective that allows for a reconceptualization of effective biosecurity practices. In true IMC fashion, these messages align to allow multiple audiences to "work together on a problem" (Vinhateiro & Cronen, 2016, p. 89)—in this case, the potentially devastating impact of ASFv on an entire industry.

This case study is informed by two sets of interviews conducted with individuals directly involved in developing and distributing crisis messages, first, for PEDv, and second, for ASFv. Individuals were selected based on their positions in the National Pork Board, American Association of Swine Veterinarians, and university extension offices. All the individuals interviewed were specialists in swine research with extensive knowledge of biosecurity. A total of twenty-seven interviews were conducted.

Context

The disease began as a frightening mystery. Piglets born vibrant and healthy on U.S. farms were dead or near death a day later. Farm workers responded initially as if the cause were a disease that they had seen previously such as transmissible gastroenteritis (TGE). As the situation worsened, further testing would reveal that the swine producers were dealing with something far harsher. Testing ultimately discovered that the piglets were dying from PEDv, a disease never before seen in the United States. This news was particularly disheartening because there is no treatment, cure, or vaccine for PEDv. Further intensifying the situation is the fact that PEDv is a resilient virus that spreads quickly. The disease can spread easily as workers, equipment, and vehicles move from building to building and farm to farm (Schultz, 2014). PEDv spread at an alarming rate, killing 100,000 piglets per day, and causing pork prices to rise sharply (Strom, 2014), before the disease was brought under control in 2015.

PEDv serves as a warning to U.S. swine producers as they prepare for an even more deadly disease, ASFv, now spreading in Africa, Asia, and Europe. Like PEDv, ASFv spreads easily and there is no known cure and no vaccine. Once infected or exposed, producers must typically euthanize their animals as a precaution against the disease spreading in the community. In a recent outbreak, for example, farmers in Nigeria were compelled to euthanized hundreds of thousands of pigs (Bugga, 2020). Such dramatic losses of animals threaten food security. Because pigs are a "fast-growing species with efficient feed conversion rates," pork is an increasingly vital source of protein worldwide (Pigs and Animal Production, 2014, para. 1). Pork production in most parts of the world has increased over the past decade. Along with this increase is a near-universal dependence on centralized pork production where hundreds or thousands of animals are reared in one location. This centralization has improved efficiency and helped to meet the growing demand. Unfortunately, the concentration of animals has also contributed to the rapid spread of diseases like PEDv and ASFv.

People facing pandemics like PEDv or ASFv need actionable information. Gerwin (2012) described actionable information in pandemics as "accurate facts and reasonable interpretations of those facts upon which an individual should rely in making reason-based decisions" (p. 630). Though the need for actionable information is glaring during pandemics, the availability of such information depends on previous experience. Both PEDv and ASFv are novel. The swine industry in the United States had no experience with PEDv. Similarly, the global swine industry has limited experience responding to ASFv. Thus, the industry faces the conflicting challenges of high uncertainty and an immediate need for information.

Because no treatment or vaccine is available yet for PEDv and ASFv, biosecurity is the most practical form of actionable information available. Biosecurity is "a strategic and integrated approach to analysing [sic] and managing relevant risks to human, animal and plant life and health and associated risks for the environment" (INFOSAN, 2010, p. 1). In pandemic conditions, the integration of security efforts to quell the spread of disease is paramount. If, for example, one country is lax, the threat of the disease spreading to other countries is intensified. Similarly, if one farm is infected and that farm fails to practice prescribed biosecurity practices, the disease is more likely to spread to neighboring farms. This need for the systematic integration of biosecurity practices to combat the global spread of disease requires a level of collaboration that may be unprecedented in other aspects of farming.

Timing of CC Communication

The National Pork Board is a central player in all biosecurity research and communication. The board played a major role in coordinating the PEDv response and is a primary resource for ASFv pre-crisis communication. As the National Pork Board and the swine industry in the United States build biosecurity defenses against ASFv, they bridge the post-crisis learning for the PEDv case into the pre-crisis planning activities for ASFv. PEDv simultaneously demonstrated the danger of novel diseases for producers and the remarkable capacity of the swine industry to collaborate in organizing a biosecurity response that included input from a broad array of stakeholders. When the diagnosis of PEDv was confirmed, industry representatives such as National Pork Board, American Association of Swine Veterinarians, and extension researchers at American universities immediately collaborated to conduct research, translate the information into suggested biosecurity practices, and create a dialogue among all stakeholders through existing and newly established networks. The industry moved through the stages of diagnosis, research, translation into practices, dialogue, and practice "in record time" (Sellnow et al., 2018, p. 132). The challenge at hand for the swine industry is to transfer the extraordinarily successful crisis response to PEDv into an equally effective crisis plan for preventing the spread of ASFv in the United States.

Use of CC Communication

The U.S. swine industry is well-positioned to apply the best practices described in chapter 2. For stage 1 of IMC, best practices call for a prompt response that establishes inclusive communication networks. The industry had in place, before the PEDv crisis, durable networks allowing producers to communicate with veterinarians and the National Pork Board. These networks were quickly adapted for managing PEDv (Sellnow et al., 2017c). Thus, these networks have a proven record and have been extended to managing pre-crisis planning for ASFv (Edwards et al., 2020). From the perspective of CC, these networks give all stakeholders in the swine industry access to information, an opportunity to be heard, and a role to play in building a biosecurity response.

The networks, discussed earlier, contribute directly to the industry's enactment of IMC's stage 2. In the second stage, the objective is for the industry to seek public information and evaluate the feedback. This stage coincides with the solicitation of feedback in the inclusive approach advocated by the best practices of crisis communication. The National Pork Board maintained a high degree of openness through constant contact with all stakeholders. For example, conference calls were used to allow producers, veterinarians, and others to respond to recommendations and discuss their experiences.

Acquiring feedback is a clearly stated and enacted function of the National Pork Board. Similarly, the Association of Swine Veterinarians, by its nature, seeks interaction with practicing veterinarians. This emphasis on feedback reflects the expectations of CC as well. The voices of stakeholders, including the farmers and employees at the smallest facilities, are heard. For example, veterinarians who interact daily with owners and farm workers express their concerns and frustrations to the American Association of Swine Veterinarians. Producers also are welcome to make their concerns known directly to the National Pork Board. The board is committed to representing its membership's concerns.

The industry's philosophy of transparency and stakeholder participation remains in place as the industry prepares for ASFv. Stage 3 of IMC articulates the need for an integrated campaign. The swine industry established a remarkably consistent narrative (Sellnow et al., 2018). The best practices of crisis communication delineate that this campaign should be tailored to the needs of various stakeholders and show compassion for those who are afflicted. The industry fulfilled this responsibility in response to PEDv through close collaboration among stakeholders, strong leadership by the National Pork Board, and transparency with media, particularly reporters whose publications specialized in swine production (e.g., *National Hog Farmer*, *Feedstuffs*, and *Pork Network*). As the industry prepares its pre-crisis narrative for ASFv, this commitment to a consistent narrative remains culture-centered. Those communicating about ASFv describe a dedication to adapting the information they share with individual farmers to fit the size of their facility, the specific role the audience plays in biosecurity, and scientific training of the listener (Edwards et al., 2020). As they prepare for ASFv, industry leaders display a clear understanding that they must analyze their audience and adapt their message to fit the needs of the wide array of stakeholders.

Stage 4 of IMC emphasizes constant monitoring and adaptation of the strategies in place. Similarly, the best practices of crisis communication advocate continuous updating as well as monitoring the community to assure that their needs are met throughout the crisis recovery period. In this case, the needs of the pork production community go beyond PEDv's post-crisis recovery to a new pre-crisis stage where preparing for ASFv is crucial. Thus, the swine industry's current objective is to leverage the resources and strategies employed against PEDv to further bolster biosecurity practices in response to the intensifying threat of ASFv. At present, this process represents cultural sensitivity through its inclusivity. Experts leading the campaign for intensified biosecurity and biosecurity planning insist that stakeholders at every level must be actively involved in the process, including farm workers, farm owners, veterinarians, and consumers (Edwards et al., 2020). If any stakeholder is ignored or underrepresented in the planning process, a weak point in the biosecurity process is inevitable. Consequently, the inclusivity stressed by the industry and the ongoing feedback it solicits in forming a narrative about ASFv biosecurity, provides a culture-centered framework for future crisis planning.

Responses to CC Messages

The IDEA model helps articulate a fitting response from those asked to join in the biosecurity response to ASFv. Initially, stakeholders need to internalize (I) the threat ASFv poses to them and participate in the networks distributing (D) invitations for dialogue. These networks provide an explanation (E) of how biosecurity needs to change based on knowledge of how ASFv is spreading in other regions. Finally, the key response is the preventive actions (A) taken on the farms, in the sale barns, in the transportation of animals, and in the preparation and delivery of feed.

Thus far, the response to ASFv warnings has been heeded. For example, states with high swine production have collaborated in simulations to test their readiness for an ASFv outbreak. In one instance, after an exercise involving fourteen states, farmers were able to identify biosecurity strengths and gaps. One animal welfare auditor for a major pork producer in Minnesota describes the industry's response in a manner reflecting the industry's need for discussion, feedback, and flexibility:

> Planning is the best way to go, and yet if African swine fever does get here, there's a good chance that the plans we have in place may not be the ones that we execute. But at least we know and have a good working knowledge of the potential obstacles we have so we can get things moving as quick as possible. (Henke, 2019, para. 17)

The widespread collaboration in such preparation efforts is promising. It provides the agility indicative of IMC through a willingness to quickly adapt plans to meet the changing needs of the industry should ASFv occur in the United States is also reassuring (Fellows, 2016).

Effectiveness of CC Messages

The messages shared throughout the industry have generated support for prevention and response plans at the farm level and for major national efforts such as import restrictions on pigs and pork products enforced by the USDA and customs agents at the border. Moreover, those who communicate directly with stakeholders about ASFv indicate that their audiences have an appreciation for the real-world stories from their peers who have experienced biosecurity failures firsthand (Edwards et al., 2020). The PEDv crisis revealed an emotional toll on the frontline farm workers who were disheartened at the death of hundreds of animals they cared for daily. Stories were collected from these workers and shared in messages to workers on other farms (Sellnow et al., 2017c). This same strategy of using stories from the firsthand experiences of workers is being used in the ASFv response (Edwards et al., 2020). Notably, these stories are not often about success but rather about the demoralizing outcomes of biosecurity failures. Swine experts generally agree on two facts: Biosecurity has improved significantly in the swine industry since PEDv and intensifying threat of ASFv, and there are likely unidentified biosecurity gaps that remain. A swine biosecurity expert summarized these points plainly when speaking about the swine industry's biosecurity progress, "Are we doing OK? Yes, but let's not break our arms patting ourselves on the back" (Hess, 2020, para. 3). The threat of ASFv is very real and more can be done to improve biosecurity. The recognition of the threat and the willingness to respond at the farm level are encouraging. The need to continue promoting these strategies is made soberingly clear by the remarks of a veterinarian from a large pork production facility, "It's probably here already: it just hasn't made its way to a pig yet" (Market report, 2020, para. 9).

Limitations of CC Approach

The swine industry is broadly committed to coordination and agility. For example, the national pork checkoff program where producers tax themselves in support of the National Pork Board is a model for other agriculture industries. The Pork Board consults regularly with its membership on myriad issues and is committed to "moving at the speed of business, focusing resources on specific projects relevant to industry needs and using the principles of project management" (Pork Checkoff, 2020, para. 1). Other industries may not have the commitment and resources to build networks with their stakeholders and advocate for safety. Furthermore, other industries may be prone to competition among organizations. Such competition may stifle the implementation of communication that is essential to the CC approach.

SUMMARY

In this chapter, the CC approach was presented and explained from the perspective of the audiences', developed messages, two-way unlimited feedback, multiple spokesperson model, and critical perspective. When critiquing the CC approach using the IDEA model, culture-centered communication involves members of the publics to determine what will trigger the internalization of the messages for these audiences, how the publics' preferences for content is satisfied in messaging, and realistic actions that will reflect the choices available to the publics within the power structure of the context in which they live. The distribution of the messages is guided by the co-researchers who share the context with their particular audience.

Through the example of ASFv, the CC approach showed when CC communication was used; how CC messages were presented (using best practices); what the responses to the CC messages were; how the CC approach facilitated effective risk communication; and limitations to the CC approach. This chapter concludes the second section of this book, focusing on the IDEA model and the three cultural approaches to risk and crisis communication within the context of IMC. In the final section of the book, the implications of emphasizing culture in risk and crisis communication are identified, along with the need for using an ethical cultural framework when communicating risk and crisis messages. We conclude with future directions for situating culture in risk and crisis communication.

Chapter 8

Implications of Emphasizing Culture in Risk and Crisis Communication

In section three of this book, we discuss the implications of emphasizing culture in risk and crisis communication. First, lessons learned from the cases illustrating the CN, CS, and CC approaches are offered within the context of IMC. Next, the consequences of differing views about what constitutes a crisis and how different responses to risk and crisis communication affect IMC are identified. Finally, strategies to enhance best practices for integrating culture are provided for practitioners, as well as business and industry leaders seeking to move from a CN to a CC orientation.

LESSONS LEARNED

The crises used to illustrate cultural approaches to risk and crisis communication were selected to represent CN, CS, and CC perspectives. The risk and crisis communication approach used by the WHO to provide messages about the ZIKv mega-crisis reflected a CN perspective. In the case of Hurricane Dorian, the approach used by the National Hurricane Center and National Weather Service reflected the CS orientation through the identification of markers that would appeal to the various publics receiving the messages. Finally, when health and industry officials developed messages about ASFv, the inclusion of the affected publics within the creation and dissemination process reflected a CC approach.

To provide a framework for discussing the lessons learned, the concept of spheres of ethnocentricity is useful (Littlefield, 2013; Littlefield & Cowden, 2006; Sellnow et al., 2009). This concept suggests that individuals pay the greatest attention to those things that are of most direct impact to them, beginning with individual concerns and moving out to family, community, region, state, nation, and world. The farther out from the center, the less interest the individual may have in the message. As Sellnow et al. (2009) suggested, "How individuals interpret, understand, or respond to risk messages is based upon their place within the spheres" (p. 38). Thus, it makes sense to use the categories of personal, family, community, region, nation, and world to explore the intersection of multiple perspectives with IMC, culture, and the IDEA model.

Integrated Marketing Communications

Organizations that use IMC effectively move through four stages. In stage 1, organizations prepare to launch a campaign promoting a product or idea to stakeholders or potential consumers. This involves horizontal and vertical integration, data integration, and internal and external integration to create coherent and consistent messaging. In many ways, these messages are designed to function in the farthest spheres from the individual and to appeal to as large a population as possible. In stage 2, data are collected to understand the consumers' characteristics and preferences. This is where external sources are identified from which information about consumers can be accessed. The spheres associated with geographic regions influence the targeted consumers. The data accessed are drawn from sources that would be specific to these regions. Stage 3 is characterized by building databases that are specific to those customers and potential consumers. Through analysis, the IMC organization uses these databases to shape its campaign for the targeted publics. At this stage, the organization begins focusing on individuals who are grouped within the databases, again keeping the spheres at the level of region or beyond. Finally, in stage 4, decision-makers in leadership positions monitor the organization's return on investment for promotions directed toward each targeted group. There is no change of spheres associated with this level of monitoring because only aggregate data would be used to determine the return on investment.

The insufficiency of the IMC model is one observation to be drawn from this study of the intersection of risk and crisis communication and culture. At no stage in the IMC process does the organization find its way to the family or personal spheres of ethnocentricity at the center, and without this level of focus, CC communication is impossible. When applied to the context of culture, the model developed by Kitchen and De Pelsmacker (2004) precludes the inclusion of CC approaches. For example, in stage 1, the organization is preparing what it proposes will be a coherent and consistent campaign to promote consumer loyalty. The focus is on creating messages intended for the universal audience. However, in the absence of including involvement from the targeted publics as co-participants in the process, efforts will be one-sided, inefficient, incomplete, and misdirected. For example, when internal communication provides the only source of information feeding decision-makers, the need to verify the veracity of the information about the target groups may result in the need to repeat research efforts. Another possibility might be the omission of information that would have provided a more complete picture of the publics receiving the messages. Based on unverified or incomplete information, efforts of the organization may be misdirected, resulting in loss of time and revenue. By using a CC approach, the views and experiences of underrepresented or marginalized groups provide the substance of what IMC organizations need to create the basis for effective campaigns.

In stage 2, the model is deficient in providing what is needed by the IMC organization seeking data from external sources to understand the consumers or potential customers. The model remains focused on developing a brand message that will reach the universal audience. But instead of focusing solely on message creation with broad appeal, stage 2 narrows the focus to identify groups within the universal audience that are recognized by decision-makers, who may be persuaded with messages tailored more to their preferences. The basis for this deficiency is the worldview of those who are collecting the data. Since the organization lacks involvement from members of the targeted publics, the data collectors will rely on established channels determined by decision-makers within the organization to retrieve the information. While this data collection will provide some specificity, information sources in the larger setting are created through established structures that reflect systemic power. If a group has been marginalized or is underrepresented, the likelihood of tracking accurate information about the group is compromised. With a CC approach in the data collection stage, access to information that more accurately describes the preferences and behaviors of the targeted publics is enhanced and clarified through the cultural agents working with the IMC organization.

Stages 3 and 4 of the IMC approach move to the administrative level as databases are created and analyzed providing descriptive information that can be used by organizational leaders as they monitor the campaign's effectiveness with each of the targeted publics. The return on investment motivates the leaders to attend to group responses, and to adjust, if necessary. Without a CC approach, the databases are created with categories determined by what the decision-makers consider to be appropriate and defined without the cultural scope necessary to give meaning to the data. In stage 4, even with an enlightened leader seeking to increase consumer loyalty and profitability, the absence of cultural awareness provided by members of the targeted publics limits effective marketing management because the messages will at best be CS based upon the leader's perspective.

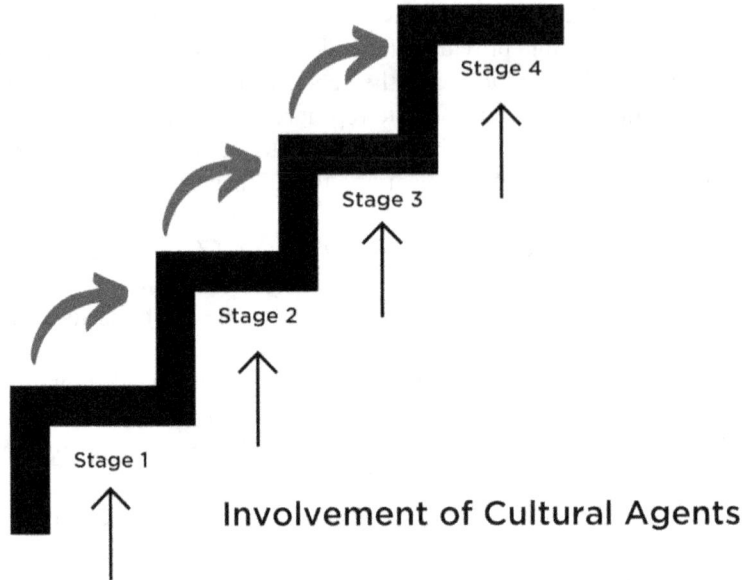

Figure 8.1 Involvement of Cultural Agents in Stages of Integrated Marketing Communications.

As the analysis presented suggests, cultural perspectives must inform each stage of the IMC process if an organization is to benefit from being truly fully integrated.

Figure 8.1 reflects the stages originally described by Kitchen and De Pelsmacker (2004) being modified as cultural agents or representatives from targeted publics are included in the stages of IMC. When cultural perspectives are added to the IMC organization's communication, the personal and family spheres of ethnocentricity are accessible; and when integrated into the decision-making process, the opportunity for successful communication increases.

Cultural Perspectives

The three approaches—CN, CS, and CC—are distinguished through descriptive categories identified in previous chapters as each was described and illustrated with specific crises. These categories included the management perspective, spokesperson model, communication flow, audience orientation, feedback, message preparation, content, cultural adaptation, and theoretical perspective. For the benefit of comparison, these categories are depicted in table 8.1.

Table 8.1 Comparison of Communication Elements in Cultural-Neutral, Culturally Sensitive, and Culture-Centered Approaches

Communication Element	Culture-Neutral	Culturally Sensitive	Culture-Centered
Management Perspective	Sender	Sender	Shared
Spokesperson model	Single	Multiple	Multiple
Communication flow	One-way	One-way	Two-way
Audience orientation	Universal	One particular	Multiple particular
Feedback	No	Limited	Full
Message preparation	Scripted	Scripted	Developed
Content	Objective	Targeted	Subjective
Cultural adaptation	Mutually exclusive	Congruent	Integrated
Theoretical perspective	Social scientific	Interpretive	Critical

Through examples from the crises, the *management perspective* of the sender dominates the CN and CS approaches, but in CC communication, the perspective is shared between sender and receiver because they work together through all phases of the process. *Spokesperson models* vary among the three options. In CN communication, a single spokesperson is used because there is no perceived need to appeal to preferences because of the message's objectivity. When using the CS approach, there may still be a single source, but the message is delivered through multiple spokespeople presenting the same message that has been tailored to appeal to each particular group. With the CC approach, multiple spokespeople interact as transceivers with the publics and with the organization to appeal to their respective cultural group.

The *communication flow* is directed toward the publics in CN and CS approaches, but because of the transceiver role of the sender and receiver in CC communication, a two-way communication process occurs. The *audience orientation* shifts across the three approaches, with the CN addressing the universal audience, CS focusing on one particular audience, and CC targeting multiple particular audiences simultaneously. Each of the approaches receives different levels of *feedback*, with CN allowing for no feedback, CS enabling limited feedback, and CC providing for full feedback. The different levels of feedback result when the process is opened to include members of the publics who are the receivers of the messages.

As messages are prepared, the CN and CS approaches rely on scripted *message preparation* reflecting the perspective of the decision-maker. However, in the CC approach, the message is developed because cultural agents are part of the process and treated as co-participants or co-researchers. The *content of messages* varies across the three approaches. With CN communication, the content is selected for its objectivity because it must appeal to the universal audience. In CS communication, the content includes targeted subjectivity tailored to what the decision-maker considers to be salient cultural characteristics that should prompt favorability among the publics. The content is CC communication is subjective, focused on the preferences and needs of the publics receiving the messages.

The *cultural adaptation* in the three approaches differs based upon the perspective of the decision-maker. As Sellnow et al. (2009) suggested, the CN approach characterizes cultural adaptation as mutual exclusivity and objectivity; and since CN messages are designed to remove culture, there is no adaptation. In the CS approach, there is construal because the specific cultural adaptation is selected by the decision-maker and portrayed in particular ways within the message. Cultural adaptation is integrated in CC messages because there is congruence between the participants in the preparation process that arrive at an agreement. Finally, the theoretical perspectives of the three approaches reflect different orientations. CN is descriptive and predictive, with the goal being generalizability. CS is interpretive, allowing for the subjectivity of the material to determine outcomes. The critical orientation of CC enables the shared voices of formerly marginalized publics to engage and address the power in the systems in which they exist and affect how they are included in the communication process.

The IDEA Model of Instructional Risk and Crisis Communication

The IDEA model provides the essential elements needed for effective instructional risk and crisis communication. Internalization of the situation must occur if there is going to be any follow-through on the part of the receiver of the message. Appropriate examples and sufficient content must be included so the receiver will understand the circumstances and the magnitude of the situation. The proposed actions must be compatible, realistic, and feasible, given the cultural context in which the receivers find themselves. Finding the right communication channel for distributing the message will have a major impact on whether it gets to the intended target publics.

The differences between the three cultural approaches within the context of the IDEA model impact how organizations striving to embrace IMC succeed in their communication efforts. Particularly, when these approaches are layered on the different spheres of ethnocentricity, the utility of the CC approach is evident. For example, using the center spheres of personal and family interests, a CC approach will appeal if the language used is informal and clearly understood; if the message is conveyed using information and examples that are meaningful and trusted as being accurate; if the spokesperson or agency presenting the message reflects the knowledge and acceptance of the publics' cultural beliefs and values; and if the actions recommended offer a progressive or holistic worldview providing for the needs of the person or family.

The further away from the center of the spheres, the more likely publics will disregard the messages unless effort is made to employ the elements of the IDEA model and identify the means to inform or persuade publics about complying with warnings about risks or crises. The example of the novel coronavirus COVID-19 illustrates this concept. When an individual or family member has contracted the virus, the internalization of messages by others in the family that emphasize positive health strategies—such as wearing masks or social distancing—will prompt them to respond as directed. The farther away from the actual experience of contracting the virus (e.g., hearing about someone across the country who has contracted the virus or died), the less urgency people feel to internalize messages, accept content as factual, and follow recommended strategies from health officials. The structure and content of risk and crisis messages can serve to save lives and livelihoods if they follow the IDEA model.

In summary, the lessons learned from the selected crises demonstrate that messages have a greater impact and are received more favorably at the personal and family level of ethnocentricity (where they will have the greatest chance of being internalized and accepted) if they are CC. The CN, CS, and CC approaches are distinct and can be compared on multiple levels. The findings suggest that the CC approach affords decision-makers with the greatest opportunity to achieve convergence. Finally, the IDEA model is designed for maximum results if the CC approach is used because the content and style of the message is created from the audience's viewpoint. Keeping this in mind, the context of a risk or crisis creates a more complex framework in which to view the CC communication approach.

CONSEQUENCES OF MULTIPLE POINTS OF CONVERGENCE

Sellnow et al. (2009) suggested that multiple perspectives exist on any given topic. Different views come from individuals who represent government, industry, science-based entities, special interest groups, politicians from different parties, talk shows, and communities, to name a few. These different perspectives constitute the discourse on any potentially controversial topic and when these perspectives are in conflict, people attempt to make sense of them. When there are different perceptions about a risk or crisis, finding points of convergence is essential to establish the basis for agreement. To inform the publics and persuade them to comply with actions that will protect them from harm or mitigate the severity of the crisis, decision-makers must strive for convergence.

Perceptions of Risk and Crisis Communication

Before one can differentiate between risks and crises, they must be able to define them. In his description of the evolution of risk and crisis communication, Palenchar (2010) traced the development of each form of communication. To clarify, he offered a range of definitions, each having its own descriptive meaning. He discovered that neither term commanded a fully agreed upon definition; so rather than identifying one meaning for each, he proposed that most people subjectively define what constitutes a crisis based upon how it affects them. Regarding risk communication, he cited Leiss (1996) who argued that risks were perceived differently by the experts than by those people who were affected by them. With crises, Palenchar suggested that they were context dependent. In other words, "one individual's crisis may be another's incident . . . with no attempt to delineate the scope or severity of a given problem" (Fishman, 1999, p. 347). Because of these different perceptions of risk and crisis, decision-makers are compelled to find the most effective way to converge the multiple perspectives into messages that will be compelling for the publics who receive them.

Decision-makers can build convergence when they are trusted by their publics. Sarbaugh (1979) suggested the three factors that contribute to trust building: the positive or negative feelings toward the other; the extent to which they believe their individual goals are compatible and mutually shared with one another, or are incompatible, and possibly conflicting; and the extent to which they believe the relationship is hierarchical or equal. In the context of risk and crisis communication, the closer the decision-makers come to the publics' personal and family spheres of ethnocentricity, the more likely they will be able to convey their intent to be well-intentioned and genuinely concerned about the well-being of the publics. If people feel that they are being manipulated or will be injured, or that the intent of the decision-maker is to create harm, they will be unlikely to trust what is being said about the risk or crisis.

When decision-makers use the IDEA model to present information to publics at their personal or family level of ethnocentricity, they demonstrate firsthand how their goals prioritize the welfare and safety of the individuals and families who make up the vulnerable publics being addressed. Once the publics see they have mutually shared goals with risk and crisis communicators, they are more likely to trust and comply with the suggested strategies. The other factor that influences trust is the relationship between the parties involved. When the decision-maker is perceived to have a higher status than the publics receiving the messages, the level of trust will be lower. Perceptions of status can be conveyed based upon income, education, race, sexual orientation, and religion, to name a few. If vulnerable publics perceive that risk or crisis strategies are designed for those with the resources to enact them (universal audience), they may not trust that the decision-makers are looking out for them (particular audience). What may be appropriate as a national strategy (nation sphere) may not be perceived as possible on a personal level (individual sphere).

When viewed from the perspective of the individual or family sphere, the intent of the risk and crisis communicator may be construed in various ways. For example, the intent of a message warning about an impending crisis may be viewed as being helpful, in that the warning signals to the individual or family that danger is approaching, and something should be done to prepare. However, if while informing the publics that all forms of public transportation have stopped and that the individual or family should leave their homes and get out of the way of the impending storm, the intent of the message might be viewed as ignoring the reality of most vulnerable individuals and families who do not own their own vehicles and would have to rely on public transportation as their way to get away from the storm. The same message calling for individuals and families to leave their homes for safety that comes on a day when the publics are celebrating a religious holiday may be viewed as disruptive or degrading. Finally, a message that warns individuals about the need to go to a safe shelter to wait out the storm but fails to provide options for those with pets who would not be welcome at the shelters may be viewed as causing injury to an animal that may be considered as one of the family. Thus, the perceived intent of the risk and crisis communicator as being other-focused and conscious of the individual and family spheres of ethnocentricity must be conveyed in CC ways in order to build trust and create convergence in the face of risks and crises.

Publics' Perceptions of Risk and Crisis Messages

In each of the crises identified in chapters 5–7, the publics did not share the same view of the situation as the decision-makers who were disseminating the risk or crisis messages. Through the following examples from each of the crises, these differing perspectives underscore how cultural factors can influence how publics perceive and respond to risk and crisis messages.

Zika Virus

The publics' responsiveness to decision-makers' messages was influenced by the cultural context of the ZIKv mega crisis. The multiple points of convergence affected the responses from those with agency, those without agency, and those who prioritized one point of view over the others. Publics with the financial ability and desire to travel had agency to heed warnings and to decide whether to expose themselves to ZIKv. As the crisis intensified, warnings were issued to "postpone travel to these areas [14 countries]" ("Washington: CDC issues," 2016) or to "cancel your vacation" ("Wisconsin: UW-Madison researchers," 2016). The tourism industry that typically appeals to the affluent was jeopardized by warnings "that this year's Carnival celebrations could aggravate the spread of the virus. Few visitors are likely to wear protective clothing on the beach or to Carnival street parties, making them vulnerable to insect bites" (Douglas, 2016). To assure potential tourists, organizers of the Summer Olympic Games indicated they would be on high alert to prevent exposure to ZIKv. In response, the traveling public, particularly pregnant women or "parents-to-be taking last-hurrah holidays" responded to these warnings by canceling their trips: "Parenting website babycenter.com asked pregnant readers with plans to travel to Zika-affected areas if they would change course. About half of the 1,118 respondents said they planned to cancel, and 27% said they were keeping their plans. The rest were undecided" ("Health Ministry issues," 2016).

For those publics living in the geographic area affected by the virus, strategic messages warning them to avoid areas where the virus was detected were ignored because for the vast majority, there was no escape. As identification of confirmed cases increased in the Americas, residents responded with a sense of panic. As Gleyse Kelly da Silva shared, "I cried for a month when I learned how God is testing us" (Romero, 2016). Because people were not able to leave their homes or move away from the virus, they could follow the recommendations to avoid traveling to regions where the virus was identified. The strategic communication messages needed to provide content describing specific steps to be taken to avoid contracting the virus.

Perhaps one of the more complex issues related to ZIKv was the possible link between the virus and microcephaly. The suspected link prompted decision-makers to issue warnings about becoming pregnant, for example: "Health Minister Alejandro Gaviria has advised Colombians to 'delay pregnancy' for the next six to eight months" (Partlow, 2016). Other warnings encouraging women to postpone pregnancy for up to years were frequent (e.g., Mercene, 2016; Ricks, 2016; "Zika virus' global spread," 2016).

When the virus was found to be sexually transmitted, warnings were issued to abstain from unprotected sex (Boddy, 2016; "First case of sexually transmitted," 2016; McNeil, 2016; Sun, Dennis & Cha, 2016; White, 2016). As the link became more definitive, some risk messages reflected sexual counseling, suggesting that "next to abstinence, condoms are the best prevention method against any sexually transmitted infections" (Glenza, 2016).

The publics responsiveness to these messages varied. More specifically, the oppositional perspectives of faith versus practical application of science affected publics differently. The risk messages encouraging women to delay pregnancy or to use contraception to avoid the sexual transmission of the Zika virus were viewed as advocating birth control. The Rev. Hector Figueroa, a priest in charge of health issues in the San Salvador Archdiocese, said: "Morality says that people shouldn't have that control over procreation." But he acknowledged that ZIKv and its connection with microcephaly was "a very delicate issue" (Partlow, 2016).

Being willing to take her chances, "Salina Velasquz Cortez[,] who has been trying to get pregnant for two years, said there is no way she will stop trying now. 'After so much time wanting to be a mother, I'm not going to give up now' because of the deputy health minister's statement. 'I think it's absurd' " (Partlow, 2016). These responses reflected the cultural context of humans being willing to be subjugated to the teachings of the church contrasted with humans being unwilling to take an action that counters the natural procreation process.

From a political perspective, the discussion centered on whether restrictions on abortion should be eased for women with ZIKv to terminate pregnancies. Ultimately, the Brazilian Health Minister Marcelo Castro said, "The government is sticking with the current law that makes abortion in the world's largest Roman Catholic country illegal except in cases of rape and risk to the mother's life" ("WHO declares Zika," 2016). The fact that the debate progressed to this point where pro-abortion forces were evident reflected the response of those who believed that law should dominate religion while science provided the link between Zika and the birth of babies with microcephaly.

Hurricane Dorian

The responses to the messages distributed to multiple publics by the NHC along with local, state, and federal entities were influenced by the cultural background of the publics receiving them. Not everyone had the same experiences with hurricanes previously. For tourists vacationing in the state or those who recently moved to Florida, naïvety and lack of experience about what to expect from a hurricane made them more responsive to warnings that use emotive language involving a potential loss of life (e.g., life-threatening). These tourists and newly arrived Floridians were more likely to comply with the evacuation message designed for the universal audience. However, for long-time residents of these regions affected by hurricanes, their previous experiences with multiple weather systems and the unpredictability of weather produce a cautious and somewhat delayed response (Church et al., 2019). These residents are more likely to respond as would a particular audience with knowledge of hurricane predictions and their destructive effects. The CS approach is well-suited to the long-time residents of Florida who will make choices based upon their perceptions of the severity of the crisis.

Tourists are more inclined to respond to the universal warnings to evacuate. In Myrtle Beach, South Carolina, the mayor attested to the compliance of the tourists to the evacuation warnings: "The evacuation for this storm was really only zone A, which is the coastal area. But we also had 100,000 visitors in town for the Labor Day weekend. So, we do feel that they did get out of town safely" (Harlow et al., 2019). Some of the responses from tourists to evacuate may have resulted from the compliance of business owners preparing for the hurricane. Rosa Flores, CNN correspondent, reported: "You know, some people are heeding the warnings and others are not . . . . If you look here in the tourist area, all of the businesses are boarded up as you go up and down the beach" (Blackwell et al., 2019). Edmonds (2019) offered a similar response: "Most people went to shelters as the Category 5 storm approached, with tourist hotels shutting down and residents boarded up their homes." With businesses and hotels closed, the message to tourists was clear: it is the time to evacuate while you still can.

The CS approach used in the NHC Bulletins that provided messages, including the hurricane's location, warning and watch explanations, emotive language, and references to local weather authorities, allowed for individual responses from the local residents that were based upon their previous experiences with hurricanes. As MacCallum et al. (2019) described:

> Most of these people that we've talked to, they say they are prepared, they have their stuff in place, they've got their shutters up, they're ready, but they just want to come out here and check it out. And a lot of them say, this isn't their first storm, so they're not too concerned not quite yet.

Chad Eatche, a resident of Cape Canaveral, Florida, concurred, "This isn't my first rodeo. I've been through a dozen hurricanes" (MacCallum et al., 2019).

Because of the CS information provided by NHC that included the geographic area next to be affected by Hurricane Dorian, the evacuation messages were less compelling due to the slow speed of the hurricane. Miguel Marquez, a CNN national correspondent, indicated that "most of the people along the coast here have evacuated along the way, but this storm has been so slow. It's creeping so slowly toward us . . . . So, you do have some people who are staying sort of here to watch, see what's happening . . . Most people say they are going to get out, but they're waiting" (Burnett et al., 2019).

Once mandatory evacuation orders were issued, the responses of residents living in the path of the hurricane were more dramatic. In South Carolina, Georgia, and Florida, at least one million people were under evacuation orders, prompting state troopers to reverse lanes enabling traffic to head inland on major coastal highways (Edmonds, 2019). In South Carolina, Governor Harry McMaster praised the reversal of traffic as the Department of Transportation officials noticed a sharp increase in traffic on I-26 Monday morning (Phillips, 2019). A National Guard official, John Anderson concurred that people were complying with evacuation orders: "We have not seen much resistance at all" (Stickings, 2019).

For those who either refused to evacuate or had nowhere to go, the CS approach acknowledged that some residents who previously had experienced hurricanes may choose to stay inside their homes and weather out the impending storm no matter what the message. In Indian River Shores, Police Chief Rich Rosell explained why his small police force remains on the barrier island to watch over those unwilling to leave:

> "Our residents expect a concierge service, and a concierge service is what they get. That's why they pay taxes." He gave advice, his cellphone number and assurance to the estimated 50 people who chose to stay in the coastal town with a population of 4,000. Those people include an elderly bed-ridden woman waiting for the storm with a caretaker. A business man who wouldn't evacuate without his prized corvette. A woman who wouldn't go to a shelter without her dog. "The last thing these residents need to feel is abandoned," Rosell says. "Their closest family members might be living 1,000 miles away. In some cases, we are the only family they've got." (Edmonds, 2019)

For those who did not evacuate, the CS messages provided descriptions of the nature and length of the hazardous impacts of the hurricane. This enabled the residents to better understand how long they would need to shelter in place.

African Swine Fever Virus

The response to ASFv exemplifies the complexity of crisis communication at the industry level. The many stakeholders involved in pork production from start to finish form a complex audience, each facet of which needs tailored messages to engage in biosecurity effectively. To maximize biosecurity in the swine industry, a constant dialogue among diagnostic laboratories and agencies, such as the National Pork Board, American Association of Swine Veterinarians, and the USDA Animal Plant Health Inspection Service, is needed. This conversation ranges from creating and testing treatments to monitoring the spread of ASFv globally and in the United States if necessary. In the field, information must be distributed by and collected from swine veterinarians, extension workers, and managers at pork production facilities. These parties play a vital role in the distribution and refinement of biosecurity information. On the front lines, feedback is needed to form recommendations and to evaluate current practices enacted by workers at swine facilities, animal haulers, feed mill managers and haulers, sale barn managers, manure haulers, and anyone else who sets foot on a farm. Additionally, consumers make up another essential element of the audience unrelated to biosecurity. Maintaining a CC approach requires the National Pork Board and others to give voice to each to these numerous and distinct groups.

On the farm level, workers face an emotional toll. During PEDv, workers expressed dismay over the death, sometimes through proactive euthanasia, of the animals they cared for. Owners or managers of facilities can often make decisions of culling animals from a distance in their corporate offices. Workers and veterinarians, however, experience the loss firsthand. Similarly, owners and operators of smaller facilities often live on site and work with the animals they own daily. As a result, the mental health of farmers who lose their animals to disease outbreaks can be emotionally devastating (Sheppard et al., 2019). Messages from individuals struggling with the loss of animals need to be considered and compassionate responses must be provided throughout the system.

Similarly, many of the stakeholders who play critical roles in the implementation of biosecurity are fully engaged in what they believe are the best practices for avoiding the spread of disease. Those who operate feed mills, for example, were implicated in the spread of PEDv, even though they had high standards for biosecurity (Schumacher, 2017). The infectious nature of the pathogen, its ability to survive for extreme lengths of time, and the possibility that it may have been introduced through imported supplements mixed with feed all contributed to feed being an unexpected source for spreading of the disease. In these cases, simply accusing operators of feed facilities of being lax in their biosecurity standards is inappropriate. Instead, such operators must be part of the conversation. In many cases, the pathogens, not the feed mill operations, contributed to the biosecurity breakdown. Thus, the operators can and should contribute to the solution of a problem they very likely did not knowingly help create.

Drivers who haul animals from facility to facility must also be part of the conversation. In the past, drivers may have helped to load animals at a facility as part of a good service initiative. With the advent of diseases such as PEDv and ASFv, drivers should no longer provide this service when moving among facilities. Interacting directly with animals makes the drivers another potential source for spreading these diseases. Thus, drivers need to be involved in helping to change the expectations farmers may have for drivers coming onto their farms. Remaining in the cab of the truck is not a sign of laziness or disregard;

doing so is rather a prime biosecurity strategy. To achieve this change in organizational culture, drivers must be allowed to express themselves and their concerns should be noted in biosecurity messages sent throughout the industry.

Veterinarians and extension workers are two of the most vibrant sources of information moving through the biosecurity network both upward to industry leadership and downward to hands-on workers. Both veterinarians and extensions workers interact regularly with individuals on the farm. They can see when language barriers, financial hardship, abusive work conditions, and other constraints impeded follow-through on biosecurity message. Veterinarians and extension workers can also see when the treatment protocols and biosecurity recommendations are or are not feasible or effective. The richness of information veterinarians and extension workers can share throughout the network can help inspire cultural advocacy to address unmet needs that likely have an impact on the extent to which biosecurity is practiced.

Finally, the complexity of science related to disease treatment and transmission can create a cultural barrier between industry recommendations and practice. For example, research may identify effective strategies for containing diseases. These strategies, however, may be more fitting for larger facilities with many more resources and much larger budgets. Thus, those working in research facilities must give voice to the broad array of farmers with whom they communicate. If recommendations are financially infeasible, adaptations or tailoring is needed. Such adaptation and tailoring works best if a diverse chorus of voices is heard throughout the industry. Similarly, translating complex science into practice requires considerable patience and feedback. Getting the science right is essential and laudable. If, however, that information is not translated into messages with recommendations that can be comprehended and enacted by diverse frontline workers, biosecurity cannot prevail. Researchers can work with veterinarians and extension workers to tailor their research into practical applications that can be understood and adapted among workers at facilities of all sizes.

Many stakeholders play vital roles in the development and implementation of biosecurity. These stakeholders are diverse in their languages, incomes, educations, and social status. Unless each stakeholder's voice is heard, the industry cannot engage in a CC approach to biosecurity. Without this sensitivity to culture, the likelihood that the messages devoted to biosecurity will induce the kind of cooperation needed is low. Thus, a commitment to culture is foundational to creating and adapting a safe industry.

Responses to Risks and Crises in IMCs

The intersection of risk and crisis communication with IMC contributes to a robust discussion. As Kitchen and De Pelsmacker (2004) described, IMC has as a goal the creation of a positive, unified brand image and awareness, understanding, value, and appreciation for the product from potential customers and consumers. These goals are similar to those of risk and crisis communicators who seek to create consistent and coherent messages and awareness and understanding of the situation facing them and appreciation for the strategies designed to save them and their livelihoods from destruction.

As the communication strategies of IMC are compared with the cultural approaches of risk and crisis communication, the benefits of using a CC model are apparent. In IMC, there are four capacities for determining the level of marketing success: (1) the ability to deliver a personal message; (2) the ability to reach a large audience; (3) the level of interaction; and (4) the credibility given by the target audience (Kitchen & De Pelsmacker, 2004). Based upon our analysis, the CC approach provides the best way for communicators to present a risk or crisis message that will reach the individual or family spheres of ethnocentricity. Conversely, if reaching a large audience is the measure of success, the CN approach that creates scripted messages for the universal audience may provide for the most objective option for IMC organizations. Clearly, within the universal audience are particular audiences, so the CC model still has utility if the format for the messages allows for multiple spokespeople to co-create the messages designed for the larger audiences. When interaction is the goal, the level best achieved by CC approach is one where the individual and family spheres of ethnocentricity are identified. Finally, as target audiences come to trust the source of the risk and crisis communication as having a helpful intent, credibility will be enhanced when members of the publics are collaborating in the creation and dissemination of the message.

Another dimension of IMC is represented in the amount of control exercised by decision-makers in all stages, but particularly in stage 4 when constant monitoring is used to adjust the marketing strategy for the greatest return on investment. Control is measured in IMC organizations by the ability to target particular audiences, and by the ability of management to adjust to the deployment of marketing tools as circumstances change (Kitchen & De Pelsmacker, 2004). The CS and CC approaches provide the greatest utility for managers seeking to target particular audiences. This is also the case with risk and crisis communicators who seek to disseminate messages to particular groups. However, in the process of targeting by IMC managers, if members of the targeted groups are involved, they can provide counternarratives to confront what would have been viewed as generalizations made by the decision-makers in their absence. Without a CC approach, the marginalized voices are ignored or limited, and their responses are not in line with expected outcomes. In addition, greater vertical integration and control by IMC managers may be possible using the CN approach because the decisions to adjust the deployment of marketing tools are made without feedback. If a CC approach were adopted instead, the power of the communication message is likely to be stronger because of the input provided by the cocreators of the marketing tool.

STRATEGIES TO ENHANCE BEST PRACTICES

The emergence of IMC resulted from the globalization of markets in the late twentieth century and early adopters embraced the multifaceted approach that used the tools of advertising, sales promotion, direct marketing, marketing public relations, e-communications, and relationship marketing. As the tools were amassed by the IMC organizations and strategic global databases were created, the resulting integrated and coordinated marketing strategies produced a marketing mix designed to reach a global audience. As Clow and Baack (2002) suggested, IMC was truly designed for the global marketplace.

Just as IMC uses all marketing tools together as the accepted norm for companies engaged in the global marketplace, the best practices of risk and crisis communication follows a similar framework as practitioners discover that they are most effective if used together in a mix that responds to the dynamic nature of risk and crisis situations. Strategic planning requires looking ahead, establishing a crisis network, and prioritizing the safety and well-being of publics. Being inclusive involves listening to public concerns, acknowledging and accounting for vulnerable populations and cultural differences, forming partnerships with the public, and meeting the needs of the media while remaining accessible. Being responsible requires the acceptance of uncertainty and public speculation, providing instruction for self-protection, tailoring messages to the affected publics, communicating with honesty, candor, openness, compassion, concern, and empathy. Taking corrective action means completing and communicating about the recovery efforts and continuously evaluating and updating crisis plans.

These essential guidelines comprise the strategies used by risk and crisis communicators as they plan for, manage, and learn from crises (Seeger, 2006; Veil et al., 2020). The tensions that are associated with using best practices shift and cluster together in different combinations throughout a crisis, resulting in the need for decision-makers to reprioritize responses and change practices when circumstances require different strategies (Littlefield, 2020b). The application of the best practices in IMC and risk and crisis communication suggests that the infusion of culture into the process will result in more effective messages and more receptive responses.

Infusing Culture into Best Practices

The CN and the CC approaches are mutually exclusive. The first approach makes every effort to remove cultural content from the message to be as objective as possible. The other infuses culture into every dimension of the message to create the greatest opportunity for internalization and connection. Sellnow et al. (2009) described mutual exclusivity as oppositional but overly simplistic because strategies in risk or crisis situations are rarely all or nothing. To move from a CN to a CC risk and crisis communication, members of the community must be included in the process (Israel, Schulz, Parker, & Becker, 2003). However, this process does not happen without conscious effort. In the following discussion, suggestions for communicators and organizations seeking to become more CC are provided.

Find the Value of Multicultural Community Involvement in Decision-Making

To gain a CC perspective, organizations must identify and involve a variety of cultural agents as part of the decision-making team, using vertical integration to communicate this strategy throughout the organization. Cultural agents assist the team in understanding cultural knowledge, attitudes, perceptions, behaviors, beliefs, values, needs, social networks, and concerns. This engagement directly impacts the quality of the communication. When identifying a cultural agent, the goal is to find someone who is trusted in the community but also has a passion for spreading key information. When working with the cultural agent, other key community leaders can be identified. The inclusion of community members requires being open and receptive to new ideas using a two-way flow of communication. From the beginning stages of efforts to be more CC, keeping the welfare of the cultural groups in mind is paramount. A key question for the decision-makers moving toward a CC approach is: How can incorporating the community concerns and issues contribute to the creation of a message that will be meaningful to the audience and achieve the intended outcomes?

Building Relationships to Create Culture-Centered Messages Takes Time

The move to become a more CC communicator requires time and should begin early in the pre-crisis stage. This external integration process begins when decision-makers identify cultural agents that are respected members of the community and invite them into the decision-making team. These cultural agents then share their knowledge of the community and provide insight about ways to engage with the community on an ongoing basis to establish presence and to build trust. Over time, the involvement of the decision-making team with members of the community expands relationships and opens channels of communication that can be used at a later time when a crisis occurs, and messages must be quickly disseminated. In all cases, follow through with the community is essential because while trust takes a long time to build, it can be destroyed in an instant if the perception of intent becomes negative.

Be Mindful of Religion and Culture

When moving to the CC approach, being mindful of religion and culture is particularly important and should be noted as data are collected integrated throughout the organization. Religious holidays, seasonal observances, and dietary and social norms for community members are influential in multicultural communities. The cultural agent becomes an essential partner in the decision-making process by revealing these religious and cultural patterns and by providing openings for the co-participants to engage appropriately with members of the community at times that are appropriate. Understanding the power religious and cultural leaders have over their followers also provides a channel for communication when crisis occurs; and information must be directed to specific groups within the community.

Be Mindful of Cultural Learning Styles and Literacy Levels

Organizations using a CN approach assume the universal audience understands their messages. This assumption is internally integrated throughout the IMC organization as it develops its messages. However, cultural learning styles and literacy levels affect the ability of different cultural groups to understand and process risk and crisis messages, particularly in times of stress or emergency. Cultural agents can be helpful in determining the best way to communicate information to particular audiences because they know their community and understand how they prefer to receive and share information. Learning how publics prefer to get information may influence whether the risk or crisis message is spoken or written. Being prepared to translate materials into the language of a cultural group may be necessary. In addition, differing literacy levels can affect the ability of communicators to disseminate information effectively. Choice of words, language structure, idioms, and acronyms can be confusing. Being conscious of how publics receive information is especially useful when following the IDEA model to construct risk and crisis messages.

Explore Different Ways to Listen and Engage Multiple Publics

To move toward a CC approach to risk and crisis communication, all levels of the organization should horizontally integrate and collaborate with their cultural agents to investigate issues that need to be addressed (or the group feels they need to be addressed). Working with cultural agents to identify cultural norms of listening and forms of engagement will create a dialogue to inform decision-makers about ways to improve the internalization experienced by members of the community when the IDEA model is used. Involving cultural agents in conversations about issues that pertain to the community will provide pertinent examples that are meaningful to the audiences who hear them. If risk and crisis communicators are trying to persuade the publics to take action, using the cultural agents to identify practical strategies will result in greater levels of compliance when crises occur, and mitigation efforts require community involvement.

Practical Applications

From a practical perspective, a CC approach requires a multicultural team, a respected cultural agent, and trustworthy, credible ways to present information that will not violate cultural norms and practices. The process of moving toward a CC approach takes time, sensitivity, attention to differences, and an understanding of competing worldviews to produce meaningful results. Seeger et al. (2003) suggested three advantages to this approach that were cited by Littlefield et al. (2006):

> Including the cultural groups will increase the competence of the decision makers because the public will provide information about matters that concern them; when organizations and groups are held accountable, they will work harder to establish legitimacy with the different publics receiving their crisis messages; and including all groups is proper in a democratic society. (p. 21)

By using a CC approach, the decision-maker will elevate the quality of messages used to communicate with multiple publics in a consistent and coherent way.

SUMMARY

In this chapter, we discussed the implications of emphasizing culture in risk and crisis communication. The lessons learned from the ZIKv, Hurricane Dorian, and ASFv crises, illustrating the CN, CS, and CC approaches were identified and offered within the context of IMC. The consequences of differing views regarding what constitutes a crisis and how different responses to risk and crisis communication will affect IMC were examined. Strategies to enhance best practices to integrate culture followed, as suggestions were provided for practitioners and business and industry leaders seeking to move from a CN to a CC orientation. The next chapter focuses on the need for an ethical cultural framework for crisis and risk communication. In addition, the principle of social utility (PSU) and the ethic of significant choice are introduced as strategies to improve ethical risk and crisis communication.

Chapter 9

The Need for an Ethical Framework

The previous chapter examined the potential implications of emphasizing culture in risk and crisis communication. This chapter provides a theoretical and practical basis for developing an ethical framework for crisis and risk communication within the context of IMC. With the convergence of multiple sources as a foundation, competing worldviews are shown to function on an equal level in a perfect world. However, in risk and crisis communication, the source of the communication is critical, particularly when considering IMC. The ethics of precedence during a crisis is weighed against the value of broadening the conversation to include the publics who are most affected by the crises when they occur.

The principle of social utility (PSU) and the ethic of significant choice are introduced as two viable ways of improving ethical risk and crisis communication. PSU suggests that whatever has social utility contributes to the survival of the group and safeguards the well-being of individuals in that group. Using PSU, this chapter provides strategies for risk and crisis communicators to navigate ethically during the pre-crisis, crisis, and post-crisis stages within IMC. In addition, the ethic of significant choice emphasizes the importance of message clarity in addressing diverse audiences. Accounting for CS and translational accuracy is pivotal to maintaining an ethical approach to risk and crisis communication, particularly as they pertain to IMC.

DEVELOPING AN ETHICAL-CULTURAL PERSPECTIVE

Ethics and ethical practices have always been part of the discussion in all aspects of communication theory and practice (Anderson, 2000). At the core of this discussion is what Farmer (2018) labeled as the "field of ethical standards," such as "teleology (the search for good), procedural aspects (such as rules of justice or fairness), and personal qualities (like virtues)" (p. 3). In most cases, Farmer suggests that developing an ethical perspective

> relies on intuition, on occasionally complex analysis or reasoning that is based on the characteristics of a rational, independent agent (the decision maker) who is guided by freely acquired values or principles that attest to his vision of what is good, evil, or just. (p. 3)

For organizations and agencies implementing IMC or risk and crisis communication, the call for ethical leadership has been widespread (Neill, 2017). Particularly in IMC organizations where vertical integration is functioning to convey a consistent top-down leadership strategy, the need for ethics training and other practices to encourage an ethical workplace environment is paramount as a basis for decision-making and resolving conflicting responsibilities to themselves and to their publics (Fitzpatrick & Gauthier, 2001). Several models of ethical decision-making reveal different approaches that managers and communicators may consider as they determine how to arrive at ethical outcomes.

Existing Models of Ethical Decision-Making

Recognition of Universal Morality

To engage in the process of ethical decision-making relying on the recognition of universal morality, Rest (1986) created a four-stage model that includes moral recognition, moral reasoning, moral intent, and reflective equilibrium. The process begins with moral recognition as the decision-maker acknowledges the presence of an issue that has moral or ethical implications. This recognition occurs because the decision-maker is aware of acceptable codes of behavior within the context where the issue presents itself. For example, in the context of crisis management, government officials are expected to provide publics with essential information that will save lives. If a government official were in a position to withhold essential information or use it for personal benefit, moral recognition occurs.

When recognition occurs, a judgment must be made through moral reasoning about what should be done to address the ethical issue. Extending the previous example, the decision-maker would need to consider available alternatives to determine conflicting interests affected by the withholding of essential information. At this point, the decision-maker gives precedence to the moral value reflecting an intent to do what is perceived as right or just. The decision to reveal the act of withholding essential information gives precedence to the values of saving lives and exposing unethical behavior. In contrast, if the decision to overlook the act of withholding the essential information were prioritized, the value of shielding the public from information that would cause panic or fear could reflect the decision-maker's perceived intent.

The final stage is reflective equilibrium (Rawls, 1971), whereby the decision-maker confirms the judgment made and either revises it or holds fast to original convictions. To close the example, if the decision-maker determines that saving lives has precedence, the moral value reflecting that choice will be upheld.

Considering Morality of Particular Audiences

In contrast, a decision-making model designed for particular audiences assumes four interrelated stages required to make an ethical decision, including "defining the situation, identifying values, selecting principles, and choosing loyalties to stakeholders" (McElreath, 1996, p. 57). Initially, an ethical situation presents itself and the decision-maker recognizes that a choice must be made about how something is communicated or accomplished. In this example, an agency or organization learns that an upcoming emergency will require a timely message conveyed to those who will be impacted by the crisis telling them what to do.

Next, values are identified to contrast the worldviews representing the different choices available to the decision-maker. For instance, the values of self-preservation and community welfare could be noted, with self-preservation encouraging individuals to use their agency to protect themselves and their families, while the value of community welfare would emphasize strategies to help those without agency to prepare for the crisis.

The principles for determining which value to prioritize are selected by comparing them against consistent criteria. In this case, the utilitarian choice to do what is best for the greatest number would be compared with the approach that most closely adheres to what the decision-maker considers as the right thing to do to uphold justice or equity.

Finally, the choice that aligns with what is in the best interest of the stakeholders becomes the decision rule by which the individual makes an ethical choice in this instance. If the decision-maker determines that selecting a communication or crisis strategy that accounts for the welfare of the entire community is the most beneficial, and includes options for those with more personal agency to protect themselves and their families, an ethical decision will have been made.

Normative Model of Ethical Issues Management

A third approach to ethical decision-making is a normative model of ethical issues management introduced by Bowen (2004), combining elements of the symmetrical model developed by Grunig and Hunt (1984) with a deontological philosophy. The tenets of rationalism and autonomy provide the foundation for this approach and use four principles of deontology—duty, dignity, respect for others, and intention—as the basis for ethical decision-making. The goal is to help managers come to the most ethical outcome. The stages of this model include issue identification; issue decision-making; engagement of autonomy; the posing of the categorical imperative; consideration of duty, respect, and intention; and symmetry.

In the issue identification stage, the item of concern is recognized based heavily on the judgment of the individual as to whether the issue is important. For example, a past action may have prompted a lawsuit and the decision-maker is in the position of determining the level of threat this lawsuit poses to the organization.

In the next stage, horizontal integration occurs as the managers meet to discuss the issue and analyze the necessary resources needed to address the issue. Because the normative model is dependent upon Kant's philosophy, the decision-makers are expected "to do what is ethical right as based on his or her duty to universal moral norms" (Bowen, 2004, p. 80). In the case of the lawsuit, doing the right thing could constitute doing what was best for the victim if the organization were other-focused; but, it also could be considered the right thing that is necessary to preserve the reputation of the organization if the organization were self-focused.

Next, the law of autonomy is applied, freeing the decision-makers to establish an impartial context in which to consider the alternatives. This stage is designed to be freeing, as managers and communicators consider a range of alternatives to find convergence, fully able to use their autonomous agency to produce the best outcomes. While values undergird this model, in the autonomy stage, the decision-makers share their views with the goal of arriving at a consensus about the most ethical option.

The fourth stage of the model applies the categorical imperative to the alternatives. The decision-makers are called upon to "act only on that maxim through which you can will that it should become a universal law" (Kant, 1785/1964, p. 88), and consider all options from all viewpoints, including those of the recipients of the actions. In other words, decision-makers must view all possible actions as if they were going to be the recipients of the outcomes. In the example, the imposition of the categorial imperative may suggest that being ethical could be settling the lawsuit out of court in favor of the victim, or it could mean going to trial to reveal the victim as making libelous claims against the organization.

When applying the categorical imperative, Bowen (2004) suggests the introduction of duty, respect, and intention compels decision-makers to consider the question, "Does this decision make us worthy of earning trust, respect, and support from our publics?" (p. 83). If the answer to this question is yes, then decision-makers may consider they have taken a rational, ethical approach to the issue at hand. For the example of the lawsuit, if settling the case outside of court will gain the trust of publics about the organization's intent to back up its product or services, then the introduction of these versions of the categorial imperative will have produced an ethical outcome.

The final stage involves the use of the symmetrical model of public relations (J. E. Grunig, 2001; Grunig & Grunig, 1992) as the means used to convey the decision to publics. The model presumes a dialogic cycle of giving and receiving information on the part of the decision-makers and the publics. Ideally, the information received from the publics will share the responses of the decision-makers. To conclude the example, by engaging in a dialog with the victim about the reasons for the lawsuit, the decision-makers may take steps to address the victim's concerns and make changes to mitigate similar lawsuits in the future.

Comparison of Existing Approaches

These three approaches to ethical decision-making reflect different perspectives, but none of them has a CC focus. The deontological and normative models presume the existence of universal moral norms, while the utilitarian model places the decision-maker in the position of identifying the principles by which an ethical decision is made. The presence of universal moral norms as a constant removes the choice from decision-makers in the first and third approaches, whereas the identification of differing worldviews and norms possibly reflecting the biases of decision-makers is possible in the second approach. Finally, the first and third approaches require the decision-maker to ethically choose from among alternatives that are reflective of and benefiting the universal value, while the second approach places the focus on loyalty to publics who are part of the situation.

All three approaches reflect the egocentric perspectives of the decision-makers as the ethical actors within the process. The decision-makers retain the agency to determine and justify their actions and communication as ethical, based upon the process they chose to guide their ethical assessment. Involvement of the publics is missing from these approaches. Even if the decision-maker in the normative model were to consider the differing worldviews of those involved in the situation as part of the symmetrical and somewhat reflective process, the locus of control remains with the decision-maker who chooses strategies in the end that are, at best, CS to the publics involved. The identification of a CC approach to ethical decision-making would provide IMCs organizations and risk and crisis communicators with an opportunity to use the IDEA model more effectively when reaching multiple publics.

CONSIDERING THE CULTURAL BASIS FOR ETHICAL PRACTICES

Ethical standards are products of contexts and societal norms of morality are established over time based upon what people in those contexts believe to be ethical behavior. Using the metaphor of culture as a fabric, Howell (1982) described ethical behavior to be "whatever strengthens or protects the fabric of a culture. . . . What strains, weakens, or tears it is unethical" (p. 180). Societal values or norms are central tendencies of behavior that a population identifies as right or good. Whether an individual acts in accordance with those norms will determine whether they are perceived as ethical or unethical. When individuals recognize that certain societal norms conflict with their own norms of morality, they may need to make personal adaptations, signaling their willingness to compromise in order to function within the ethical parameters of the context. When individuals following different societal norms of morality are willing to make these personal adaptations, Howell (1982) suggests that a third culture is created, one where "ethical systems can adjust to each other without damage to the fabrics of the participating cultures" (p. 181). This is the context where the CC approach can function effectively.

The tendency to compromise what is perceived as ethical behavior is complicated because every culture has the egocentric tendency to assume superiority based upon its own set of values. When making decisions about how to implement IMC or create and disseminate a risk or crisis message, if the moral perspective of the decision-maker is perceived as superior to the moral perspective of the consumers or publics, an unequal power relationship develops, much like a parent and child, and the result of the effort is likely to be unsuccessful. The conflict between societal norms of morality makes ethics central to both the decision-making process for IMC organizations and the message creation and dissemination process for risk and crisis communicators.

Convergence of Multiple Sources

In a perfect world, Sellnow et al. (2009) illustrated that when issues arise, many bodies of knowledge contribute to the convergence that is required to produce consensus decision-making. These bodies of knowledge represent different sources of information and worldviews coming from different cultural perspectives. In the larger system of discourse, the information is presented, and consumers of that information make sense of it. To arrive at a decision about the best option, individuals must weigh many variables, including source credibility, veracity, and compatibility with prior knowledge and experiences.

Based upon how the multiple bodies of knowledge converge, members of different publics will form their opinions about who and what they will believe.

The challenge for decision-makers is intensified when bodies of knowledge associated with differing societal norms of morality are in conflict. Deciding whether or not the government, industry, special interest group, media network, or neighborhood leader is acting in the best interests of the publics or sharing information that will lead to increased safety or security, based upon whether their actions or words are perceived to be ethical, makes the roles of the decision-maker or risk and crisis communicator more complicated. To be successful, decision-makers must find ways to negotiate their egocentric perspectives with conflicting societal norms, while not destroying the ethical fabrics of the discerning publics.

Challenges of Precedence in IMC

With multiple perspectives, consumers and publics must give precedence to the information that is perceived as most credible, compatible, and relevant to their circumstances. As the context changes, so does the available information. Perelman and Olbrechts-Tyteca (1958/1971) suggested that opposing arguments are best analyzed holistically because the contexts where they are introduced "[shift] each moment as argumentation proceeds" (p. 460). Having access to all sources of the information, and discounting distracting or political alignments is necessary for individuals to make decisions. Some sources of information may be scientific or technical, coming from established entities reflecting paternalistic views about what and how something should be done, while others may be personal and based upon the lived experiences of people within given contexts. As the argumentation proceeds, strengths and weaknesses of claims will be revealed and opposing points may begin to converge with neither position being completely right or completely wrong. The emergence of a single conclusion resulting from multiple perspectives is the goal of risk and crisis communicators.

The belief that consumers and publics are capable of making choices about how to respond based on the information they have available to them reflects the presence of spheres of ethnocentricity, as these individuals will internalize information addressing matters that directly affect them. Thus, giving precedence is derived from having access to multiple sources of information and applying theoretical approaches having their origins in consequentialist theory, including the utilitarian and deontological perspectives.

Utilitarianism as a Basis for Precedence

Consequentialism is the basis for situational ethics found to be prevalent among decision-makers embracing utilitarianism (Bowen, 2004; Pratt, 1991).

Consequentialist theory is subjective and presumes that community benefit should take precedence over individual values. This theory is the basis for utilitarianism, which supports acting for the greater good, not for what may be the preference of an individual making the decision. The presumed consequences of the action provide the basis for making an ethical decision. The intersection of utilitarianism and culture in the process of ethical decision-making requires a CC approach because to determine the greatest good, the multiple sources of knowledge from the marketplace of ideas must be shared and compared before precedence can be given to the one with the greatest convergence as being the most ethical.

Deontology as a Basis for Precedence

Non-consequentialism assumes objectivity and presumes there is one *right* or *moral* position that should be upheld. Theoretically, this represents a deontological perspective that morality or moral rightness is universal; and that all humans have autonomy and "every person is equal with all others" (Kant, 1785/1964, p. 203). Individuals have agency; and, in fact, a moral obligation to act in such a way that is moral, no matter what the consequences of that action might be (Sullivan, 1989). The intersection of deontology and culture in the process of decision-making represents a CN approach because proponents believe there is only one source of knowledge that matters; and that knowledge stems from the individual who determines morality and chooses to communicate or act from a singular perspective of determining what is or is not ethical. This approach presumes there is a *right* decision, reflecting a very ethno-European, elitist perspective.

Ethics of Precedence

These two opposing views of ethics place the decision-maker in the position of having to select which perspective has precedence while making choices about how to use IMC when launching a campaign or employing best practices in risk and crisis situations. The placement of decision-makers situated in the role of determining the process by which choices are made, and the decision not to broaden the conversation to include the publics who are impacted by those decisions, has been the object of critique among communication ethicists who view the exclusion of audiences from the process as paternalistic. Tinker (2019) characterized paternalism as

> the limitation, influence, or judgment of choices, whether physical, psychological, interpersonal, cultural, social, professional, or political of one person, public, or organization by another. Paternalism reifies ontological relations

between communicative agents as hierarchical, parent-child interactions . . . . It diminishes responsibility or agency on the part of the paternalized. (pp. 315)

The position of the communicator seeking to use a CC approach when making ethical choices can avoid paternalism and resist defaulting to egocentric decision-making. The PSU confronts paternalism and includes multiple actors to engage in the process (Howell, 1982).

Principle of Social Utility

When using the PSU as a criterion to evaluate ethical decision-making, Howell (1982) suggested that whatever "contributes to the survival of the group" and "safeguards the well-being of individuals in that collective" has social utility (p. 188). In other words, the proposed action or communication must promote or maintain the existence of the group and do no harm to those who belong to the group. The most direct way for decision-makers to meet these criteria for ethical decision-making involves including members of the affected groups as co-decision-makers in the determination of shared issues of concern, shared norms and values, shared acceptable options, and shared consequences.

Deontologists would argue that existing models of ethical decision-making already consider the views of members of publics through the feedback they provide when interacting in the communication process. They claim: "every person is equal with all others" (Kant, 1785/1964, p. 203) and deserves dignity and self-respect. However, this presumption is disputed because marginalized publics who may have access to communication channels do not have direct access to the systems and contexts in which ethical decisions are made and are left out of the decision-making process. Dutta (2008) critiqued the dominant approach in the context of health communication because of its "systematic omission of the structural contexts that encompass the health experiences of individuals, groups, and communities" (pp. 53–54). Similarly, the exclusion of vulnerable publics from decision-making in risk and crisis situations, or when launching IMC, reflects the omission of their voices in the process. Engaging the publics in the decision-making process through a CC approach produces ethical consequences and empowers previously marginalized publics to be more engaged in matters affecting their lives and livelihoods. Dutta (2008) supported this: "The culture-centered approach privileges the dialogue between the researcher/practitioner and the community as a way of knowing" (p. 46).

A criticism of social utility is its reliance on situational ethics (Pratt, 1991). Deontologists argue that without universal or generally applicable moral norms, each situation must be viewed independently. Without moral guidance, the decision is without value. In addition, critics suggest because utilitarianism requires that any actions must benefit the greatest number of people, proponents give precedence to the majority, and put the needs of the minority at risk. This oppositional perspective presupposes that consequences must be mutually exclusive. However, that is not the case when applied to IMC or risk and crisis communication where decisions can be made to create and disseminate messages to multiple publics, including those who embrace a deontological perspective.

STRATEGIES TO IMPROVE ETHICAL RISK AND CRISIS COMMUNICATION

Sellnow et al. (2009) suggested that whenever decision-makers determine what to communicate, when to communicate, how to communicate, or to whom to communicate about a risk or crisis, they are making ethical choices with ethical implications. Whether suggesting crisis response strategies to victims of a natural disaster, or warning consumers about unsafe or unhealthy food products, decision-makers often are criticized for making choices having ethical consequences that put competing worldviews at odds. Similarly, Kitchen and De Pelsmacker (2004) suggested that companies using IMC have been criticized for being "deceptive, manipulative, offensive, and for influencing people to buy products or services they do not need" (p. 38). Together, these criticisms are not unique to risk and crisis communication or IMC, as all forms of communication have elements that can be construed as harmful or unethical. Thus, strategies to improve ethical risk and crisis communication are essential.

Using Social Utility as Ethical Model of Decision-Making

To use the PSU as an ethical model of decision-making, the process begins with the assumption that moral norms of behavior are societally determined. These norms reflect convergence based upon the beliefs and behaviors of the group that have developed and perpetuated as acceptable within the society. Within this context, individuals choose whether to follow the societal norms, using their personal control as a basis for this decision. Landau et al. (2015) defined personal control as, "[a] person's belief that he or she is capable of obtaining desired outcomes, avoiding undesired outcomes, and achieving goals" (p. 695). Thus, when a member of the group exercises personal control and chooses to adhere to societal norms, that adherence is regarded as ethical behavior. In contrast, if an individual chooses not to adhere to societal norms or exercises personal agency, using "skills, knowledge, and other capabilities that enable the self to initiate action, expend effort in the service of goals, and persist in the face of adversity" (Landau, 2015, p. 695), that behavior is viewed as unethical.

Applying this assumption to existing models for ethical decision-making poses an immediate challenge stemming from the fact that organizations using IMC and communicators applying the essential guidelines for ongoing risk and crisis communication (Veil et al., 2000) have established norms that preclude marginalized groups from engaging in decision-making. Thus, within these cultures, using personal agency to change the process might be viewed as unethical. However, to create a third culture (Howell, 1982) where convergence can exist supporting multiple perspectives and safeguarding the well-being of all, a CC approach to ethical decision-making is needed.

In the pre-crisis stage, before any decision-making takes place, the relevant participants in the process must be identified by existing decision-makers within the structures currently operating in the context. The identification process should include cultural agents who are members of and reflect the concerns of the publics being affected by the decisions. These cultural agents have the trust of the communities they represent and will assist in the process of conveying the positive intent of the entity to share in the decision-making process. These cultural agents also will identify additional members of the communities who have leadership roles and can assist in conveying the message or campaign to the publics.

The purpose of identifying these people is to create a group of co-decision-makers who become familiar with each other and develop a relationship based upon mutual support and acceptance. As Sarbaugh (1979) suggested, to know and accept the normative beliefs and values of others within the multiple sources of information needed to find convergence is essential to effective intercultural relationships. The PSU relies on the foundation of these relationships. Knowing and accepting beliefs and values is reflective of personal control because when participants have all the information available to them, they can find points of convergence and move toward mutually acceptable goals. The creation of this group of co-decision-makers is best suited for the pre-crisis stage because it takes time to identify the participants, to reveal all of the multiple sources of information, and to arrive at a place where trust and open dialogue is possible. Once in place, the CC process of ethical decision-making continues through four stages: recognition of a shared concern, examination of shared and conflicting perspectives, identification of shared acceptable options, and assessment of shared impacts or consequences.

In stage 1, the decision-makers recognize a shared issue that requires attention. The issue may be identified by one or more of the members who have differing levels of knowledge about the situation. The issue must have ethical implications, which suggest that responses to the issue are in conflict.

Stage 2 provides for an examination of both shared and conflicting perspectives related to the issue. In this stage, multiple spheres of knowledge inform the discussion without prioritization. The basis for comparison of these perspectives is the PSU, which examines each viewpoint using two criteria: (1) Will the proposed communication or action support the survival or existence of the cultural group being affected? (2) Will the proposed communication or action safeguard all members of the group from harm?

Once the available information has been examined, stage 3 calls for the identification of the shared available options. Here, the decision-makers select the best alternative that reflects the shared acceptance of the group. In traditional models, decision-makers have the authority to make the final decision; but in the CC model, established hierarchies are challenged in order to find a shared ethical outcome that allows for the most positive outcome for all involved.

Once shared acceptable options are identified, CC organizational responses are issued and results noted. The impact of context may modify the process due to the immediacy of the crisis or critical situation. However, when trusted relationships have been established, the CC team is able to mobilize quickly to respond. The fourth stage is entered once the crisis has subsided. Here, an assessment of shared impacts or consequences is determined based on the criteria previously identified. Ultimately, new shared interests of concern may emerge initiates a cyclical return to stage 1.

Applying Social Utility to IMC

IMC requires organizations to take stock of existing resources to create a coherent and consistent message for loyal customers and potential clients. Consumers are "at the center of the marketing enterprise" (David, 2004, p. 187). The stages of IMC move from stage 1—tactical coordination of organizational leadership, shared information, consistent external messaging, transparent internal communication, and shared data—to stage 2—gathering of external information from agencies and consumers to learn more about their preferences and feedback. Once acquired, global databases are created and used to plan and implement marketing strategies in stage 3. Finally, from the vantage point of senior leadership, the ongoing integration of financial and strategic planning necessitates ongoing evaluation and monitoring to assure that the organization is getting an appropriate return on investment. Within these stages, the infusion of cultural agents was suggested in the previous chapter as necessary to modify IMC as a CC endeavor. It is within this context that using social utility to achieve ethical decision-making is discussed.

Because customers are the focus of marketing, companies using IMC have the potential to demonstrate paternalism in the decision-making process if they are led by individuals who have the authority to make final decisions and exclude customers and targeted publics. If the circle of decision-making excludes representatives from the publics or groups of consumers the company is seeking to influence, the ethics of the company will be challenged by those who do not share its value structure. Thus, before ethical decision-making can occur, representatives from the targeted groups must be brought into the decision-making process as co-decision-makers. Once accomplished, the stages of ethical decision-making can be followed through the stages of IMC.

In stage 1 of IMC, representatives from the targeted groups can be part of the process of recognizing issues with ethical implications within all aspects of vertical, horizontal, internal, external, and data integration. These cultural representatives can assist in the recognition of shared issues among the leadership of the company, so when conflicting perspectives are examined and acceptable shared options are identified, these ethical practices can be vertically transmitted throughout the organization. Cultural representatives can assist the departments within the company as they recognize issues in their areas, examine shared and conflicting perspectives, and identify shared options to use in the campaign that can be shared horizontally across different units. Including cultural representatives in the communication processes will acknowledge consistency when recognizing shared issues, examining shared and conflicting perspectives, identifying acceptable options as ethical, and sharing these decisions as internal and external messages during the planning process. Finally, within the data collected by different units, including representatives from the targeted groups will help data collectors to recognize ethical issues involved with using data about cultural groups, examine conflicting and shared perspectives about data use, identify acceptable shared options for collecting and using data, and explain the meanings that may or may not come from the data for all units in the organization as it plans the campaign.

When redefining the scope of the marketing communication in stage 2 of IMC, all aspects of stage 1 continue, with the addition of gathering extensive information about current and potential customers. The organization will benefit from including members of the groups in the development of surveys and other means of data collection, and the results will produce more accurate and meaningful information for the organization as it prepares to market its global campaign. Following the process of recognition, examination, and identification will produce decisions reflecting the ethic of social utility because actions will support the survival or existence of the group and will safeguard the well-being of the individuals in the group.

The ethical issues at play in stage 3 of IMC reflect the building of global databases and accessibility to that information. Following the stages of recognition, examination, and identification, when members of the targeted group are involved in the process of determining what information is being used to create the databases and how the data will be used in the planning and implementation phases of the campaign, the potential for finding issues with ethical implications is great. In addition, determining who will have access to cultural information can cause conflict if the use of that information may threaten the survival or existence of the cultural group or cause harm to individuals in that group.

The questions of use and access become part of the ongoing evaluation that is characteristic of stage 4 of IMC. As the CEO monitors the performance of the campaign with an eye for those strategies that are most cost-effective and produce the greatest return on investment—without involvement from members of the targeted groups to recognize potential issues with ethical implications, examine shared and conflicting perspectives, and identify options that have shared acceptance—there can be no assessment of the shared consequences and impacts of the decisions used to implement IMC throughout the organization. If companies using IMC employ the CC approach to ethical decision-making, they will enhance their reputation and demonstrate enhanced CSR.

For the IMC organizations, there is an ethical obligation to acknowledge the legitimacy of other views about risk and to include them in a comprehensive risk dialogue that comes through a CC approach. In addition to applying the PSU, the ethics of significant choice is essential in arriving at decision-making.

Ethic of Significant Choice in IMC

Within the marketplace of ideas, multiple points of knowledge present views reflecting beliefs, values, and perspectives that are in conflict. Streifel et al. (2006) suggested that to make sense of these different messages, consumers and publics must determine which is most compatible and consistent with their views: "The presence of many perspectives is the best environment for a good decision because the individual has many options from which to choose" (pp. 390–391). Once presented with complete information on an issue with ethical implications, consumers can make a significant choice on whom to believe or what to do. As Sellnow et al. (2009) suggested: "There is an ethical obligation to provide all the relevant information whenever individuals face a significant choice" (p. 155).

Nilsen (1974) defined the ethic of significant choice as one made "based on the best information available when the decision must be made" (p. 45). More specifically, Nilsen explained the need for decision-makers to consider significant choice when communicating with different publics: "When we communicate to influence the attitudes, beliefs, and actions of others, the ethical touchstone is the degree of free, informed, and critical choice on matters of significance in their lives that is fostered by our speaking" (1974, p. 46). Streifel et al. (2006) offered the impact of significant choice on ethical communication:

> Significant choice is founded on the principle that when a group has vital information that publics need in order to make important decisions, that information must be disseminated as completely and accurately as possible. To do otherwise is unethical by many ethical standards. (p. 391)

Thus, clarity, accuracy, and sufficiency of information are essential to an ethical crisis response.

Message Clarity

At times, the line between what is fact and what is public relations may be blurred, resulting in messages that obfuscate what may be the recognition of the shared issue that provides for convergence among different perspectives. Clearly identifying the origins and sources of the information available through news organizations and public relations professionals is essential to assure that publics understand the context of the messages being transmitted (Wulfemeyer & Frazier, 1992). When companies use IMC to include video news releases (VNRs), these messages can take the appearance of typical news stories. However, as Wulfemeyer and Frazer (1992) explain, "Unlike typical TV news stories, VNRs are not produced by a news organization. They are produced on behalf of a client in an attempt to obtain free air time" (p. 151).

Other common ethical issues facing communication professionals that challenge message clarity for the consumer involve: "targeting of minors; truthfulness in communication; challenges to professional integrity; altering of research data; working for questionable clients; and workplace practices such as office politics, competitive bidding, and billing practices" (Neill, 2017, p. 121). Additionally, as social media and other traditional forms of media blur the line between news and public relations, transparency and message clarity has suffered.

Cultural Sensitivity and Translational Accuracy

When considering multiple sources of knowledge, the use of scientific and unfamiliar terminology, including acronyms, complicates the publics' understanding of the arguments and creates communication issues having ethical implications. Commonly, to identify shared linguistic ties and to shorten explanations, we use terms (e.g., acronyms, abbreviations, code words) that signal we have a common language when communicating. However, when consumers or publics do not share the common code system, they have no idea what is being presented, they are placed in an ethical dilemma of acting like they know what is being said or losing face or being embarrassed if they ask a question.

Communication accommodation theory explains how people adjust to each other to achieve social or communication goals (Gasiorek, 2013). The affective function accounts for accommodations involving social distance and social identity, and the cognitive function of the theory suggests that when adjustments are made that help people understand what is being communicated, they are being accommodative. If communication adjustments do not aid in comprehension, they are nonaccommodative (Gallois et al., 2005).

In the case of risk and crisis, cognitive accommodation is exacerbated due to the lack of universal acceptance for terms associated with emergencies, disasters, and crises (Federici & Sharou, 2018). The use of terms associated with risk and crisis is particularly relevant when translation is involved because vulnerable communities typically are also underserved and lack resources to provide translators to communicate messages in times of crisis. To help explain how misunderstandings could occur, Sarbaugh (1979) suggested that when two people do not share a common language code, there must be a translator who understands the native codes of both people.

In addition, the lived experiences of marginalized publics shape their perceptions of the magnitude of a crisis. For example, for those who have experienced a flood from a major river that washes away a village, their reaction will be much more intense than that of a person who has experienced a flood as the rise of a slow-moving river that will flood basements. Communicators cannot assume the publics will understand the information that is being presented to them. An ethical approach in this context depends on the development of content focused on helping publics, not confusing them.

SUMMARY

In this chapter, a theoretical and practical basis for developing an ethical framework for crisis and risk communication within the context of IMC was presented. The ethics of precedence during a crisis is weighed against the value of broadening the conversation to include the publics who are most affected by the crises when they occur. The PSU and the ethic of significant choice were introduced as ways to improve ethical risk and crisis communication, and strategies for risk and crisis communicators to navigate ethically during the pre-crisis, crisis, and post-crisis stages within IMC illustrated the need to account for cultural sensitivity and translational accuracy when maintaining an ethical approach to risk and crisis communication. In the final chapter, we conclude with the belief that a CC approach is advantageous when communicating risk and crisis messages to multiple publics in the context of IMC. While beneficial, challenges to the successful implementation of a CC approach are offered, as well as directions for future study.

Chapter 10

Future Directions for Situating Culture in Risk and Crisis Communication

The previous chapter examined a theoretical basis for developing an ethical cultural framework for crisis and risk communication within the context of IMC. Because competing sources of information reflect different worldviews, a way to determine precedence in decision-making must prevail, necessitating a model that applies the PSU and accounts for the ethic of significant choice. This chapter concludes with a final word on the utility of a CC approach in the context of the world today. In addition to discussing the benefits of this approach, limitations are presented that compromise the ability of decision-makers to maintain the same ethical approach in all situations. Areas for future study close the chapter, with an example of one CC organization that revealed to the academy and to practitioners the transformative power of giving voice to those who previously had been excluded from the systems that affecting their lives and livelihoods.

ADVANTAGES OF A CULTURE-CENTERED APPROACH

The CC approach to risk and crisis communication produces advantages over CN and CS alternatives. Across the board, the benefits of CC communication come from shared management, multiple spokespersons, two-way communication flow, the inclusion of multiple particular audiences, full feedback, developed messages, subjective content, integrated cultural adaptation, and a critical theoretical orientation. These benefits of a CC approach provide several advantages when developing and disseminating risk and crisis messages.

Focus on Particular Audiences

The CC approach focuses on collaboration among audiences, rather than only on the sender's worldview. Being audience focused places the emphasis on understanding the cultural preferences of the multiple receivers of messages. By removing the focus from the sender, the ethnocentricity of decision-makers is challenged and neutralized. If decision-makers internalize the need for involving their publics in message creation and dissemination, their personal spheres are expanded to include multiple perspectives. The inclusion of potential customers, consumers, and multiple publics into the process of culturally communicating risk and crisis messages puts them in the shared position of mutual influence over the basis upon which messages are developed and launched. In so doing, messages are designed for particular audiences, where they enter their personal spheres of ethnocentricity for family and community and are internalized.

Focus on Cultural Variables

The CC approach also promotes the development of a more robust understanding of the cultural variables that affect how publics perceive risk and crisis messages and how those messages are processed by different publics. The complexity of culture is revealed through the use of language or code systems, the development of relationships based upon the intent of the participants, the knowledge and acceptance of normative beliefs and values, and the understanding of differing worldviews. How people view their agency through progressive, fatalistic, or holistic perspectives shapes how they regard the nature of life, purpose of life, and their place in the world around them.

Focus on Strategy over Tactics

The CC approach provides decision-makers with a strategic orientation when conveying messages carefully to achieve intended outcomes. To be strategic, an organization creates a plan or goal that represents a broader outcome. With a strategy in place, tactics are steps taken to achieve the overarching goal. Without the strategy, tactics can be unfocused and used without a clear reasoning and often without coordination or accountability. Once a strategy or goal is identified, appropriate tactics can be used to achieve it. Thus, as organizations expand their messaging to a global market, IMC compels organizations to become more strategic because of the focus on reaching a broader range of potential customers. In each of the four stages of IMC, the goal of creating consistent, coherent, and coordinated messages benefits the organization when CC communication is used. When seeking to create awareness of a crisis, an organization gains knowledge about how publics prefer to receive information. When establishing the credibility of the information, identifying opinion leaders to speak on behalf of the organization can be beneficial. A CC approach actively involves diverse publics in every phase of the crisis and at every stage of IMC. When creating the tactical coordination of a campaign, the publics can direct the organization to the underlying issues that may otherwise be overlooked and ensure that the mix of elements in the message is consistent with audience preferences. When redefining the scope of the campaign with audience and consumer preferences, the inclusion of the publics helps the organization to focus on sources of data that reflect a more accurate perspective of the potential consumers or multiple publics. As organizations move into stage 3 of IMC, where the application of information technology results in data about customer preferences, the availability of members of the publics being surveyed can help to sort and validate the data based upon personal experience. Finally, as leaders make financial and strategic decisions based upon return on investment, the inclusion of the publics in the decision process will influence how the decisions are received.

Focus on Enhanced Instructional Messages

The CC approach contributes positively to the enhancement of the dissemination of instructional risk and crisis messages. Having access to cultural insights may trigger examples that are relevant to those receiving the messages, thereby enhancing the internalization of why the risk or crisis situation should be included within their personal sphere of ethnocentricity, prompting attention and interest on the immediate message. IMC's *outside-in* orientation begins with an understanding of the consumers and potential customers and works back to the organization where the development of campaigns and information originates. The pre-crisis or early relational stage provides the opportunity when time is available to build the trust needed for when a crisis actually occurs, and communication must be disseminated. IMC inherently points to the CC approach because the potential customers, consumers, and publics are the focus of their campaigns and communication and if they are integrated into the decision-making process, there is a greater likelihood those publics will respond as desired by the decision-makers. Every organization seeking to reach its publics is able to use IMC if they recognize that their multiple publics have different needs and perspectives. By incorporating co-participants from the publics being addressed into the decision-making process leading to the creation and dissemination of messages through appropriate and preferred channels to particular audiences, organizations can achieve greater impact. The best practices associated with strategic planning, inclusivity, responsible communication, and corrective action are evident when the CC approach is adopted.

Focus on the IDEA Model

Another advantage of the CC approach is its focus on elements of the IDEA model, because through the use of internalization, explanation, action, and distribution, instructional messages are developed to be readily internalized, easily understood, realistically actionable, and appropriately disseminated. In IMC, stage 1 establishes the basis for the campaign through the mutual sharing of information within the organization. Not until the organization moves to stage 2 does the emphasis shift to learning more about potential customers or consumers. This knowledge enables the decision-makers to identify certain themes that may resonate with the potential consumers; but at best, the response is CS because the decision-makers determine which themes will be prioritized and how the messages will be tailored to fit their views. As the organization becomes more committed to IMC, the decision-makers begin creating and managing databases in order to make cost-effective decisions. Without incorporating customers, consumers, and publics in the process, a CC campaign is impossible.

Focus on Ethics and Corporate Social Responsibility

Organizations using a CC approach experience more ethical decision-making because CC communication contributes to the survival and well-being of all affected individuals and it strives to do no harm to any individual. For all practical purposes, CC communication produces ethical consequences and empowers marginalized publics. By including members of the affected publics in the decision-making process, the ethic of significant choice is enacted. The more inclusive the process, the more information can be processed. Because the CC approach is rooted in a focus on the communities that comprise the receivers of risk and crisis messages, when culturally diverse publics share in the processes associated with the creation and dissemination, the ethical basis upon which the communication decisions are made will be more positively perceived. At the highest levels of the IMC organization, the introduction of CSR provides a vehicle for the decision-makers to vertically integrate the CC model throughout its structure. The CC communication used in CSR challenges the "sender-based model in favor of a knowledge sharing orientation" (Chaudhri, 2016, p. 421). When members of the affected publics are brought into the CSR decision-making process, the result is mutually respectful, dialogic, and values-based relationships needed to develop a loyal following: "Inclusion, openness, tolerance, empowerment, and transparency are advanced as normative dimensions of stakeholder dialogue" (Chaudhri, 2016). This approach is also highly ethical because "dialogue elevates publics to the status of communication equal with the organization" (Botan, 1997, p. 196).

In summary, these six advantages of using a CC approach focus on the audiences who receive risk and crisis messages, including a more robust understanding of the cultural variables influencing their perceptions. With a CC perspective, organizations are able to focus their tactics on global strategies using enhanced instructional messages reflecting the IDEA model that are designed to reach and influence those most affected by risks and crises. Finally, more ethical decision-making and the resulting enactment of corporate social responsibility provide foundational advantages for organizations seeking to build and strengthen their relationships with their consumers, potential customers, and publics.

LIMITATIONS OF A CULTURE-CENTERED APPROACH

Despite the identified advantages of a CC approach, three limitations should be identified. By no means do we argue that these are sufficient to persuade decision-makers to reject the CC approach, but they represent alternative perspectives that should be considered and addressed.

Loss of Authority

The CC approach reduces the authority decision-makers traditionally exercise over the process of message development and dissemination. Previously, vertical integration in IMC resulted in the perspective of the decision-maker being transferred throughout the organization from the top-down to the various departments and units that implement the decision-maker's vision. While the decision-maker's authority over the narrative may have allowed for input, the control was not shared equally. If decision-makers are unwilling to give up authority to co-participants from the publics affected by the messages, the CC approach will be unable to function. At every level of the organization, the infusion of different perspectives into the processes inherent in the generation of ideas, the gathering of data, and decision-making has benefits, but without buy-in from those who will lose control, the approach will be impossible to implement.

Loss of Control

The introduction of a CC approach in an organization requires time and coordination because co-participants from outside of the organization must be brought into the process at all levels. Initially, the identification of co-participants depends on building relationships and trust between entities that may have traditionally been on less-than-positive terms due to historical or cultural issues. Selecting and inviting these co-participants requires a cultural awareness on the part of the organization's leaders about how to proceed in an appropriate way from the perspective of the co-participants. Once integrated into the organization, when decisions or changes to previous decisions need to be made, adjustments will require negotiation as the different perspectives are shared before arriving at convergence about the best approach. This process will require an awareness on the part of the organization's leaders about the cultural norms of the co-participants about time orientation and the deliberative process. For example, in the Pueblo culture, factionalism is perceived as a positive way to arrive at a collective decision (Littlefield & Ball, 2004). While the introduction of strongly conflicting views may be perceived by outsiders as disruptive, within the Pueblo community, a lasting decision cannot be reached without going through this conflict. Understanding that the decision-making process may be impacted by the introduction of different perspectives may be perceived as a loss of control over the time needed to complete the process. Thus, the climate of the organization must recognize and appreciate a new level of cultural awareness if a CC approach is going to be successfully implemented.

Impact of Urgency

The CC approach may not always function well in times of immediate crisis when circumstances demand an immediate response to save lives and livelihoods. For example, within the crisis phase when chaos is affecting how agencies and publics respond to changing circumstances and dangers, the need may require one message from a recognized leader with the authority to respond. In these cases, a CS or CN message may need to override the CC approach. For example, in the case of Hurricane Dorian, the National Weather Service issued a warning for residents to evacuate immediately in the face of what would be a devastating landfall. Similarly, the WHO declared an international public health alert about ZIKv to mobilize local public health agencies to begin their specific campaigns to particular audiences in their regions. So, unless an organization had already integrated a CC approach within its structure, the context of crisis may be too immediate to allow for collaborative decision-making; resulting in the need for one-way, scripted messages designed for a universal audience.

The loss of authority and control over the process are limitations to be addressed by organizations seeking to introduce the CC approach to their decision-making process within IMC or risk and crisis messaging. In addition, the urgency of a crisis may require a CN or CS approach if the CC process has not already been implemented and successfully utilized prior to the onset of a crisis.

FUTURE AREAS FOR STUDY

This book focuses on the utility of a CC approach in organizations using IMC, as well as how the creation and dissemination of risk and crisis messages can be enhanced by including the publics in the process. Through three crisis scenarios, the CN, CS, and CC approaches have yielded support for moving from a process that removes cultural content to one that incorporates cultural content for audiences to internalize, understand, and act in ways that will save their lives and livelihoods. The application of the IDEA model to risk and crisis communication inherently enhances the effectiveness of the message and gives voice to those communities that have been overlooked. But where do we go from here?

First, there is benefit in exploring ways to open up the decision-making process in organizations to those populations who are the focus of the messages. IMC speaks to developing campaigns for the global marketplace. However, in most public relations organizations, little effort is made to go beyond stage 1 where the organization conceptualizes and identifies the central components of the campaign. Future studies should explore and compare how messages by different organizations are created and for which audiences they are directed. Through the examination of one-sided, inefficient, incomplete, or misdirected messages, and their comparison with developed, coherent, and consistent messages developed for multiple audiences, practitioners and scholars can identify ways to open the decision-making process in risk and crisis situations. Dutta (2008) made a similar call for the inclusion of multiple voices: "Communication here is envisioned not simply in the realm of messages, but as a process that brings forth dialogic spaces where multiple voices can be heard" (p. 263).

Future studies that explore the four stages of IMC before and after the introduction of cultural co-participants in the decision-making process may yield further support for the integration of a CC approach to communication. For example, in stage 1, the focus on developing the message or campaign may be impacted by how the intended audiences prefer to receive information, from whom they prefer receiving that information, and when that information is disseminated. In stage 2, the sources from which data are gathered about the intended audiences may yield different outcomes. Similarly, once data are sorted and stored in databanks, how they are combined and compared by upper management and applied based upon return on investment may be impacted when influenced by multiple perspectives.

Different types of crises may be studied to further determine if the CC approach is equally effective in all circumstances. For example, natural disasters may require a different cultural approach from that of a technological, or human-made crisis. The environment for organizational misdeeds or workplace violence to occur may be mitigated when a CC structure is present and multiple perspectives are engaged regularly. The IDEA model focuses on particular elements that engage audiences in ways that lead to a desired response. Studying different crises while applying the CC approach may provide further insight into the IDEA model's applicability.

Finally, through this examination of a CC approach to risk and crisis communication, we integrated IMC into the decision-making process. Specifically, in chapter 2, we demonstrated how aspects of best practices in risk and crisis communication are reflected in the stages of IMC; and in chapter 8, the involvement of cultural agents in each stage of IMC was illustrated as an enhancement for organizations seeking to increase customer loyalty and brand identification. Further examination of how the integration of cultural perspectives into decision-making in the marketplace may yield insight into the creation of more effective messages to save lives in times of risk or crisis.

The ECHO Example

An example of such CC integration in an organization is the Emergency and Community Health Outreach (ECHO) program founded in 2004 in St. Paul, Minnesota (ECHO, 2004) to address the growing needs of Minnesota's Limited English-speaking communities. ECHO Minnesota—a nonprofit organization dedicated to connecting immigrant and refugee communities to health, safety, emergency preparedness, and civic engagement—provides multilingual and cultural-specific education, television broadcasts, web-based videos, outreach, phone lines, and training to multiple publics. ECHO is supported by a network of over 200 organizations and agencies, including the Saint Paul-Ramsey County Public Health, Hennepin County Public Health Protection, and the Minnesota Department of Health.

The need for ECHO was prompted by the large number of immigrants and refugees settling in Minnesota. For many of the 325,000 estimated to have relocated to the region, at least a third were international, many speaking no English, and two-thirds of them not comprehending English well enough to understand written information. In the event of a terrorist attack or a major disease outbreak, the emergency response system communicating only in English would fail to deliver life-saving information to large numbers of people with limited English-language skills. Through a CC approach, ECHO was formed to provide public health education and emergency communication in multiple languages (McDonald, 2020).

Because immigrants and others with Limited English proficiency rely on listening to programs delivered on Public Broadcasting System (PBS) as a way to learn to speak English (PBS, 2020), ECHO uses television and other media to disseminate information in seven different languages (English, Hmong, Khmer, Lao, Somali, Spanish, and Vietnamese). To reach a larger audience, ECHO also established www.echominnesota.org where people who miss the television broadcasts can view the programs at a convenient time for them. Organizations like ECHO should be replicated because they demonstrate the transformative power of the CC approach to risk and crisis communication.

IN CLOSING

As the world continues to reel from challenges imposed by the most significant public health emergency in over a century, the COVID-19 pandemic provides a backdrop for the application of a CC approach to communicating about the current crisis and raises questions about how agencies and governments communicate with multiple publics. As the virus spread and entered the personal and family spheres of ethnocentricity, the publics affected by the virus internalized the message and wanted to know more about what was happening. Unfortunately, for those not directly affected by family or as essential workers, internalization was deflected by messages that the virus was a hoax or politically motivated. The explanations about the virus and its impacts varied, depending upon the source of the information. The governmental spokespersons associated with the administration provided messages that minimized the impact, while the health and science experts presented explanations that laid out a more threatening forecast based upon verifiable facts and rates of infection and death. These mixed messages confused the publics, resulting in inconsistent responses and actions that undercut the public health strategies designed to control the virus. Media outlets had different perspectives, leaving the dissemination of information for the public to be overwhelming and confusing (Littlefield, 2020a). The effective use of the IDEA model would have been helpful if used collaboratively by government and public health officials in response to the pandemic.

With regard to the components of IMC, in the absence of consistent messages from the top decision-makers about the coronavirus, vertical integration of information sharing within the government and public health community about how to manage the virus was ineffective. The horizontal integration between agencies and departments was hindered because of conflicting goals pertaining to reopening the economy versus controlling the virus. For example, when the president did not follow the guidelines developed by public health agencies (e.g., wearing of a mask in public) based on scientific data, those managing the external communication were placed in an impossible situation. Collecting data about those affected by the virus was mishandled when the number of tests for the virus was inaccurately associated with the number of positive cases (Littlefield, 2020a). The absence of a consistent, coherent, and solid plan to fight COVID-19 illustrated how the application of IMC could have yielded a more effective public health campaign.

A CN approach was used by the administration as it launched the Coronavirus Task Force to issue messages to a universal audience. What made the situation unique was the reliance of the president on information that was not always verifiable. While President Trump controlled the information being presented to the publics—only calling upon a limited number of public health officials like Dr. Anthony Fauci and Dr. Deborah Birx, when he deemed it necessary to make a point he had initiated—he created a narrative that challenged the preeminence of scientific knowledge. The marginalization of the news media that questioned his information or motives was evident at the daily briefings as he called out individual journalists and demeaned their publications. In the context of a political campaign, his stories reflected his values and lacked empathy with the growing number of families affected by the deaths of their loved ones. The resistance to the administration came from the media and from science and public health experts who provided fact checks on what the administration was presenting as counternarratives to a reliance on science (Littlefield, 2020a). Using the cultural approach to unpack the dynamics of the official communication of the administration offers insight into how the absence of multiple perspectives can impact the creation and dissemination of messages.

Whether in the application of the IDEA model to the messaging of the administration about the coronavirus, or the introduction of IMC to the process of developing a consistent and coherent public health campaign, or through the lens of a cultural approach to message creation and dissemination, when communication practitioners and scholars seek a more robust understanding of risk and crisis communication, the intersection of the elements discussed in this book will provide insight that can enhance the quality of messages designed to save lives and livelihoods now and in the future.

References

Abram, S. (2016, January 29). Despite Zika virus, travel agencies are still booking flights. *The Daily News of Los Angeles*. Retrieved from www.lexisnexis.com

Abramson, N. R., & Moran, R. T. (2018). *Managing cultural differences: Global leadership for the 21st century* (10th ed.). Routledge.

African Swine Fever. (2020, June 18) World Organization for Animal Health. Retrieved from https://www.oie.int/en/animal-health-in-the-world/animal-diseases/african-swine-fever/

Andersen, K. E. (2000). Developments in communication ethics: The Ethics Commission, Code of Professional Responsibilities, and Credo for Ethical Communication. *Journal of the Association for Communication Administration, 29*, 131–144. https://eric.ed.gov/?id=EJ603209

Anderson, M. (2019, June 13). Mobile technology and home broadband 2019. *Pew Research Center*. https://www.pewresearch.org/internet/2019/06/13/mobile-technology-and-home-broadband-2019/

Anthony, K. E., & Sellnow, T. L. (2016). The role of the message convergence framework in medical decision making. *Journal of Health Communication, 21*(2), 249–256. doi:10.1080/10810730.2015.1064497

Anthony, K. E., Sellnow, T. L., & Millner, A. G. (2013). Message convergence as a message-centered approach to analyzing and improving risk communication. *Journal of Applied Communication Research, 41*(4), 346–364. doi:10.1080/00909882.2013.844346

Arnett, R. C., DeIuliis, S. M., & Corr, M. (2017). *Corporate communication crisis leadership: Advocacy and ethics*. Business Expert Press.

Arpan, L. M. (2002). When in Rome? The effects of spokesperson ethnicity on audience evaluation of crisis communication. *Journal of Business Communication, 39*(3), 314–339.

Associated Press. (2019, November 15). Hurricane Dorian responsible for $3.4 billion in losses on Bahamas, report says. *The Weather Channel*. https://weather.com/news/news/2019-11-15-hurricane-dorian-bahamas-losses-report.

Atlantic hurricane best track (HURDAT version 2). (2020, May 25). United States National Hurricane Center. https://www.nhc.noaa.gov/data/hurdat/hurdat2-1851-2019-052520.txt

Avila, L., Steward, S., Berg, R., & Hagen, A. (2020, April 20). Hurricane Dorian (AL052019). Tropical Cyclone Report. *National Hurricane Center*. https://www.nhc.noaa.gov/data/tcr/AL052019_Dorian.pdf

Bahamas Information Services. (2020, February 29). NEMA update: Death toll rises to 74 post-hurricane Dorian. *The Government of the Bahamas*. http://www.bahamas.gov.bs/wps/portal/public/gov/government/news/nema%20update

Bankoff, G. (2017). Living with hazard: Disaster subcultures, disaster cultures and risk-mitigating strategies. In G. S. Schenk (Ed.), *Historical disaster experiences: Towards a comparative and transcultural history of disasters across Asia and Europe* (Transcultural Research. Heidelberg Studies on Asia and Europe in a Global Context), (pp. 45–59). Springer.

Barack Obama seeks USD 1.8 billion to fight Zika virus. (2016, February 9). *Tangerine Zee News*. Retrieved from www.lexisnexis.com

Baxter, L. A. (2006). Relational dialectics theory: Multivocal dialogues of family communication. In D. O. Braithwaite & L. A. Baxter (Eds.). *Engaging theories in family communication: Multiple perspectives* (pp. 130–145). Sage.

Baxter, L. A., & Montgomery, B. M. (1996). *Relating: Dialogues and dialectics*. Guilford Press.

Beech, P. (2020). World Health Organization: What does it do and how does it work? *World Economic Forum*. https://www.weforum.org/agenda/2020/04/world-health-organization-what-it-does-how-it-works/

Bennett, M. J. (1993). Towards ethnorelativism: A developmental model of intercultural sensitivity. In R. M. Paige (Ed.), *Education for the intercultural experience* (2nd ed., pp. 21–71). Intercultural Press.

Bevins, V. (2016, January 27). The World: Virus is expected to reach U.S.; Mosquito-borne Zika, linked to birth defects, is spreading, the World Health Organizaiton says. *Los Angeles Times*. Retrieved from www.lexisnexis.com

Bi, Y., Fu, G., Chen, J., Peng, J., Sun, Y., Wang, J., ... & Tian, F. (2010). Novel swine influenza virus reassortants in pigs, China. *Emerging Infectious Diseases, 16*(7), 1162. doi:10.3201/eid1607.091881

Blackwell, V., Baldwin, B., Gray, J., Todd, B., Flores, R. (2019, September 2). Hurricane Dorian Moving Dangerously Close to Florida Coast . . . Aired 2:30-3p ET. *CNN*. https://advance-lexis-com.ezproxy.net.ucf.edu/api/document?collection=news&id=urn:contentItem:5WYN-6PC1-JB20-G0HS-00000-00&context=1516831.

Blackwell, V., Newton, P., Maxouris, C. (2019, September 7). The Bahamas death toll is rising as 70,000 residents left homeless by Hurricane Dorian seek food and shelter. *CNN*. https://web.archive.org/web/20190907150416/https:www.cnn.com/2019/09/07/us/hurricane-dorian-bahamas-saturday-wxc/index.html

Blitzer, W., Burnett, E., Sater, T., Oppmann, P., Marquez, M., Griffin, D., Elam, S., Raju, M., Collins, K. (2019, September 3). Gov. Roy Cooper (D-NC) is Interviewed About Preparations as Dorian Moves Dangerously Close to U.S.

After Battering Bahamas . . . Aired 7-8p ET. *CNN.* https://advance-lexis-com.ezproxy.net.ucf.edu/api/document?collection=news&id=urn:contentItem:5X03-5101-DXH2-62SN-00000-00&context=1516831

Bloom, B. S. (1956). *Taxonomy of educational objectives, Handbook I: The cognitive domain.* David McKay.

Boddy, N. (2016, February 4). Zika outbreak in territory 'unlikely.' *Canberra Times* (Australia). Retrieved from www.lexisnexis.com

Bolkan, S., & Griffin, D. J. (2018). Catch and hold: Instructional interventions and their differential impact on student interest, attention, and autonomous motivation. *Communication Education, 67*(3), 269–286. doi:10.1080/03634523.2018.1465193

Botan, C. (1997). Ethics in strategic communication campaigns: The case for a new approach to public relations. *Journal of Business Communication, 34,* 188–202.

Bowen, S. A. (2004). Expansion of ethics as the tenth generic principle of public relations excellence: A Kantian theory and model for managing ethical issues. *Journal of Public Relations Research, 16*(1), 65–92. doi:10.1207/s1532754xjprr1601_3

Brandus, P. (2020, June 4). What makes 2020 so uniquely awful? It distills a century of horrors in one year. *USA Today.* https://usatoday.com/story/opinion/2020/06/04

Brazil fears birth defects linked to mosquito-borne virus. (2016, January 6). *The Maltese Independent.* Retrieved from www.lexisnexis.com

Bugga, H. (2020, July 2). Nearly a million pigs killed after an outbreak of African Swine Fever. *Mercy for Animals.* https://mercyforanimals.org/nearly-a-million-pigs-killed-after-outbreak

Burnett, E., Marquez, M., Todd, B., Sater, T., Oppmann, P., Sidner, S., Young, R., Collins, K. (2019, September 2). Millions Facing Mandatory Evacuation From Florida To Georgia As Hurricane Moves "Dangerously Close" To U.S. . . . Aired 7-8p ET. *CNN.* https://advance-lexis-com.ezproxy.net.ucf.edu/api/document?collection=news&id=urn:contentItem:5WYW-5V11-DXH2-64VD-00000-00&context=1516831.

Carmon, A. F. (2013). Is it necessary to be clear? An examination of strategic ambiguity in family business mission statements. *Qualitative Research Reports in Communication, 14*(1), 87–96. doi:10.1080/17459435.2013.835346

Cavanagh, G., & Wambier, C. G. (2020). Rational hand hygiene during the coronavirus 2019 (COVID-19) pandemic. *Journal of the American Academy of Dermatology, 82*(6), e211. doi:10.1016/j.jaad.2020.03.090

Cénat, J. M., Mukunzi, J. N., Noorishad, P. G., Rousseau, C., Derivois, D., & Bukaka, J. (2020). A systematic review of mental health programs among populations affected by the Ebola virus disease. *Journal of Psychosomatic Research, 131,* Advanced online publication. 109966. doi:10.1016/j.jpsychores.2020.109966

Chaudhri, V. (2016). Corporate social responsibility and the communication imperative: Perspectives from CSR managers. *International Journal of Business Communication, 53*(4), 419–442. doi:10.1177/2329488414525469

Christophel, D. M. (1990). The relationships among teacher immediacy behaviors, student motivation, and learning. *Communication Education, 39,* 323–340. doi:10.1080/03634529009378813

Church, R., Van Dam, D., Oppmann, P., Thomas, D., Stewart, A., Javaheri, P. (2019, September 4). Hurricane Dorian Pummeled Bahamas For 48 Hours . . . Aired 2-3a ET. *CNN.* https://advance-lexis-com.ezproxy.net.ucf.edu/api/document?collection=news&id=urn:contentItem:5X03-5101-DXH2-62TM-00000-00&context=1516831

Claeys, A. S., & Schwarz, A. (2016). Domestic and international audiences of organizational crisis communication. *The Handbook of International Crisis Communication Research, 43*, 224–235.

Clark, L. S., Demont-Heinrich, C., & Webber, S. A. (2004). Ethnographic interviews on the digital divide. *New Media & Society, 6*(4), 529–547. doi:10.1177/146144804044333.

Clow, K., & Baack, D. (2007). *Integrated advertising, promotion, and marketing communications* (3rd ed.). Pearson.

Coombs, W. T. (1998). An analytical framework for crisis situations: Better responses from a better understanding of the situation. *Journal of Public Relations Research, 10*(3), 177–192. doi:10.1207/s1532754xjprr1003_02

Coombs, W. T. (1999). Information and compassion in crisis responses: A test of their effects. *Journal of Public Relations Research, 11*(2), 125–142. doi:10.1207/s1532754xjprr1102_02

Coombs, W. T. (2019). *Ongoing crisis communication: Planning, managing, and responding* (5th ed.). Sage.

Coronavirus disease (COVID-19) pandemic. (2020). World Health Organization. https://www.who.int/emergencies/diseases/novel-coronavirus-2019

Cox Media Group National Content Desk. (2019, September 5). Hurricane Dorian live updates: Eye of storm close to North Carolina coast. *Dayton Daily News (Ohio).* https://advance-lexis-com.ezproxy.net.ucf.edu/api/document?collection=news&id=urn:contentItem:5X0G-F431-DXVP-V43D-00000-00&context=1516831.

David, P. (2004). Extending symmetry: Toward a convergence of professionalism, practice, and pragmatics in public relations. *Journal of Public Relations Research, 16*(2), 185–211. doi:10.1207/s1532754xjprr1602_3

Delaney, B. (2020, July 3). The nightmare that is 2020 is only halfway done. Are these the worst days of our lives? *The Guardian* (U. S. Edition).

Dewey, J. (1938). *Experience and education.* University of Chicago Press.

Douglas, B. (2016, January 21). Zika virus: Health experts fear Carnival celebrations will lead to spread; Millions of tourists, probably not wearing protective clothing will descend on Brazil's coastal cities during the peak breeding season for mosquitos. *The Guardian.* Retrieved from www.lexisnexis.com

Duffy, J., & Brasileira, A. (2016, January 24). Zika virus outbreak linked to World Cup. *The Sunday Herald* (Glasgow). Archived at https://web.archive.org/web/20190806042427/https://www.heraldscotland.com/news/14226384.zika-virus-outbreak-in-brazil-linked-to-world-cup

Dutta, M. J. (2008). *Communicating health: A culture-centered approach.* Polity.

Edmonds, L. (2019, September 2). Virginia becomes FIFTH state to declare emergency as Hurricane Dorian approaches East Coast - hours after Category 4 storm slammed into the Bahamas killing at least five people and ravaging the island.

MailOnline. https://advance-lexis-com.ezproxy.net.ucf.edu/api/document?collection=news&id=urn:contentItem:5WYN-6VG1-JCJY-G1KH-00000-00&context=1516831.

Edwards, A. L., Sellnow, D. D., Sellnow, T. L., Iverson, J., Parrish, A., & Dritz, S. (2020). Communities of practice as purveyors of instructional communication during crises. *Communication Education*, 1–22. (published online). doi:10.1080/03634523.2020.1802053

Eisenberg, E. M. (1984). Ambiguity as strategy in organizational communication. *Communication Monographs, 51*(3), 227–242. doi:10.1080/03637758409390197

Emergency and Community Health Outreach (ECHO). (2004). Bridging refugee youth & children's services. http://brycs.org/clearinghouse/2560

Farmer, Y. (2018). Ethical decision making and reputation management in public relations. *Journal of Media Ethics, 33*(1), 2–13. doi:10.1080/23736992.2017.1401931

Federici, F. M., & Sharou, K. A. (2018). Moses, time, and crisis translation. *Translation and Interpreting Studies, 13*(3), 486–507. doi:10.1075/tis.00026.fed

Fellows, K. L. (2016). Integrated marketing communication and public health campaigns: Let's quit together. In J. M. Persuit & C. L. McDowell Marinchak (Eds.), *Integrated marketing communication: Creating spaces for engagement* (pp. 111–128). Lexington Books.

Feng, S., Shen, C., Xia, N., Song, W., Fan, M., & Cowling, B. J. (2020). Rational use of face masks in the COVID-19 pandemic. *The Lancet Respiratory Medicine, 8*(5), 434–436. doi:10.1016/S2213-2600(20)30134-X

Ferro, S. (2013, August 29). Why it's so hard to predict hurricanes. *Popular Science*. https://www.popsci.com/science/article/2013-08/why-predicting-hurricanes-still-imprecise-science/

First case of sexually transmitted Zika virus in the US reported. (2016, February 3). *The Sun* (Nigeria). Retrieved from lexisnexis.com

Fisher, W. R. (1978). Toward a logic of good reasons. *Quarterly Journal of Speech, 64*, 376–384.

Fischer, D., Posegga, O., & Fischbach, K. (2016). Communication barriers in crisis management: A literature review. *Twenty-Fourth European Conference on Information Systems (ECIS)*, Istanbul, Turkey. https://researchgate.net/publication/301770566_Communication_Barriers_in_Crisis_Management_A_Literature_Review

Fisher, W. R. (2017). Narration as a human communication paradigm: The case of public moral argument. In C. R. Burgchardt & H. A. Jones (Eds.), *Readings in rhetorical criticism* (5th ed., pp. 262–283). Strata Publishing, Inc.

Fishman, D. A. (1999). Valujet Flight 592: Crisis communication theory blended and extended. *Communication Quarterly, 47*, 345–357. doi:10.1080/01463379909385567

Fitzpatrick, K., & Gauthier, C. (2001). Toward a professional responsibility theory of public relations ethics. *Journal of Mass Media Ethics, 16*(2&3), 193–212. Lawrence Erlbaum Associates, Inc.

Flammia, M., & Sadri, H. A. (2011). Intercultural communication from an interdisciplinary perspective. *US-China Education Review, 8*(1), 103–109. https://files.eric.ed.gov/fulltext/ED519428.pdf

Forney, T., & Torres, A. (2019, September 3). Cocoa Beach residents heed Hurricane Dorian's warnings. https://www.local10.com/weather/2019/09/03/cocoa-beach-residents-heed-hurricane-dorians-warnings/

Frisby, B. N., & Buckner, M. M. (2018). Rapport in the instructional context. In M. L. Houser and A. M. Hosek (Eds.), *Handbook of instructional communication: Rhetorical and relational perspectives* (2nd ed., pp. 126–137). Routledge.

Frisby, B. N., Veil, S. R., & Sellnow, T. L. (2014). Instructional messages during health-related crises: Essential content for self-protection. *Health Communication, 29*(4), 347–354. doi:10.1080/10410236.2012.755604

Frymier, A. B., & Shulman, G. M. (1995). "What's in it for me?": Increasing content relevance to enhance students' motivation. *Communication Education, 44*(1), 40–50. doi:10.1080/03634529509378996

Gallois, C., Ogay, T., & Giles, H. (2005). Communication accommodation theory. In W. B. Gudykunst (Ed.), *Theorizing about intercultural communication* (pp. 121–148). Sage.

Gasiorek, J. (2013). "I was impolite to her because that's how she was to me": Perceptions of motive and young adults' communicative responses to underaccommodation. *Western Journal of Communication, 77*(5), 604–624. doi:10.1080/10570314.2013.778421

Gerwin, L. E. (2012). The challenge of providing the public with actionable information during a pandemic. *The Journal of Law, Medicine & Ethics, 40*, 630–654. doi:10.1111/j.1748-720x.2012.00695.x

Getchell, M., Sellnow-Richmond, D. D., Woods, C., Williams, G., Hester, E., Seeger, M., & Sellnow, T. (2018). Competing and complementary narratives in the Ebola crisis. In H. D. O'Hair (Ed.), *Risk and health communication in an evolving media environment* (pp. 316–334). Routledge.

Gill, G. S. (2019). When all else fails: Amateur radio becomes lifeline of communications during a disaster. *International Journal of Emergency Services, 9*(2), 109–121. doi: 10.1108/IJES-10-2018-0054

Glenza, J. (2016, February 2). First Zika virus case contracted in US was sexually transmitted, officials say; First case of Zika virus contracted in US mainland, confirmed in Texas, is only second documented example of virus being passed through sexual contact. *The Guardian*. Retrieved from www.lexisnexis.com

Grunig, J. E. (2001). Two-way symmetrical public relations: Past, present, and future. In R. L. Heath (Ed.), *Handbook of public relations* (pp. 11–30). Sage.

Grunig, J. E., & Grunig, L. A. (1992). Models of public relations and communication. In J. E. Grunig (Ed.), *Excellence in public relations and communications management* (pp. 285–325). Lawrence Erlbaum Associates.

Grunig, J. E., & Hunt, T. (1984). *Managing public relations*. Holt, Rinehart, & Winston.

Gudykunst, W. B., & Ting-Toomey, S. (1988). *Culture and interpersonal communication*. Sage.

Hall, E. T. (1976). *Beyond culture*. Doubleday.
Hardy, B. W., Tallapragada, M., Besley, J. C., & Yuan, S. (2019). The effects of the 'war on science' frame on scientists' credibility. *Science Communication, 41*(1), 90–112. doi:10.1177/1075547018822081
Harlow, P., Collins, K., Healy, P., Blitzer, W., Savidge, M., Sater, T., Griffin, D. Newton, P. (2019, September 5). Dorian Unleashes Heavy Rain and Tornadoes on the Carolinas . . . Aired 7-8p ET. *CNN*. https://advance-lexis-com.ezproxy.net.ucf.edu/api/document?collection=news&id=urn:contentItem:5X0H-3CR1-DXH2-60NB-00000-00&context=1516831
Haskell, T. L. (1990). Objectivity is not neutrality: Rhetoric vs. practice in Peter Novick's That Noble Dream. *History and Theory, 29*(2), 129–157. doi:10.2307/2505222.
Health Ministry issues Zika travel warning. (2016, February 4). *The Saudi Gazette*. Retrieved from www.lexisnexis.com
Henke, J. (2019, September 24). 14 States Ask, 'What If African Swine Fever Hits the U.S.?' Pork producers are also role-playing the ASF scenario. *Successful Farming*. https://www.agriculture.com/news/livestock/14-states-ask-what-if-african-swine-fever-hits-the-us
Hess, A. (2020, March 12). African swine fever: Top 5 biosecurity strategies. *National Hog Farmer*. https://nationalhogfarmer.com/animal-health/african-swine-fever-top-5-biosecurity-strategies
Hewlett, B. S., & Hewlett, B. L. (2007). *Ebola, culture and politics: The anthropology of an emerging disease*. Cengage Learning.
Hofstede, G. (1991). *Cultures and organizations: Software of the mind*. McGraw-Hill.
Hofstede, G. (2001). *Culture's consequences: Comparing values, behaviors, institutions and organizations across nations* (2nd ed.). Sage.
Howell, W. S. (1982). *The empathic communicator*. Wadsworth Publishing Company.
Humayun, H., & Ehlinger, M. (2019, September 4). Bahamas PM: Dorian "the greatest national crisis in our country's history." *CNN*. Archived https://web.archive.org/web/20190904092449/https://www.cnn.com/us/live-news/hurricane-dorian-september-2019/h_6b44454d1eceb9b8cd2d42ec8b70ab10
Hurricane Dorian updates: Seven fatalities confirmed, more deaths expected. (2019, September 3). *The Tribune*. http://www.tribune242.com/news/2019/sep/03/hurricane-dorian-tuesday-updates/
INFOSAN. (2010). Biosecurity: An integrated approach to manage risk to human, animal and plant life and health. *Food and Agriculture Organization of the United Nations*. https://www.who.int/foodsafety/fs_management/No_01_Biosecurity_Mar10_en.pdf?ua=1
Ishii, S., Klopf, D., & Cooke, P. (2006). Our locus in the universe: World view and intercultural communication. In L. E. Samovar, R. E. Porter, & E. R. McDaniel (Eds.), *Intercultural communication: A reader* (11th ed., pp. 32–38). Thomson Wadsworth.
Israel, B. A., Schultz, A. J., Parker, E. A., & Becker, A. B. (2001). Community-based participatory research: Policy recommendations for promoting a

partnership approach in health research. *Education for Health, 14*(2), 182–197. doi:10.1080/13576280110051055

Jahoda, G. (1984). Do we need a concept of culture? *Journal of Cross-Cultural Psychology, 15*(2), 139–151. doi:10.1177/0022002184015002003

Jester, B., Uyeki, T. M., Jernigan, D. B., & Tumpey, T. M. (2019). Historical and clinical aspects of the 1918 H1N1 pandemic in the United States. *Virology, 527,* 32–37. doi:10.1016/j.virol.2018.10.019

Johnson, N. P., & Mueller, J. (2002). Updating the accounts: Global mortality of the 1918-1920 'Spanish' influenza pandemic. *Bulletin of Historical Medicine, 76*(1), 105–115. doi:10.1353/bhm.2002.0022

Jordan, D. (2019, December 17). The deadliest flu: The complete story of the discovery and reconstruction of the 1918 pandemic virus. *Centers for Disease Control and Prevention.* http://www.cdc.gov/flu/pandemic-resources/reconstruction-1918-virus.html

Kaiser Family Foundation. (2020, December 11). COVID-19: Confirmed cases & deaths by country as of 11 December. kff.org/coronavirus-covid-19/fact-sheet/coronavirus-tracker/

Kant, I. (1964). *Groundwork of the metaphysic of morals* (H. J. Paton, Trans.). Harper & Row (Original work published 1785).

Keaton, J., & Cheng, M. (2016, January 29). Zika virus 'spreading explosively,' WHO warns. *The Vancouver Province* (British Columbia). Retrieved from www.lexisnexis.com

Kitchen, P. J., Brignell, J., Li, T., & Jones, G. S. (2004). The emergence of IMC: A theoretical perspective. *Journal of Advertising Research, 44*(1), 19–30. doi:10.1017/S0021849904040048

Kitchen, P. J., & DePelsmacker, P. (2004). *Integrated marketing communications: A primer.* Routledge.

Klopf, D. W. (2000). *Intercultural encounters: The fundamentals of intercultural communication* (5th ed.). Morton Publishing.

Kluckhohn, F., & Strodtbeck, F. (1961). *Variations in value orientations.* Row, Peterson.

Kotler, P. (2005). *Marketing management* (13th ed.). *Harvard business review.* Prentice Hall.

Krathwohl, D. R., Bloom, B. S., & Bertram, B. M (1973). *Taxonomy of educational objectives, the classification of educational goals, Handbook II: Affective domain.* David McKay.

Landau, M. J., Kay, A. C., Whitson, J. A. (2015). Compensatory control and the appeal of a structured world, *Psychological Bulletin, 141*(3), 694–722. doi:10.1037/a0038703

Lasker, R. D., & Weiss, E. S. (2003). Broadening participation in community problem solving: A multidisciplinary model to support collaborative practice and research. *Journal of Urban Health, 80*(1), 14–47. doi:10.1093/jurban/jtg014

Lasker, R. D., Weiss, E. S., & Miller, R. (2001). Partnership synergy: A practical framework for studying and strengthening the collaborative advantage. *The Milbank Quarterly, 79*(2), 179–205. doi:10.1111/1468-0009.00203

Leiss, W. (1996). Three phases in the evolution of risk communication practice. *Annals of the American Academy of Political and Social Science, 545*, 85–94. doi:10.1177/0002716296545001009

Lester, P. M. (2013). *Visual communication: Images with messages.* Cengage.

Lindell, M. K., & Perry, R. W. (2004). *Communicating environmental risk in multi-ethnic communities.* Sage.

Linnenbrink, E. A., & Pintrich, P. R. (2002). Motivation as an enabler for academic success. *School Psychology Review, 31*, 313–327. https://psycnet.apa.org/record/2002-18945-003

Lipsitch, M., Swerdlow, D. L., & Finelli, L. (2020). Defining the epidemiology of Covid-19—studies needed. *New England Journal of Medicine, 382*(13), 1194–1196. doi:10.1056/NEJMp2002125

Little, B. (2020, July 7). Why the 1918 flu became 'America's forgotten pandemic.' http://www.history.com/news/1918-americas-forgotten-pandemic.

Littlefield, R. S. (2013). Communicating risk and crisis communication to multiple publics. In A. J. DuBrin (Ed.), *Handbook of research on crisis leadership in organizations* (pp. 231–251). Edward Elgar Publishing Ltd.

Littlefield, R. S. (2015). Improving how we communicate about infectious disease risks. *Microbe, 10*(5), 1–4.

Littlefield, R. S. (2020a). Controlling the narrative: Mixed messages and presidential credibility. In D. O'Hair and M. J. O'Hair (Eds.), *Communicating science in times of crisis: Coronavirus* (in press). John Wiley & Sons Limited.

Littlefield, R. S. (2020b). The tensions of strategic communication decision-making: An exploratory examination of theory and practice. *Journal of International Crisis and Risk Communication, 3*(2), 81–112. doi:10.30658/jicrcr.3.2.4

Littlefield, R. S., & Ball, J. A. (2004). Factionalism as argumentation: A case study of the indigenous communication practices of Jemez pueblo. *Argumentation & Advocacy, 41*(2), 87–101.

Littlefield, R. S., Beauchamp, K., Lane, D., Sellnow, D. D., Sellnow, T. L., Venette, S., & Wilson, B. (2014). Instructional crisis communication: Connecting ethnicity and sex in the assessment of receiver-oriented message effectiveness. *Journal of Management and Strategy, 5*(3), 16–23. doi:10.5430/jms.v5n3p

Littlefield, R. S., & Cowden, K. (2006). *Rethinking the single spokesperson model of crisis communication: Recognizing the need to address multiple publics.* Paper presented to the Public Relations Division of the National Communication Association, San Antonio, TX.

Littlefield, R. S., Cowden, K., Farah, F. M., McDonald, L. R., & Sellnow, T. L. (2006). *10 tips for risk and crisis communicators when working and conducting research with Native and New Americans.* North Dakota Institute for Regional Studies.

Littlefield, R. S., Cowden, K., & Hueston, W. (2007). *Crisis and risk communication: 10 tips for public health professionals communicating with Native and New Americans.* North Dakota Institute for Regional Studies.

Littlefield, R. S., & Thweatt, T. S. (2004). The use of cultural agents as data collectors in Bosnian, Roma, Sudanese, and Somali groups. *Journal of Intercultural Communication Research, 33*(2), 77–87.

MacCallum, M., Heinrich, J., Paul, J., Harrigan, S., Reichmuth, R., Coleman, C. (2019, September 2). National Hurricane Center Gives Latest Briefing On Category 4 Hurricane Dorian . . . *Fox News Network.* https://advance-lexis-com.ezproxy.net.ucf.edu/api/document?collection=news&id=urn:contentItem:5WYN-PJS1-JB20-G15P-00000-00&context=1516831.

MacCormaic, R. (2016, January 25). Travel alert for pregnant women over Zika virus; Mosquito-borne virus spreads in Brazil, Mexico and other Latin American states. *The Irish Times.* Retrieved from www.lexisnexis.com

Maercker, A., Ben-Ezra, M., Esparza, O. A., & Augsburger, M. (2019). Fatalism as a traditional cultural belief potentially relevant to trauma sequelae: Measurement equivalence, extent and associations in six countries. *European Journal Psychotraumatol, 10*(1), 1657371. doi:10.1080/20008198.2019.1657371

Market report: The risk of African Swine Fever in the U.S. and Australia-June 2020. (2020, July 8). *The Pig Site.* https://thepigsite.com/articles/market-report-the-risk-of-african-swine-fever-in-the-us-and-australia-june-2020

Markus, H. R., & Kitayama, S. (1991). Culture and the self: Implications for cognition, emotion, and motivation. *Psychological Review, 98,* 224–253. doi:10.1037/0033-295X.98.2.224

Mazer, J. P. (2017). Instructor message variables. In *Handbook of instructional communication* (pp. 40–55). Routledge.

McBride, J. (2019, September 1). Dorian spaghetti models: The hurricane's path and track. *Heavy.* https://heavy.com/news/2019/08/dorian-spaghetti-models/

McDonald, L. (2020). ECHO: Emergency and Community Health Outreach Factsheet. www.cidrap.umn.edu/sites/default/files/public/php/47/47_factsheet_O.pdf

McElreath, M. P. (1996). *Managing systematic and ethical public relations campaigns* (2nd ed.). Brown & Benchmark.

McKendree, A. G. (2016). Integrated marketing communication and crisis communication: The American Red Cross. In J. M. Persuit & C. L. McDowell Marinchak (Eds.), *Integrated marketing communication: Creating spaces for engagement* (pp. 129–142). Lexington Books.

McNeil, D. G., Jr. (2016, January 26). Two cases suggest that Zika virus could be spread through sexual contact. *The New York Times.* Retrieved from www.lexisnexis.com

Mercene, R. (2016, February 2). Miaa moves to prevent entry of Zika as WHO declares its spread an international emergency. *Business Mirror* (Philippines). Retrieved from www.lexisnexis.com

Merrill, S. C., Moegenburg, S., Koliba, C. J., Zia, A., Trinity, L., Clark, E., ... & Smith, J. M. (2019). Willingness to comply with biosecurity in livestock facilities: Evidence from experimental simulations. *Frontiers in Veterinary Science, 6,* 156. https://www.frontiersin.org/articles/10.3389/fvets.2019.00156/full

MMC Learning. (2019). Integrated Marketing Communications. Retrieved from http://multimediamarketing.com/mkc/marketingcommunications/

Moriarty, S. E. (1994). PR and IMC: The benefits of integration. *Public Relations Quarterly, 39*(3), ABI/INFORM Collection, 38. http://connection.ebscohost.com/c/articles/9412092109/pr-imc-benefits-integration

Mushengyezi, A. (2003). Rethinking indigenous media: Rituals, "talking" drums and orality as forms of public communication in Uganda. *Journal of African Cultural Studies, 16*(1), 107–177. doi:10.1080/1369681032000169302

National Oceanic and Atmospheric Administration. (2019). Hurricane Dorian. *National Hurricane Center and Central Pacific Hurricane Center*. https://nhc.noaa.gov/archive/2019/DORIAN.shtml?

National Public Radio (NPR). (2019, August 28). Florida governor declares state of emergency as Hurricane Dorian gains force. https://www.npr.org/2019/08/28/754984058/dorian-will-hit-florida-as-category-2-hurricane-new-forecast-says

Neill, M. S. (2017). Ethics education in public relations: Differences between stand-alone ethics courses and an integrated approach. *Journal of Media Ethics, 32*(2), 118–131. doi:10.1080/23736992.2017.1294019

Neuliep, J. W. (2003). *Intercultural communication: A contextual approach* (2nd ed.). Houghton Mifflin.

Nilson, T. R. (1974). *Ethics of speech communication* (2nd ed.). The Bobbs-Merrill Company, Inc.

Officials study virus link to birth defects. (2016, January 28). *China Daily*. Retrieved from www.lexisnexis.com

O'Neil, P. D. (2014). Emergency evacuation orders: Considerations and lessons from Hurricane Sandy. *Journal of Emergency Management, 12*(3), 219–227. doi:10.5055/jem.2014.0174.

Palenchar, M. J. (2010). Historical trends of risk and crisis communication. In R. L. Heath & H. D. O'Hair (Eds.), *Handbook of risk and crisis communication* (pp. 31–52). Routledge.

Partlow, J. (2016, January 24). Women warned over Zika outbreak. *The Washington Post*. Retrieved from www.lexisnexis.com

Perelman, C., & Olbrechts-Tyteca, L. (1971). *The new rhetoric: A treatise on argumentation* (J. Wilkinson, & P. Weaver, Trans.). University of Notre Dame Press (Original work published 1958)

Persuit, J. M. (2013). *Social media and integrated marketing communication: A rhetorical approach*. Lexington Books.

Persuit, J. M. (2016). Integrated marketing communication and public relations: Epideictic rhetoric, Kairos, and Ireland's Vote Yes. In J. M. Persuit & C. L. McDowell Marinchak (Eds.), *Integrated marketing communication: Creating spaces for engagement* (pp. 71–86). Lexington Books.

Peters, E., Västfjäll, D., Slovic, P., Mertz, C. K., Mazzocco, K., & Dickert, S. (2006). Numeracy and decision making. *Psychological Science, 17*(5), 407–413. doi:10.1111/j.1467-9280.2006.01720.x

Pew Research Center. (2019, June 12). Social media fact sheet. *Pew Research Center*. Retrieved from: https://www.pewresearch.org/internet/fact-sheet/social-media/

Phillips, P. (2019, September 3). McMaster on Dorian: This is a serious storm, heed the warnings.' *WCSC*. https://www.wmbfnews.com/2019/09/03/mcmaster-dorian-this-is-serious-storm-heed-warnings/

Pigs and animal production. (2014). Food and Agriculture Organization of the United Nations. http://www.fao.org/ag/againfo/themes/en/pigs/production.html

Piller, I., Zhang, J., & Li, J. (2020). Linguistic diversity in a time of crisis: Language challenges of the COVID-19 pandemic. *Multilingua, 39*(5), 503–515. Advanced online publication. doi:10.1515/multi-2020-0136

Pork Checkoff. (2020). Pork Checkoff 2020 strategic vision overview. https://www.pork.org/wp-content/uploads/2020/03/Strategic-Vision-and-Framework.pdf

Pratt, C. B. (1991). Public relations: The empirical research on practitioner ethics. *Journal of Business Ethics, 10*, 217–224.

Public Broadcasting Service. (2020, April 29). How teachers are trying to reach English language learners during pandemic. https://www.pbs.org/newshour/education/how-teachers-are-trying-to-reach-english-language-learners-during-pandemic

Public Safety and Homeland Security. (2019, August 29). Hurricane Dorian Communications Status Report. https://fcc.gov/document/hurricane-dorian-communication-status-report-august-29-2019

Puerto Rico declares public health emergency over zika virus. (2016, February 8). *Caribbean News Now*, Grand Cayman, Cayman Islands. Retrieved from www.lexisnexis.com

Randar, M. T. (1973). Social work from a social science perspective. *Social Science, 48*(2), 82–86.

Rani, K. U. (2016). Communication barriers. *Journal of English Language and Literature, 3*(2), 74–76. https:research_gate.net/profile/usha_kumbakonam/publication/304038097_Communication_Barriers/

Ravazzani, S. (2016). Exploring internal crisis communication in multicultural environments. *Corporate Communications: An International Journal, 21*(1), 73–88. doi:10.1108/CCIJ-02-2015-0011

Rawls, J. (1971). *A theory of justice*. Harvard University Press.

Reiss, J., & Sprenger, J. (2014). Scientific objectivity. *Stanford Encyclopedia of Philosophy*. https://plato.stanford.edu/entries/scientific-objectivity/

Rest, J. R. (1986). *Moral development. Advances in research and theory*. Praeger.

Rhone, N., & Hansen, Z. (2019, August 29). State of emergency for 12 South Georgia counties ahead of Hurricane Dorian. *Atlanta Journal-Constitution*. https://www.ajc.com/atlanta-news-metro-ajc/hurricane-dorian-intensifies-moves-toward/USpZM6x5jBYVHCEsh6WWHP/#

Richmond, V. P. (1990). Communication in the classroom: Power and motivation. *Communication Education, 39*, 181–195. doi:10.1080/03634529009378801

Richmond, V. P., Houser, M. L., & Hosek, A. M. (2018). Immediacy and the teacher-student relationship. In M. L. Houser and A. M. Hosek (Eds.), *Handbook of instructional communication: Rhetorical and relational perspectives* (2nd ed., pp. 97–111). Routledge.

Ricks, D. (2016, January 24). 3 people in New York test positive for mosquito-borne Zika virus; They traveled to endemic parts of the world that have infected insects; One person is said to be fully recovered, two others are recovering. *Newsday* (New York). Retrieved from www.lexisnexis.com

Ricks, D., & Chayes, M. (2016, January 29). 7 Zika virus cases in NY, 'no risk' of spread now, officials say. *Newsday* (New York). Retrieved from www.lexisnexis.com

Risk and Social Policy Group. (2020, June 22). COVID-19 technical report: Wave one. www.riskandsocialpolicy.org

Rogers, E. M. (2003). *The diffusion of innovations* (5th ed.). Free Press.

Romero, S. (2016, January 2). In Brazil, epidemic of malformed infants; Government suspects Zika virus of causing microcephaly in babies. *News*; p. 6. Retrieved from www.lexisnexis.com

Rowan, K. E. (1991). Goals, obstacles, and strategies in risk communication: A problem-solving approach to improving communication. *Journal of Applied Communication Research, 19*(4), 300–329. doi:10.1080/00909889109365311

Rykiel, E. J., Jr. (2001). Scientific objectivity, value systems, and policymaking. *BioScience, 51*(6), 433–436. https://watermark.silverchair.com/51-6-433.pdf

Samovar, L. A., Porter, R. E., McDaniel, E. R., & Roy, C. S. (2014). *Intercultural communication: A reader* (14th ed.). Cengage Learning.

Sarbaugh, L. E. (1979). *Intercultural communication*. Hayden Book Company, Inc.

Schultz, D. E. (1993, January 18). Integrated marketing communications: Maybe definition is in the point of view. *Marketing News, 27*(2), 17. http://connection.ebscohost.com/c/articles/17598990/integrated-marketing-communications-maybe-definition-point-view

Schultz, D. E., & Kitchen, P. J. (2000). *Communicating globally: An integrated marketing approach*. Macmillan Press Ltd.

Schultz, K. (2014, September 18). Preventing PEDV spread. *National Hog Farmer*. https://www.nationalhogfarmer.com/business/preventing-pedv-spread

Schumacher, L. L., Huss, A. R., Cochrane, R. A., Stark, C. R., Woodworth, J. C., Bai, J., ... & Gauger, P. C. (2017). Characterizing the rapid spread of porcine epidemic diarrhea virus (PEDV) through an animal food manufacturing facility. *PLOS ONE, 12*(11), e0187309.

Schwartz, S. H. (1992). Universals in the content and structure of values: Theoretical advances and empirical tests in twenty countries. In S. H. Schwartz (Ed.), *Advances in experimental social psychology* (vol. 25, pp. 1–66). Academic Press.

Search for survivors of Hurricane Dorian continues in Bahamas. (2019, September 9). *The Guardian*. https://www.theguardian.com/world/2019/sep/09/search-for-bodies-and-survivors-continues-after-hurricane-dorian-in-bahamas

Seeger, M. W. (2006). Best practices in crisis communication: An expert panel process. *Journal of Applied Communication Research, 34*(3), 232–244. doi:10.1080/00909880600769944

Seeger, M. W., Sellnow, T. L., & Ulmer, R. R. (2003). *Communication and organizational crisis*. Praeger.

Sellnow, D. D. (2018). *The rhetorical power of popular culture: Considering mediated texts*. Sage.

Sellnow, D. D., Iverson, J., & Sellnow, T. L. (2017a). The evolution of the operational earthquake forecasting community of practice: The L'Aquila communication crisis as a triggering event for organizational renewal. *Journal of Applied Communication Research, 45*(2), 121–139. doi:10.1080/00909882.2017.1288295

Sellnow, D. D., Johannesen, B., Lane, D. R., & Sellnow, T. L. (2020). No heat, no electiricity, no water, Oh no!: An IDEA model experiment in instructional risk communication. Paper presented at the International Communication Association conference (held virtually).

Sellnow, D. D., Johanssen, B., Sellnow, T. L., & Lane, D. R. (2019a). Toward a global understanding of the effects of the IDEA model for designing instructional risk and crisis messages: A food contamination experiment in Sweden. *Journal of Contingencies and Crisis Management, 27*(2), 102–115. doi:10.1111/1468-5973.12234

Sellnow, D. D., Jones, L. M., Sellnow, T. L., Spence, P., Lane, D. R., & Haarstad, N. (2019b). The IDEA model as a conceptual framework for designing earthquake early warning (EEW) messages distributed via mobile phone apps. In *Earthquakes- impact, community vulnerability and resilience*. IntechOpen.

Sellnow, D. D., Lane, D. R., Sellnow, T. L., & Littlefield, R. S. (2017b). The IDEA model as a best practice for effective instructional risk and crisis communication. *Communication Studies, 68*(5), 552–567. doi:10.1080/10510974.2017.1375535

Sellnow, D. D., & Sellnow, T. L. (2014). Instructional principles, risk communication. In T. L. Thompson (Ed.), *Encyclopedia of health communication* (pp. 1181–1182). Sage.

Sellnow, D. D., & Sellnow, T. L. (2019). The IDEA model for effective instructional risk and crisis communication by emergency managers and other key spokespersons. *Journal of Emergency Management, 17*(1), 67–78. doi:10.5055/jem.2019.0399

Sellnow, D. D., Sellnow, T. L., & Martin, J. M. (2019c). Strategic message convergence in communicating biosecurity: The case of the 2013 porcine epidemic diarrhea virus. *Communication Reports, 32*(3), 125–136. doi:10.1080/08934215.2019.1634747

Sellnow, T. L., Parker, J. S., Sellnow, D. D., Littlefield, R. S., & Helsel, E. M. (2017c). Improving biosecurity through instructional crisis communication: Lessons learned from the PEDv outbreak. *Journal of Applied Communications, 101*(4), COVC-COVC. doi:10.4148/1051-0834.1298

Sellnow, T. L., & Seeger, M. (2001). Exploring the boundaries of crisis communication: The case of the 1997 Red River Valley flood. *Communication Studies, 52*(2), 153–167. doi:10.1080/10510970109388549

Sellnow, T. L., & Seeger, M. W. (2013). *Theorizing crisis communication* (Vol. 4). Wiley.

Sellnow, T. L., Sellnow, D. D., Helsel, E. M., Martin, J. M., & Parker, J. S. (2018). Risk and crisis communication narratives in response to rapidly emerging diseases. *Journal of Risk Research, 22*(7), 897–908. doi:10.1080/13669877.2017.1422787

Sellnow, T. L., Ulmer, R. R., Seeger, M. W., & Littlefield, R. S. (2009). *Effective risk communication: A message-centered approach.* Springer.

Sellnow, T. L., & Vidoloff, K. (2009). Getting crisis communication right. *Food Technology, 63*(9), 40–45. file:///C:/Users/ro265358/Downloads/FoodTechnology MagazineArticle.pdf

Sellnow-Richmond, D. D., George, A. M., & Sellnow, D. D. (2018). An IDEA model analysis of instructional risk communication in the time of Ebola. *Journal of International Crisis and Risk Communication Research, 1*(1), 135–159. doi:10.30658/jicrcr.1.1.7

Sheppard, R., Sellnow, T. L., Sellnow, D. D., & Parrish, A. J. (2019, October 3–5). Innovations in crisis communication theory to aid in the comprehension and compliance with urgent biosecurity messages. Crisis6—Innovations in Risk and Crisis Communication, Leeds, United Kingdom.

Simon, R., & Teperman, S. (2001). The World Trade Center attack: Lessons for disaster management. *Critical Care, 5*(6), 318–320. doi:10.1186/cc1060

Simpson, E. J. (1972). *The classification of educational objectives in the psychomotor domain.* Gryphon House.

Slovic, P. (1986). Informing and educating the public about risk. *Risk Analysis, 6*(4), 403–415. doi:10.1111/j.1539-6924.1986.tb00953.x

Sohn, Y. J., & Edwards, H. H. (2018). Strategic ambiguity and crisis apologia: The impact of audiences' interpretations of mixed messages. *International Journal of Strategic Communication, 12*(5), 552–570. doi:10.1080/1553118X.2018.1512111

Solomon, R. C. (2003). On fate and fatalism. *Philosophy East and West, 53*(4), 435–454. doi:10.1353/pew.2003.0047

South Carolina Emergency Management Division (SCEMD). (2019, August 31). Gov. Henry McMaster declares state of emergency to prepare for potential impact from Hurricane Dorian. https://scemd.org/news/gov-henry-mcmaster-declares-state-of-emergency-to-prepare-for-potential-impact-from-hurricane-dorian/

Southern California Earthquake Center. (2020). Los Angeles, CA. Retrieved from http:// www.shakeout.org/home.html

Spence, P. R., Lachlan, K. A., & Burke, J. M. (2008). Crisis preparation, media use, and information seeking: Patterns across Katrina evacuees and lessons learned for crisis management. *Journal of Emergency Management, 6,* 11–23. doi:10.5055/jem.2010.0030

Stickings, T. (2019, September 3). Hurricane Dorian causes a 'historic tragedy' in the Bahamas after stalling over the islands for 40 HOURS killing at least five people - but fears for the US recede as storm weakens to a category three with 120mph winds. *MailOnline.* https://advance-lexis-com.ezproxy.net.ucf.edu/api/document?collection=news&id=urn:contentItem:5WYN-PXN1-F021-62J1-00000-00&context=1516831

Streifel, R. A., Beebe, B. L., Veil, S. R., & Sellnow, T. L. (2006). Significant choice and crisis decision making: MeritCare's public communication in the Fen-Phen case. *Journal of Business Ethics, 69,* 389–397. doi:10.1007/s10551-006-9097-2

Strom, S. (2014, July 4). Virus plagues the pork industry, and environmentalists. *The New York Times*. Retrieved from http://www.nytimes.com/2014/07/05/business/PEDv-plagues-thepork-industry-and-environmentalists.html?_r=0

Sullivan, R. J. (1989). *Immanuel Kant's moral theory*. Cambridge University Press.

Sun, L. H., Dennis, B., & Cha, A. E. (2016, February 3). U.S. identifies a case of Zika spread by sex. *The Washington Post*. Retrieved from www.lexisnexis.com

Tando Jr., E. C., Lim, Z. W., & Ling, R. (2018). Defining "fake news": A typology of scholarly definitions. *Digital Journalism, 6*(2), 137–153. doi:10.1080/21670811.2017.1360143

Tierney, K. J. (1999). Toward a critical sociology of risk. *Sociological Forum, 14*(2), 215–242.

Ting-Toomey, S., & Chung, L. C. (2005). *Understanding intercultural communication*. Roxbury.

Tinker, A. (2019). Communication ethics and the rejection of paternalism in John Stuart Mill's on Liberty. *Communication Quarterly, 67*(3), 312–333. doi:10.1080/01463373.2019.1596140

Triandis, H. C. (1993). Collectivism and individualism as cultural syndromes. *Cross-Cultural Research: The Journal of Comparative Social Science, 27*, 155–180. doi:10.1177/106939719302700301

Ulmer, R. R., & Sellnow, T. L. (1997). Strategic ambiguity and the ethic of significant choice in the tobacco industry's crisis communication. *Communication Studies, 48*(3), 215–233. doi:10.1080/10510979709368502

United States Department of Agriculture (USDA). (2020). *Joint Statement on the International Swine Fever Forum*. https://www.aphis.usda.gov/aphis/newsroom/news/sa_by_date/sa-2019/asf-forum

United States Department of Health and Human Services (USDHHS). (2018). *History of 1918 Flu Pandemic*. cdc.gov/flu/pandemic-resources/1918-commemeration/1918-pandemic-history.htm

Veil, S. R., Anthony, K. E., Sellnow, T. L., Staricek, N., Young, L. E., & Cupp, P. (2020). Revisiting the best practices in risk and crisis communication: A multi-case analysis. In H. D. O'Hair & M. J. O'Hair (Eds.), *The handbook of applied communication research* (vol. 1, pp. 377–396). John Wiley & Sons, Inc.

Vickery, K. (2016, February 6). Fears of northern exposure. *Northern Territory News* (Australia). Archived at https://web.archive.org/web/20200605142013/ https://www.territorystories.nt.gov.au/bitstream/10070/261300/33/Northern%20Territory%20News_20160206_page22_NTNews_News_22.PDF

Vignoles, V. L., Owe, E., Becker, M., Smith, P. B., Easterbrook, M. J., Brown, R, et al. (2016). Beyond the 'East-West' dichotomy: Global variation in cultural models of selfhood. *Journal of Experimental Psychology, 145*(8), 966–1000. doi:10.1037/xge0000175

Vinhateiro, C., & Cronen, V. E. (2016). Integrated marketing communication and social media: "Coordinated management of meaning" and entrepreneurship. In J. M. Persuit & C. L. McDowell Marinchak (Eds.), *Integrated marketing communication: Creating spaces for engagement* (pp. 87–110). Lexington Books.

Washington: CDC issues Zika-virus guidance for docs with pregnant patients. (2016, January 20). *U. S. Official News: Plus Media Solutions.* Retrieved from www.lexisnexis.com

Washington: Interim guidelines for pregnant women during a Zika virus outbreak—United States, 2016. (2016, January 19). *U.S. Official News: Plus Media Solutions.* Retrieved from www.lexisnexis.com

Washington: Zika virus expected to spread North through U.S.: WHO. (2016, January 25). *U.S. Official News: Plus Media Solutions.* Retrieved from www.lexisnexis.com

Weather.gov. (2019, September 6). Hurricane Dorian, September 6, 2019. https://www.weather.gov/mhx/Dorian2019

Weick, K. E. (1988). Enacting sensemaking in crisis situations. *Journal of Management Studies, 25*(4), 305–317. doi:10.1111/j.1467-6486.1988.tb00039.x

Wenger, E., McDermott, R. A., & Snyder, W. (2002). *Cultivating communities of practice: A guide to managing knowledge.* Harvard Business Press.

Wexler, M. N. (2009). Strategic ambiguity in emergent coalitions: The triple bottom line. *Corporate Communications: An International Journal, 14*(1), 62–77. doi:10.1108/13563280910931081

White, S. (2016, February 1). Shrunken head virus hits Brits on holiday who are warned not to try for a baby; The health alert comes as the Zika virus, which can cause severe birth defects, tears its way through south and Central America. *The Daily Record.* Retrieved from www.lexisnexis.com

WHO declares Zika virus a global health emergency. (2016, February 2). *Mail & Guardian.* Retrieved from www.lexisnexis.com

Wisconsin: UW-Madison researchers find Zika virus in Colombia, look for ways to stop it. (2016, January 26). *U. S. Official News: Plus Media Solutions.* Retrieved from www.lexisnexis.com

World Health Organization. (2015a, October 21). Zika virus infection—Brazil and Colombia. *Disease Outbreak News: Emergencies preparedness, response.* Retrieved from www.who.int/csr

World Health Organization. (2015b, November 27). Zika virus infection—El Salvador. *Disease Outbreak News: Emergencies preparedness, response.* Retrieved from www.who.int/csr

World Health Organization. (2015c, December 21). Zika virus infection—Honduras. *Disease Outbreak News: Emergencies preparedness, response.* Retrieved from www.who.int/csr

World Health Organization. (2016a, January 27). Zika virus infection—Dominican Republic. *Disease Outbreak News: Emergencies preparedness, response.* Retrieved from www.who.int/csr

World Health Organization. (2016b, January 28). WHO to convene an international health regulations emergency committee on Zika virus and observed increase in neurological disorders and neonatal malformations. https://www.who.int/news-room/detail/28-01-2016-who-to-convene-an-international-health-regulations-emergency-committee-on-zika-virus-and-observed-increase-in-neurological-disorders-and-neonatal-malformations

World Health Organization. (2016c, February). Zika: Strategic response framework & joint operations plan January–June 2016. https://www.who.int/emergencies/zika-virus/strategic-response-framework.pdf?ua=1

World Health Organization. (2016d, February 1). WHO statement on the first meeting of the International Health Regulations (2005) (IHR 2005) Emergency Committee on Zika virus and observed increase in neurological disorders and neonatal malformations. https://www.who.int/news-room/detail/01-02-2016-who-statement-on-the-first-meeting-of-the-international-health-regulations-(2005)-(ihr-2005)-emergency-committee-on-zika-virus-and-observed-increase-in-neurological-disorders-and-neonatal-malformations

World Health Organization. (2016e, February 5). Zika situation report. https://www.who.int/emergencies/zika-virus/situation-report/5-february-2016/en/

World Health Organization. (2016f, February 12). Zika virus infection—United States of America. *Disease Outbreak News: Emergencies preparedness, response.* Retrieved from www.who.int/csr

World Health Organization. (2016g, May 13). Pregnancy management in the context of Zika virus infection: Interim guidance update. https://www.who.int/csr/resources/publications/zika/pregnancy-management/en/

World Health Organization. (2018, July 20). Zika virus. https://www.who.int/news-room/fact-sheets/detail/zika-virus2016

World Health Organization. (2019, July). Zika Epidemiology Update. https://www.who.int/emergencies/diseases/zika/zika-epidemiology-update-july-2019.pdf?ua=1

World Health Organization. (2020). Emergencies preparedness, response: Zika virus infection. *Disease Outbreak News.* https://who.int/csr/don/archive/disease/zika-virus-infection/en/

Wulfemeyer, K. T., & Frazier, L. (1992). The ethics of video news releases: A qualitative analysis. *Journal of Mass Media Ethics, 7,* 151–168. doi:10.1080/10627260801894405

Zika spurs global alarm. (2016, February 9). *Al-Ahram Weekly.* Retrieved from www.lexisnexis.com

Zika virus' global spread alarms WHO. (2016, January 30). *The Nation* (Thailand). Retrieved from www.lexisnexis.com

Zillman, D. (2006). Exemplification effects in the promotion of safety and health. *Journal of Communication, 56,* S221–S237. doi:10.1111/j.1460-2466.2006.00291.x

Index

Page references for figures are italicized.

Abaco Islands, 56
Abramson, Neil R., 92
aedes aegypti mosquito, 54, 80, 87
Africa, 57, *58*, 117
African Swine Fever virus (ASFv), 115, 116; biosecurity threat, 57, 61, 116–21, 135–37; context, 57, 116; effects, 57, 62, 65, 117, 136; information sources, 137; response to, 135, 137; timeline of crisis, *58*; transmission and treatment, 57, 116–17, 136, 137; use of culture-centered approach, 5, 73, 118, 121. *See also* culture-centered approach (CC)
Alves, Herique, 86
American Association of Swine Veterinarians, 57, 116, 118, 119, 135
American College of Obstetricians and Gynecologists, 84
American Indian: Nations, 48, 49; Pueblo culture, 168; Tribal Elder, 49; women, 48
American Red Cross, 83
Anderson, John, 106, 135
Arnett, Ronald C., 32
Arpan, Laura M., 21

ASFv. *See* African Swine Fever virus (ASFv)
Asia, 57, *58*, 117
Atlantic Ocean, 54–56, 98, 99, 103
audience: particular, 23, 44, 47, 71, 72, 78, 79, 89, 92, 94–96, 107, 115, *127*, 131, 134, 138, 141, 147, 164, 168; universal, 21, 23, 71, 72, 76–79, 82, 87, 89, 92, 94, 115, 124, 125, *127*, 131, 134, 138, 147, 164, 168, 172
audience-focused communication. *See* culture-centered approach (CC)
Australia, 2

Baack, Donald, 139
Bahamas, 5, 54–56, 91, 98, 103, 109
Beech, Peter, 88
best practices. *See* essential guidelines for ongoing risk and crisis communication; risk and crisis best practices
Birx, Deborah, 172
Bowen, Shannon A., 147, 148
Brazil, 53–55, 80, 85, 86, 133

California Department of Public Health, 84

Canada, 56, 58, 98
Canadian Blood Services, 83
Cape Canaveral, Florida, 134
Caribbean, 53, 55, 86, 87
Caribbean Public Health Agency (CARPHA), 83
Carnival, 132
Castro, Marcelo, 133
Category 5 hurricane, 5, 55, 99, 134
Catholic Church, 85–88, 93, 133
CC. *See* culture-centered approach (CC)
CDC. *See* U. S. Centers for Disease Control and Prevention (CDC)
Central America, 53
China, 57, 61
Chung, Leeva C., 9
Clow, Kenneth, 139
CN. *See* culture-neutral approach (CN)
code systems. *See* culture
Colombia, 132
communication accommodation theory, 160
communication model, 113
communities of practice, 65, 67
consequentialism. *See* ethics
Cooper, Roy, 105, 107
corporate social responsibility, 158, 166
Cortez, Salina Velasquz, 133
COVID–19, 102; code systems used, 66–67; competing narratives, 61, 63, 65–66, 171–72; context, 2, 61; coronavirus task force, 172; self-protection, 67–68, 105
crisis, 130; crisis phase, 24, 30, 68, 80, 99; post-crisis phase, 24, 80–81, 82, 99, 118, 119; pre-crisis phase, 24, 30, 68, 80, 99, 113, 118, 119, 155
Crosby, Alfred W., 1
CS. *See* culturally sensitive approach (CS)
cultural agent, 21, 22, *114*, *126*, 141–42, 155, 156, 170
culturally sensitive approach (CS): communication approach, 4, 5, 6, 47, 50, 73, 76, 94, *127*; content, 47, 127; context, 49, *53*; cultural adaptation, 21, 48, 93, 94–95, 102, *127*, 128; effectiveness, 106–7; IDEA model, application of, 72; interpretive perspective, 95, *127*, 128; managerial/elite perspective, 92–93, *127*; multiple-spokesperson model, 94, *127*; power, 48, *53*; resistance, 49, *53*, 100, 102, 105–6; scripted message, 93, *127*; stories and values, 49, *53*, *127*. *See also* Hurricane Dorian
culture, 7, 96; best practices, 140–42; categories of, 92, 95, 111; code systems, 9, 9, 21, 44, 47–48, 66, 92, 96, 102, 159, 160; effects on communication, 8, 10; individual agency, 37, 38, 60; knowing and accepting normative beliefs and values, 9, 45, 48, 155; perceived relationship and intent, 8, 45, 131, 155; taxonomy, 8–9, 36, 44–45, 47–48, 66, 92–93, 131, 155; worldview, 9, 45, 46, 48, 60
culture-centered approach (CC): audience focus, 3, 11, 22, 30, 31, 41, 111–*12*, *114*, *127*, 140; best practices, 36, 140–42, 164; communication approach, 4, 50–53, 112–13, 119, *127*; community involvement, 3–4, 110, 115, 140, 153; comparison with CN and CS, 163–67; context, 51, *53*; critical perspective, 113–14, 116, *127*, 128*;* dimensions of, 4, 5, 6, 43, 52; effectiveness, 120–21, 124, 142, 167–68; health communication in, 42, 153, 169; IDEA model, application of, 72–73; managerial perspective, *127*, 163; message development, 111–*12*, *127*; multiple spokesperson model, 113, 114, 116, *127*, 138; power, 50, 52, *53*, 114; resistance, 42, 52, *53*, 120; stories and values, 52, *53*, 121; timing of,

118. *See also* African Swine Fever virus (ASFv)
culture-centered model. *See* culture-centered approach (CC)
culture-neutral approach (CN): audience focus, *127*; characteristics of, 19, 21, 43, 82; communication approach, 4, 5, 43–47, 73, 75, 77, 79, 80–81, *127*; content, 10, 44, 77, 78, 81, 84, 88, 89, 97, *127*; context, 45, *53*; effectiveness of, 41, 78–79, 87–88, 89, 166; ethnocentric perspective, 41–42, 77; IDEA model, application of, 7, 8, 72, 75, 78, 89; managerial-elite perspective, 75, 76, 81, *127*; power, 44, *53*; resistance, 46, *53*, 87; scripted message, 75, 76–77, 81, 82, *127*; single-spokesperson model, 75, 77, *127*; social science perspective, 78, *127*, 128; stories and values, 45, *53*. *See also* Zika virus (ZIKv)

Da Silva, Gleyse Kelly, 132
decision-makers, 2, 9–11, 15, 19, 24, 34, 42, 50, 51, 59–60, 70–72, 76, 77, 84, 92–96, 102, 110, 111, 114, 125, 128, 130, 138, 142, 149–51, 153, 167, 171
decision-making, 3, 24, 34, 41, 49–51, 59–60, 72–73, 76, 77, 110, 111, *158*, 164–65, 169; cultural, 140–42; ethical models, 146–49, 154–58; principle of social utility, 6, 145, 153, 154–56; tensions of strategic communication, 41, 139
deontology. *See* ethics
DePelsmacker, Patrick, 111, 124, 126, 137, 154
DeSantis, Gov. Ron, 55
diffusion process, 20, 95
Disease Outbreak News. *See* World Health Organization (WHO)
Dutta, Mohan, 15, 46, 47, 50–53, 110, 153, 169

Eatche, Chad, 134
Ebola, 80, 105
ECHO. *See* Emergency and Community Health Outreach (ECHO)
Edmonds, Lauren, 134
El Salvador, 80, 82, 86
Emergency and Community Health Outreach (ECHO): culture-centered, 170–71; origin, 170
essential guidelines for ongoing risk and crisis communication, 31, 36; need for inclusivity, 31–*33*, 83–84, 139, 141; recovery, 31, 35, 84–85, 139; responsible communication, 31–32, *34*, 84, 119, 139; strategic planning, 29, 30, 31, 82–83, 139
ethical behavior. *See* ethics
ethic of significant choice. *See* ethics
ethics: behavior, 150, 159; categorial imperative, 148; consequentialism, 151–52; culture, dimensions of, 6, 159; deontology, 148, 149, 152, 153; ethno-relativity, 48; law of autonomy, 148; leadership, 146; model for CC decision-making, 6, 146, 166; morality of particular audiences, 147; normative model of ethical issues management, 147–48; precedence, 151, 152; significant choice, 6, 65–66, 145, 158–59; situational, 151; standards of, 150; symmetrical model of public relations, 149; universal morality, 146, 149; utilitarianism, 151–52, 154. *See also* decision-making
ethno-relativity. *See* ethics
Europe, 57, *58*, 61, 117
European Centre for Disease Surveillance and Control, 83

Facebook, 64
factionalism, 168
Farmer, Yanick, 145
fatalistic worldview. *See* culture, individual agency

Fauci, Anthony, 172
Figueroa, Rev. Hector, 133
Fisher, Walter, 89
Flores, Rosa, 134
Florida, 55, 56, 103, 109, 133, 135; Division of Emergency Management, 107
France, 80

Frazer, Lowell, 159
Gaviria, Alejandro, 132
Georgia, 55, 135
Gerwin, Leslie E., 117
Great Depression, 2
Great Shake Out Earthquake Drill, 67
Greenland, 99
Grunig, James E., 148
Gudykunst, William B., 8
Guillain-Barré syndrome, 80

H1N1 virus, 1, 102
Hofstede, Geert, 8
holistic worldview. *See* culture, individual agency
Hong Kong, 63
Howell, William S., 150, 153
Humane Society of Grand Bahama, 56
Hunt, Todd, 148
Hurricane Dorian: context, 5, 54, 55, 56, 97, 109; path of, 55, 97, *98*, 99, *100*, 103, 105, 134; responses to, 133, 135, 168; timeline, 56, 97, *98–99*, 168. *See also* culturally sensitive approach (CS)
Hurricane Katrina, 102
Hurricane Maria, 64

IDEA model of instructional risk and crisis communication, 4, 73, 96, 114, 129, 169; action, 5, 59, 60, 67–68, 71, 78, 96, 104–5, 115, 120, 128; distribution, 5, 60, 63–65, 70–72, 78, 97, 101–2, 107, 120, 122, 128; explanation, 5, 60, 65–67, 78, 96, 102–4, 115, 120, 128, 130, 171;

internalization, 5, 60, 61–63, 69, 72, 78, 87, 96, 99–*101*, 107, 115, 120, 122, 128, 171; learning domains, 60, 141; need for integration, 68
IMC. *See* integrated marketing communication (IMC)
instructional communication, 61, 68, 165
integrated marketing communication (IMC): advantages of, 14–16; application of culture, 3, 4, 7; audience focus, 3, 10, 11, 15, 19; barriers to, 16–17; components of, 8, 13; definition, 10; implementation strategies, 10, 17–19, 76, 139, 154; levels of integration, 12–14; levels of market success, 18, 138; limitations of, 88–89, 124; objectives of, 3, 11, 13, 69, 137–38; origin, 10–11; stage 1 IMC, *12*, 27, 31–*32*, 70, 118, 124, *126*, 156, 157, 166, 169; stage 2 IMC, *12*, 28, 32–*33*, 70–71, 91–95, 118–19, 124, 125, *126*, 156, 157, 166, 169; stage 3 IMC, *12*–13, 28, *34*–35, 71, 110, 119, 124, 125, *126*, 156–58; stage 4 IMC, *12*, 13, 28, *35*–36, 71, 111, 114, 119, 124, 125, *126*, 138, 158
interacting arguments, 23, *127*, 128, 129, 150–51; congruence, 23, *127*, 128; convergence, 23, 64, 129, 130, 150, 159; dominance, 23; mutual exclusivity, 23, *127*, 128; with publics, 39
intercultural communication, 8–9, 21
international public health emergency, 53, 80, 83
International Sanitary Conferences, 88
Ishii, Satoshi, 9
Isreal, Barbara A., 112

Jahoda, Gustav, 7
Japan, 62
Jordan, DeAndre, 2

Kansas, 1
Kant, Immanuel, 148
Kemp, Gov. Brian, 55
Kitchen, Phillip J., 12, 111, 124, 126, 137, 154
Klopf, Donald W., 9, 21, 77
knowing and accepting normative beliefs and values. *See* culture

Landau, Mark J., 154
Latin America, 79, 87
learning domains. *See* IDEA model of instructional risk and crisis communication
Leiss, William, 130
Lexis-Nexis, 79
Littlefield, Robert S., 19, 21, 33, 95, 142

MacCallum, Martha, 134
Machowsky, Lauren, 86
Magley, Joanne, 106
marginalization, 43–45, 48–49, 51, *53*
Marquez, Miguel, 134
Marsh Harbour International Airport, 56
McKendree, Amanda G., 11
McMaster, Gov. Henry, 55, 106, 135
media: digital, 102; legacy, 63; social, 10, 20, 63, 64, 159
Merrick, Rosemary Saponaro, 86
Mexico, 58
Miami, Florida, 97
microcephaly, 53–55, 84–86, 93, 132, 133
Micronesia, 54
Minnesota, 120, 170
Minnis, P. M. Hubert, 56
Moran, Robert T., 92

narrative paradigm, 89
National Health Information Center, 83
National Hurricane Center (NHC), 54, 97–100, 102–4, 106, 134
National Pork Board, 57, 115–16, 118, 119, 121, 135, 136
National Weather Channel, 54

National Weather Service, 54, 97, 100, 168
New Orleans, 102
New York, 101
NHC. *See* National Hurricane Center (NHC)
NHC Bulletins, 99–102, 104, 134
Nigeria, 117
Nilsen, Thomas R., 158
North America, 53, 57
North Carolina, 105, 107
North Dakota, 64
Norwegian Cruise Line, 86

Olbrechts-Tyteca, Lucie, 23, 89, 151
Oswaldo Cruz Foundation, 84
Outer Banks, North Carolina, 56

PAHO. *See* Pan American Health Organization (PAHO)
Palenchar, Michael, 130
Pan American Health Organization (PAHO), 54, 55, 82, 83
Passieux, Stefanie, 107
paternalism, 151–53
PEDv. *See* Porcine Epidemic Diarrhea virus (PEDv)
perceived relationship and intent. *See* culture
Perelman, Chaim, 23, 89, 151
Persuit, Jeanne, 11
PEW Charitable Reserve Center, 64
polio, 80
Porcine Epidemic Diarrhea virus (PEDv), 57, *58*, 65, 116–21, 136
principle of social utility (PSU). *See* decision-making
progressive worldview. *See* culture, individual agency
projective cognitive similarity, 77
PSU. *See* principle of social utility (PSU)
Public Broadcasting System (PBS), 171
Public Health Emergency of International Concern, 54

publics, 3, 6, 10, 11, 21, 33, 36–38, 61, 72, 151; consumers, 3, 33, 92, 110, 111, 151; customers, 3, 10, 18, 110, 111; Hispanic, 1–2; marginalized, 42, 44, 45, 47, 50–52, 78, 79, 125, 128, 153, 160, 166; Spanish-speaking, 92, 102, 171; stakeholders, 10, 27, 67, 116, 119, 120, 136, 137, 167; vulnerable, 31, 33, 84, 92, 94, 111, 114, 131, 139, 153, 160
Puerto Rico, 64

Quagliariello, John, 105

rational world paradigm, 71, 72, 81–82, 89
Red River, 64
Red Scare, 1
relational dialectics theory, 19
Rest, James R., 146
risk and crisis best practices: account for cultural differences, 29, 30, 119, 140–42; continuously evaluate and update, 29, 30, 35, 84; proactive strategies, 29, 30; strategic planning, 29, 30, 82–83; strategic responses, 29, 30, 33
risk communication, 130
Rogers, Everett, 95
Rosell, Rich, 135

Samovar, Larry A., 22
Sarbaugh, Lawrence, 8, 155
SARS, 102
Schultz, Don E., 12
Seeger, Matthew W., 30, 33, 142
Sellnow, Deanna D., 78, 96, 113, 114
Sellnow, Timothy L., 19, 23, 30, 78, 96, 113, 114, 124, 129, 150, 154, 158
Smith, Russell, 86
South America, 53
South Carolina, 55, 56, 106, 134, 135; Myrtle Beach, 134
Southern California Earthquake Council, 67

Spanish Flu, 1
spheres of ethnocentricity, 6, 50, 76, 87, 123–24, 128–31, 138, 151, 165
spokesperson models: multiple spokespersons, 22; responses to, 21–22; role of, 19, 20; single spokesperson, 20–21, 22
St. Paul, Minnesota, 170
Streifel, Renae A., 158, 159
Summer Olympic Games, 85–88, 132
Sweden, 64
Swine Flu, 80

Thweatt, Tatyana, 21
Ting-Toomey, Stella, 8, 9
Tinker, Andrew, 152
transceivers, *112*–13
Trump, Donald, 2, 172

Uganda, 54, 55, 62
United Nations, 56, 88
U. S. Centers for Disease Control and Prevention (CDC), 83
U. S. Department of Agriculture (USDA), 102, 135
U. S. Department of Public Safety and Homeland Security, 102
U. S. Food and Drug Administration (USFDA), 102
utilitarianism. *See* ethics

Van Dam, Derek, 106
Veil, Shari, 30–33, 84
Vidoloff, Kathleen, 30
Virginia, 55
Volusia County, Florida, 106

Weick, Karl E., 20
White House, The, 83
Wilkinson, Phillip, 86
World Health Organization (WHO): best practices, 82–85; credibility, 79, 81–82, 88; effectiveness, 87–88; failures of IMC, 75; messages, 5, 79, 88, 105; role of, 88. *See also* culture-

neutral approach (CN); Zika virus (ZIKv)
worldview. *See* culture
World War I, 1
World War II, 88
World Wide Web, 8
Wulfemeyer, K. Tim, 159

Zika virus (ZIKv), 5; background, 53–54, 79; effects, 54; mitigation strategies, 85–87, 131–33; timeline of exposure, 55, 80–81, 82; transmission of, 54, 132, 133; use of best practices, 82–85

About the Authors

Robert S. Littlefield is Founding Director and Professor in the Nicholson School of Communication and Media at the University of Central Florida. Littlefield's research focuses on alternative perspectives of risk and crisis held by vulnerable publics and the need for a culture-centered approach including these groups into contexts where risk and crisis messages are developed and distributed to broader constituencies. Most recently, he introduced the Tensions of Strategic Communication Decision Making (TSCD), an applied theory describing how decision makers respond to the tensions they experience in risk and crisis situations. He has several books to his credit, including *Risk and Crisis Communication: Navigating the Tensions Between Organizations and the Public*. The author or co-author of over seventy-five journal articles, Littlefield has nearly 100 conference presentations to his credit. He is the former editor of *Communication Studies*, and a recipient of the Jack Kay Award for Community Engagement and Applied Communication Scholarship presented by the Central States Communication Association. His research has been funded, in part, by grants from the U.S. Department of Homeland Security, the U.S. Department of Agriculture, and the U.S. Department of Education.

Deanna D. Sellnow is Professor of Strategic Communication and an Assistant Director of the Nicholson School of Communication and Media at the University of Central Florida. Her research focuses on strategic instructional communication in a variety of contexts, including risk, crisis, and health. She has conducted numerous funded research projects with agencies, such as the Centers for Disease Control, U.S. Department of Agriculture, the World Health Organization, National Oceanic and Atmospheric Administration, and the U.S. Geological Association. She has published in a wide range of national and international journals, and is the author of several books, including *The Rhetorical Power of Popular Culture, Communicate!* and *Effective Speaking in a Digital Age*. She is the current editor of *Journal of Communication Pedagogy* and former President of Central States Communication Association.

Timothy L. Sellnow is Professor of Strategic Communication and Director of Graduate Studies in the Nicholson School of Communication and Media at the University of Central Florida. Sellnow's research focuses on risk and crisis communication. In addition to serving frequently as a corporate consultant, he has conducted funded research for the Department of Homeland Security, the U.S. Department of Agriculture, the Centers for Disease Control and Prevention, the Environmental Protection Agency, the U.S. Geological Survey, and the World Health Organization. He has served in an advisory role for the National Academy of Sciences, the Federal Emergency Management Agency, and the U. S. Food and Drug Administration. He has published many refereed journal articles and coauthored six books on risk and crisis communication. Sellnow is the former editor of *Journal of Applied Communication Research*, and a recipient of the National Communication Association's Gerald M. Phillips award for Distinguished Applied Communication Research.

www.ingramcontent.com/pod-product-compliance
Lightning Source LLC
Chambersburg PA
CBHW070830300426
44111CB00014B/2513